JOURNAL FOR THE STUDY OF THE OLD TESTAMENT
SUPPLEMENT SERIES
387

Circumscribing the Prostitute

The Rhetorics of Intertextuality, Metaphor
and Gender in Jeremiah 3.1–4.4

Mary E. Shields

T&T CLARK INTERNATIONAL
A Continuum imprint
LONDON • NEW YORK

Copyright © 2004 T&T Clark International
A Continuum imprint

Published by T&T Clark International
The Tower Building, 11 York Road, London SE1 7NX
15 East 26th Street, Suite 1703, New York, NY 10010

www.tandtclark.com

British Library Cataloguing-in-Publication Data
A catalogue record for this book is available from the British Library

Typeset and edited for Continuum by Forthcoming Publications Ltd
www.forthcomingpublications.com

Printed on acid-free paper in Great Britain by The Bath Press, Bath

ISBN 0-8264-6999-X

CONTENTS

ACKNOWLEDGMENTS

As with any large undertaking, this book would not have been possible without many people's support along the way. In particular, I wish to thank the following. First, I am grateful to Carol A. Newsom, my original dissertation adviser, who was a wonderful mentor and who pushed me to strive for excellence. And I am also grateful to the wise counsel of the other readers of my dissertation, on which this book is based: David M. Gunn, John H. Hayes and Gail R. O'Day. Next, I would like to thank Philip Davies, editor of the *JSOT* Supplement series, for his patience, perseverance and unfailing good cheer. J. Cheryl Exum provided critical insights for the revision process. Duncan Burns, the copy-editor of this book, shepherded me through the final editing process. I am ever grateful to him for his painstaking work.

I am grateful to the members of our weekly research group from Capital University, Erica Brownstein and Suzanne Marilley for their support, accountability and friendship.

There are three people in particular from Trinity Lutheran Seminary who have been of immense help and support as I have worked on this manuscript. First, I wish to thank Joy A. Schroeder, Assistant Professor of Church History, who read and commented on drafts, pushing me to greater clarity. Her gifts of time, keen perception, friendship and sense of humor are invaluable resources. In addition, I wish to thank two Bible division research assistants: Brian Miller, for his computer wizardry, for putting in many hours tracking down footnotes, and for doing the countless little jobs that needed to be done in order to tie up the loose ends before the initial submission of the manuscript; and Steve Bond, for his close editing, for his great suggestions and for his work in tracking down the final bits and pieces needed at the end of the editing process. Finally, I thank my colleagues at Trinity, particularly those in the Bible Division, for their support and encouragement, and for making Trinity the kind of environment where research can flourish.

I wish also to thank the publishers at E.J. Brill for granting permission to use material from my article, 'Circumcision of the Prostitute: Gender, Sexuality, and the Call to Repentance in Jeremiah 3.1–4.4' (*BibInt* 3 [1995], pp. 61-74), which contained a much earlier reading of this text.

I dedicate this book to my parents, Ed and Grace Shields.

ABBREVIATIONS

ATANT	Abhandlungen zur Theologie des Alten und Neuen Testaments
ATD	Das Alte Testament Deutsch
BDB	Francis Brown, S.R. Driver and Charles A. Briggs, *A Hebrew and English Lexicon of the Old Testament* (Oxford: Clarendon Press, 1907)
BHS	*Biblia hebraica stuttgartensia*
Bib	*Biblica*
BibInt	*Biblical Interpretation: A Journal of Contemporary Approaches*
BKAT	Biblischer Kommentar: Altes Testament
BWANT	Beiträge zur Wissenschaft vom Alten und Neuen Testament
BZAW	Beihefte zur *ZAW*
CBQ	*Catholic Biblical Quarterly*
G	Greek Septuagint (LXX)
HAT	Handbuch zum Alten Testament
HSM	Harvard Semitic Monographs
IEJ	*Israel Exploration Journal*
Int	*Interpretation*
JBL	*Journal of Biblical Literature*
JFSR	*Journal of Feminist Studies in Religion*
JJS	*Journal of Jewish Studies*
JLA	*The Jewish Law Annual*
JSOT	*Journal for the Study of the Old Testament*
JSOTSup	*Journal for the Study of the Old Testament*, Supplement Series
KAT	Kommentar zum Alten Testament
MT	Masoretic text
NICOT	New International Commentary on the Old Testament
OTL	Old Testament Library
RSV	Revised Standard Version
S	Syriac
SBL	Society of Biblical Literature
SBLDS	SBL Dissertation Series
THAT	Ernst Jenni and Claus Westermann (eds.), *Theologisches Handwörterbuch zum Alten Testament* (2 vols.; Munich: Chr. Kaiser, 1971–76)
TLZ	*Theologische Literaturzeitung*
VT	*Vetus Testamentum*
WBC	Word Biblical Commentary
ZAW	*Zeitschrift für die alttestamentliche Wissenschaft*

Introduction

> The matrix of any idea is reality—people cannot conceive of something they
> have not themselves experienced or at least that others have before them
> experienced. Thus, images, metaphors, myths all find expression in forms
> which are 'prefigured' through past experience. In periods of change people
> reinterpret these symbols in new ways, which then lead to new combina-
> tions and new insights.
>
> —Gerda Lerner

This book is a study of the rhetoric of Jer. 3.1–4.4. Intertextuality, metaphor and gender are the primary threads from which the prophet weaves a
rich and complex rhetorical tapestry designed to convince the people that
their political and religious actions have been wrong and that they must
change their ways before it is too late. On first reading, the most noticeable
thread is metaphor. The move from accusation to promise in Jer. 3.1–4.4 is
mirrored by a move from female metaphors to male metaphors. The passage begins with marriage imagery: God as the husband, and Israel as the
wife who acts like a whore (3.1-5). Sister imagery is used next to portray
the 'rivalry' in prostitution between Judah and the Northern Kingdom
(vv. 6-11). When the text moves to the possibility of repentance, however,
the portrait changes to father-son imagery: God as the father and Israel as
the repentant and obedient son (vv. 14-18; 3.21–4.4). The last shift, to circumcision as a sign both of human repentance and of God's promise,
occurs in 4.1-4.

In addition to shifts in metaphor, there are also shifts in mode of address,
from feminine direct address to masculine direct address. Like the shifts in
imagery, the direct address is used rhetorically to pressure the audience
into identifying in one way as opposed to another (e.g. to identify as the
proper sons to God as father rather than as unfaithful wife to God as husband).

The shifts in imagery and direct address in Jer. 3.1–4.4 correspond to
equally significant shifts in intertexts. For the purposes of this study, intertextuality will be defined broadly: (1) as an examination of the interaction
and/or play among texts; (2) the reinterpretation of old symbols in new

contexts; and (3) the interaction between a text and cultural conventions and ideals. As the use of the term 'interaction' indicates, intertextuality is a two-way bridge; there is play between the texts, or, to put it another way, dialogue back and forth. Thus, rather than looking at issues of influence alone, study of intertextuality incorporates the role of the reader and the ways in which the historical, political and social contexts of both author and reader (including the implied reader and the present-day reader) enter into dialogue and thus produce different interpretations.

When dealing with the intertextual relationships between Jer. 3.1–4.4 and other biblical texts, the following terms will be used: 'host text', which is the focus of study (in this case, 3.1–4.4), and 'intertext', which is the text alluded to or quoted by the host text.[1] While the term 'intertext' will not be used with regard to intertextuality of culture, cultural conventions and ideals are nevertheless 'intertexts' with which the 'host text' of 3.1–4.4 interacts. Jeremiah 3.1 begins with a citation of a divorce law (also found in Deut. 24.1-4) and ends with allusions to the patriarchal covenant with Abraham and its attendant sign, circumcision, in Jer. 4.1-4. In addition, there are interplays with other texts (e.g. Isa. 2.2-4; Hos. 10 and 14), as well as play with cultural and religious conventions and ideals, particularly those revolving around gender relationships.

Gender is the third rhetorical thread running through the text of Jer. 3.1–4.4. As I will show, using material from traditions familiar to his audience and interweaving it in new ways with metaphors which play upon well-accepted cultural conventions of gender and sexuality, allows the prophet to place pressure on a male audience to choose one behavior over another. One of the aims of this book is to show that the gender construction, that is, the ways in which gender both constructs and is constructed by the text, is primarily responsible for the effectiveness of the rhetoric on both the affective and cognitive levels. I argue that the gender rhetoric itself (that is, the rhetoric which uses imagery pertaining to gender and/or sexual roles) places strong pressure on a male audience to identify themselves along the lines the prophet is advocating.

The gender rhetoric is not without problems, however. The switch from female to male imagery and direct address relies on a construction of gender and sexuality which I will argue is harmful for both genders. More-over, the deity is implicated in the prophet's construction of gender and

---

1.   These terms are taken from the work of Mary Orr, *Claude Simon: The Inter-textual Dimension* (University of Glasgow French and German Publications; Somerset: Castle Cary Press, 1993), p. 25.

sexuality, often in problematic ways. In my reading of Jer. 3.1–4.4, I aim not only to highlight the rhetorical strategies and their effectiveness, but also to expose the problems which the gender construction specifically poses for prophet, deity and audience alike.

In this book, an extensive revision and update of my doctoral dissertation, I will combine discussion of literary and rhetorical theory which illumines this text with detailed analysis of the text itself. The guiding questions for the study as a whole will be: What conventions about gender (both male and female) are brought into play in both the metaphorical and the intertextual aspects of the passage? What is the significance of the shift from husband–wife metaphors to father–son metaphors? How do these shifts reflect the cultural conventions associated with gender? How do the intertexts function rhetorically? What is their power? What gender conventions do the intertexts bring into play?

Before beginning to address these questions, however, it is necessary to deal with three introductory matters which will provide the necessary background to the following analysis: the limits of the passage; the larger context, which sets up the first instance of intertextuality in Jer. 3.1 and introduces the primary metaphors which construct 3.1–4.4; and the overall structure of the unit.

1. *The Limits and Unity of the Passage*

Jeremiah 3.1–4.4 falls within two larger sections: chs. 2–6 and 2.1–4.2/4. Since the time of Bernhard Duhm, most scholars identify Jeremiah 2–6 as a collection of the earliest, genuinely jeremianic material.[2] In terms of

2.   See, for example, Bernhard Duhm, *Das Buch Jeremia* (Tübingen: J.C.B. Mohr [Paul Siebeck], 1901), p. 15; Sigmund Mowinckel, *Zur Komposition des Buches Jeremia* (Norske Videnskapsakademie, Oslo. Hist.-Filos. Klasse, Skrifter 1913, No. 5; Oslo: J. Dybwad, 1914), p. 20—for the earliest scholars to propose this idea. Other early scholars in this line are F. Hitzig, *Der Prophet Jeremiah* (Leipzig: Weidmannsche Buchhandlung, 1841), pp. x, 8, 25; Heinrich Ewald, *Die Propheten des Alten Bundes* (Göttingen: Vandenhoeck & Ruprecht, 2nd edn, 1868 [1841]), II, p. 69; Karl Heinrich Graf, *Der Prophet Jeremia* (Leipzig: T.O. Weigel, 1862), p. 54; and C.F. Keil, *The Prophecies of Jeremiah* (2 vols.; Edinburgh: T. & T. Clark, 1873), I, p. 21. Accepting uncritically the historicity of the so-called biographical sections of Jeremiah, and on the basis of the content of those sections, scholars since the time of Duhm have tried to reconstruct the original words of Jeremiah which appeared on the *Urrolle* destroyed by King Jehoiakim as well as the second scroll, both mentioned in Jer. 36. W. Rudolph, in his classic commentary (*Jeremia* [HAT, 12; Tübingen: J.C.B. Mohr (Paul Siebeck),

content, however, chs. 2–6 are usually divided into two units: (1) 2.1–4.2/4; and (2) 4.3/5–6.30, the latter of which William L. Holladay classifies as the 'foe from the north' cycle.[3] Jeremiah 3.1–4.4 falls within the former division: 2.1–4.2/4. The introductory formula of 2.1 clearly indicates the beginning of a new section, as does the change of content and direct address to Israel. Jeremiah 2 sets the reader up for the legal citation and rhetorical questions of 3.1.

Although 3.1–4.4 is a sub-unit of the larger rhetorical unit of 2.1–4.4, there are several reasons to treat ch. 3 separately from ch. 2. The first is formal: Jer. 3.1 begins with לֵאמֹר, which a majority of scholars sees as a truncated introductory formula.[4] On the basis of the formal similarities between Jer. 3.1 and Hag. 2.11,[5] I prefer to read לֵאמֹר as it stands, as an indicator of a citation. Nevertheless, the word itself indicates a division between what precedes and what follows. An even more convincing reason for seeing 3.1–4.4 as separate from ch. 2 is the way in which 3.1-5, rather than ch. 2, functions in governing the whole of 3.1–4.4. Jeremiah 3 contains the actual quotation and the metaphorical basis for the following appeals. Moreover, the chapter revolves around the question raised by vv. 1-5—namely: Can YHWH take Israel back?—as well as the related question, if YHWH can take Israel back, what are the conditions for such a return? In short, the rhetorical argument of 3.1–4.4 is determined by the rhetorical question and metaphors of 3.1 rather than the rhetoric of ch. 2.

3rd edn, 1968], pp. xvii, 1), is one of those who has cemented this view. Following Mowinckel, he categorizes 3.1-5 + 3.19–4.4 as part of 'die Sprüche Jeremias' (p. xiv) and places it in the Urrolle along with 1.4–6.30 (excluding 3.14-18 and 5.18-20, dating the poem itself to the time of Josiah). An exhaustive study of this problem through the early 1960's is that of C. Rietzschl, *Das Problem der Urrolle: Ein Beitrag zur Redaktionsgeschichte des Jeremiabuches* (Gütersloh: Gerd Mohn, 1966). Finally, the recent commentary by William L. Holladay (*Jeremiah 1* [Hermeneia; Philadelphia: Fortress Press, 1986]) is an example of this ongoing search. Holladay presents quite a sophisticated view of the development of Jer. 3. According to him, Jeremiah himself reworked the material in this chapter several times: Jer. 3.1-2, 4-5, 12, 18bβ, 19, 21a, 22-23 was originally addressed to the North; it was subsequently expanded by 3.2ab and 4.3-4 for the *Urrolle* and finally, 3.3 and 20 were added for the second scroll (pp. 63-73). I think that the search for the *Urrolle* is doomed to failure, simply because it is impossible ever to get back to an original author's work and/or intent. Any attempts to do so are inevitably highly speculative.

3.   William J. Holladay, *The Architecture of Jeremiah 1–20* (London: Associated University Press, 1976), pp. 30-34.

4.   See, for example, Rudolph, *Jeremia*, p. 22.

5.   See the discussion in Chapter 1.

While the designation of Jer. 3.1 as the starting place of the larger unit is relatively straightforward, there is some disagreement over the ending, whether at 4.2 or 4.4. There is universal agreement, however, that with 4.5 the theme changes dramatically. Those who maintain that the material begun in 3.1 ends with 4.2 usually claim that 4.3-4 serve as the opening to the so-called 'foe cycle' in 4.5–6.30.[6] Others see continuity between 4.1-2 and 4.3-4.[7] Formally, there is a division between vv. 2 and 3: an introductory formula. Yet there are some important reasons for maintaining that 4.3-4 should be included as the conclusion to the material begun in 3.1. First, 4.3-4 elaborates and radicalizes the conditions for return given in 4.1-2. Moreover, the circumcision imagery of 4.3-4 fits most closely with the citation of the promise to Abraham from Genesis in 4.1-2, since circumcision is the sign of that promise. Finally, v. 4b emphasizes once again what has been emphasized throughout the passage, namely, the conditional nature of God's promise to take Israel back. In its context, v. 4b also serves as a transition to the threatening oracles of 4.5–6.30.

In terms of the text's unity, redactional approaches have to this point dominated scholarship, the most recent example being that of Mark Biddle, *A Redaction History of Jeremiah 2.1–4.2*.[8] While the central questions governing my study necessitate a different approach, that is, one which treats the larger unit as a whole, these studies have nevertheless been important for showing how Jer. 3.1–4.4 is actually a multi-layered text. Such studies correctly indicate that there are 'voices' from several historical periods contributing to the final form of the text. Yet, *contra* Duhm *et al.*, those voices are not simply strung together.[9] Rather, taking into consideration the insights of those such as Paul Volz, who look for meaning and

---

6.   See, e.g., Hitzig, *Der Prophet Jeremia*, p. 25; Keil, *The Prophecies of Jeremiah*, I, p. 21; and Jeremiah Unterman, *From Repentance to Redemption: Jeremiah's Thought in Transition* (JSOTSup, 54; Sheffield: JSOT Press, 1987).

7.   Cf. Rudolph, *Jeremia*, p. xiv; and J.G. McConville, *Judgment and Promise: An Interpretation of the Book of Jeremiah* (Winona Lake, IN: Eisenbrauns, 1993), pp. 27-41. Carl Heinrich Cornill also sees an integral connection between 4.3-4 and 3.19-25. He argues that YHWH's answer to 3.19-25 is only found in 4.3-4 (*Das Buch Jeremia* [Leipzig: Chr. Herm. Tauchnitz, 1905], p. 45).

8.   Mark Biddle, *A Redaction History of Jeremiah 2.1–4.2* (ATANT, 77; Zürich: Theologischer Verlag, 1990).

9.   Assuming that the original oracles were very short, Duhm characterizes Jer. 2.1–4.4, with the exception of 2.4-13, 3.6-12a, 14-18, and a few smaller additions, as 'ein Serie von eng mit einander verbundenen kleinen Dichtungen Jeremias…die sämtlich in demselben Metrum geschrieben sind und in vortrefflicher Disposition Ein Thema behandeln' (*Das Buch Jeremia*, p. 15).

coherence in longer sections of the text,[10] this study will presuppose such a coherence between sections.

In terms of contextualizing Jer. 3.1–4.4, the work of Rudolph Smend is also particularly helpful. Smend's summary of Jeremiah's prophecy and his discussion of the book is structured primarily around the content of chs. 2 and 3, where he also makes the initial connection (which has often been noticed since Smend's time) between chs. 3 and chs. 30 and 31.[11] He suggests different viewpoints for this similar material, with ch. 3 looking forward and chs. 30–31 responding to the past. According to Smend, ch. 3 (with the exception of 3.14-18) addresses future events and portrays the fate of Judah as conditional. In contrast, the entire argument of chs. 30–31 presupposes the exile and discusses YHWH's re-establishment of Judah and Jerusalem through conquering Judah's enemies.[12] Although he does not go

---

10. Paul Volz, *Der Prophet Jeremia* (KAT, 10; Leipzig: A. Deichertsche Verlagsbuchhandlung, 2nd edn, 1928 [1920]), p. xxxiv. His notion that the prophets were writing prophets and not simply oral communicators has been taken up in recent scholarship, most notably in *Swallowing the Scroll: Textuality and the Dynamics of Discourse in Ezekiel's Prophecy* (JSOTSup, 78; Bible and Literature Series, 21; Sheffield: Almond Press, 1989], pp. 29-45, in which Ellen Davis raises the issue of the relationship between oral and written material in the prophets. In her second chapter, Davis deals with the development of prophetic speech from oral to written forms. Specifically, she maintains that Ezekiel was the first prophet to use primarily written forms of communication (p. 39). However, she suggests that prophets began to use a combination of written and oral speech as early as Isaiah (p. 38). On this basis, and for several other reasons as well, much of what Davis says could be applied to Jeremiah (see especially her discussion of van der Ploeg, p. 39). For instance, she cites several anthropological and archaeological studies which suggest that the Israelite and Mesopotamian societies of the seventh and sixth centuries BCE were essentially literate societies, which would lend credence to the application of her thesis to Jeremiah. Within the book of Jeremiah itself there are also some indications that written communication was used alongside verbal communication (cf. ch. 36, his letters to the exiles in chs. 27–29, etc.). Thus, I agree with Davis that writing could have begun early, and therefore propose that we need to rethink the long-held presupposition of the prophets as producers of very short, undeveloped oracles.

11. Rudolf Smend, *Lehrbuch der Alttestamentlichen Religionsgeschichte* (Freiburg: J.C.B. Mohr, 2nd edn, 1899), pp. 244-53.

12. Debate has long raged over the respective dates of Jer. 3 and 30–31, with scholars dividing into two general groups: (1) those dating the 'original' portions of both to Jeremiah and positing a pre-exilic timeframe (exactly which verses of each are 'original' differs from scholar to scholar); and (2) those dating the majority of ch. 3 to pre-exilic times, while dating chs. 30–31 to the exile and positing a different author.

so far as to say that chs. 30–31 are a reinterpretation of ch. 3, his discussion foreshadows such a view.

Smend's astute literary characterization is also helpful in thinking about the structure of the book as a whole. I agree with Smend that there is likely both early and later material in chs. 3 and 30–31, and that their final forms took shape in the exilic period. Yet his insight raises questions as to whether two similar collections of oracles were placed in different literary and rhetorical contexts as a structuring mechanism for the book. If so, their use in two such disparate contexts also reveals the equal applicability of a similar message to two different historical/political situations.[13] Smend's work thus raises the issue of intertextuality (or intratextuality) within the book of Jeremiah itself. Additionally, it emphasizes ways in which the voices in the book as a whole are in dialogue with each other.

While relying on the insight that there are various voices from different dates incorporated into Jer. 3.1–4.4, my main concern, however, is not redactional; that is, my focus is not on the separation and dating of those voices. Rather, my concern lies with investigating how the various voices contained in the 3.1–4.4 are in dialogue with each other—how, for instance, the exilic voice in 3.14-18 engages the earlier verses, builds on previous interpretation and provides a reinterpretation for a different historical situation. Thus, developing a line of thought hinted at in Smend's work, I will be reading 3.1–4.4 as a coherent multi-layered unit.

2. The Context: Jeremiah 2

If Jer. 3.1–4.4 is a complex unit, its integral relationship to ch. 2 nevertheless needs to be addressed, since it sets the stage for 3.1–4.4 in several ways. An outline of ch. 2 will help to provide a framework for the discussion of each of these context-setting features. The chapter can be divided into five parts: (1) vv. 1-3 (Israel's faithfulness in the wilderness); (2) vv. 4-13 (Israel's religious disloyalty); (3) vv. 14-19 (Israel's political disloyalty); (4) vv. 20-28 (a return to Israel's religious disloyalty); and (5) vv. 29-37, (a return to Israel's political disloyalty). As can be seen from this outline, vv. 4-37 contrast the people's present behavior with their original loyalty (חסד) at the time YHWH established his[14] covenant relationship with them.

---

13. I will deal with this idea in greater detail in my analysis of Jer. 3.14-18.

14. As will be shown below, YHWH is consistently pictured in male terms and as a male deity in the text of Jeremiah. Hence the term, 'his'.

The above designation, 'Israel', is problematic throughout Jer. 2.1–4.4; therefore a few words need to be said regarding how this work will be using the term. J.G. McConville rightly notes 'how elusive the idea of Israel is in the rhetoric' of Jeremiah 2.[15] At times it seems as if Israel means the historic people, that is, the term incorporates both the previous Northern Kingdom and present-day Judah (e.g. vv. 6-7, 21). McConville argues that this identification predominates in the chapter: 'the Judah that is addressed by Jeremiah can be seen as an embodiment of the historic people, and that indeed is one of the burdens of the chapter'.[16] However, there are a few places where Israel and Judah are differentiated, for example, vv. 14-18, 36. Here the interpretation is connected with the identification of Assyria. McConville's conclusion is the one adopted here, namely, that the Assyria to which the text alludes is not merely metaphorical, but is the former empire which conquered the Northern Kingdom, Israel. In this case the references to Israel serve a specific purpose for a pre-exilic Judean audience: 'It is the actual memory of past discomfiture through falsely placed trust in Empire which gives force to the warning not to make the same mistake again'.[17]

The same issue arises in connection with Jer. 3.6-11 where the two kingdoms, personified as two sisters, are differentiated for similar reasons to those proposed by McConville for Jeremiah 2: the former Northern Kingdom is presented as a bad example which Judah should cease following.[18] For the purposes of this study, with the exception of the discussion of 3.6-11, 'Israel' will refer to the historic designation which encompasses both the Northern Kingdom and Judah. Here, then, is one link between ch. 2 and 3.1–4.4. There are others as well.

Jeremiah 2 creates the context for 3.1–4.4 in the following ways: furnishing a disputational backdrop which sets up the legal citation in 3.1, establishing a link between Israel's behavior and the land, introducing the primary metaphors with which 3.1–4.4 will play, and presenting the discourses[19] against which Jeremiah is preaching. In addition, two rhetorical

15. McConville, *Judgment and Promise*, p. 33.

16. McConville, *Judgment and Promise*, p. 29.

17. McConville, *Judgment and Promise*, p. 31. For a thorough discussion of the various positions which commentators take on this issue, see pp. 29-33.

18. See the full discussion in Chapter 3.

19. Following Bruce Lincoln, I define discourse as any use of language, written or verbal, which assumes a speaker and a hearer, in which the speaker intends to influence the hearer. Any discourse is inherently rhetorical: it persuades the audience toward one version of reality over others. My definition of discourse is intentionally broad, and

devices used in 3.1–4.4 are introduced in ch. 2: argument from absurdity, which portrays the people's behavior as unnatural, and rhetoric using images of overstepped boundaries.

The first of these context-setting features requires further elaboration. The juridical context is visible through the form of Jeremiah 2: that of a disputation (רִיב, v. 9), specifically YHWH's covenantal dispute against Israel. On the basis of supposed legal connotations of the root רִיב (cf. Jer. 2.9), it has been generally accepted that 2.4-37 takes the form of a lawsuit.[20] More recently, however, Michael de Roche has argued persuasively that 'lawsuit' does not accurately reflect the type of interactions involved between the two parties in the 'contention' (רִיב).[21] Rather, his designation, 'disputation', acknowledges the fact that a contention between two parties need not be decided in a courtroom situation, and takes into account that no such situation may be assumed in any of the so-called 'רִיב oracles'.[22] Whether one presumes a courtroom situation or not, however, there are strong marks of a serious dispute between two parties in Jeremiah 2: YHWH and Israel. Jeremiah 2 thus establishes the larger, disputational perspective for the following chapter, and the citation of a law in 3.1 situates 3.1–4.4 within that context.

allows for a variety of types or modes of discourse to be present in any given social setting. When I talk about the discourses against which the prophet is speaking I am indicating not only the behaviors against which the prophet preaches, but also the rhetoric behind those behaviors. For a more complete description of discourse and its functions see Bruce Lincoln, *Discourse and the Construction of Society* (New York: Oxford University Press, 1989), esp. pp. 3-11; and Fred W. Burnett, 'Postmodern Biblical Exegesis: The Eve of Historical Criticism', in Gary A. Phillips (ed.), *Post-Structural Criticism and the Bible: Text/History/Discourse* (Semeia, 51; Atlanta: Scholars Press, 1990), pp. 51-80 (65-66).

20. Cf. H.B. Huffmon, 'The Covenant Lawsuit in the Prophets', *JBL* 78 (1959), pp. 285-95. Cf. also Rudolph, *Jeremia*, pp. 13-23; A. Weiser, *Der Prophet Jeremiah* (ATD, 20/21; Göttingen: Vandenhoeck & Ruprecht, 1960), pp. 11-23.

21. Michael de Roche, 'YHWH's *Rîb* against Israel: A Reassessment of the So-Called "Prophetic Lawsuit" in the Preexilic Prophets', *JBL* 102 (1983), pp. 563-74. Note that Dwight R. Daniels takes de Roche's argument one step further, arguing that there should not even be a genre designated 'prophetic lawsuit' ('Is there a "Prophetic Lawsuit" Genre?', *ZAW* 99 [1987], pp. 339-60).

22. De Roche defines the difference between a רִיב and a lawsuit in the following manner: 'a *rîb* is a contention, while a lawsuit is a particular way of solving a contention. The important mark that distinguishes the lawsuit from the other means of solving a *rîb* is the function of a third party as a binding arbiter' ('YHWH's *Rîb* against Israel', p. 569). See pp. 569-70 for his discussion of Jer. 2 in particular.

Through a series of images, each heaped upon the next, the text of ch. 2 portrays YHWH's innocence and the people's guilt. The rhetorical effect of the dispute is to convince the reader that Israel is guilty. By the time the reader of Jeremiah reads the questions of 3.1, which imply that Israel wishes 'to return' to YHWH, the impossibility of such return is well-grounded. The citation of the law makes explicit what is implicit in ch. 2 —according to the law as applied to the metaphorical relationship between YHWH and Israel, YHWH cannot take Israel back. To anticipate the discussion of 3.1–4.4, the rest of ch. 3 then takes up the question of the law: Does the law, in metaphorical terms, really apply to relations between YHWH and Israel? Is there any possibility that, contrary to law, YHWH can take Israel back? And finally, under what circumstances could YHWH allow Israel to return?

The second important connection between 2.4-13 and 3.1–4.4 is the importance of the land. With regard to 2.7, Walter Brueggemann has pointed out that where 'YHWH's action leaves the land fruitful and good, Israel's action leaves it defiled and abominable'.[23] Jeremiah 3.1-5 picks up this theme, developing and deepening the significance of those connections. Together with the legal context of ch. 2, the legal citation of 3.1, which makes reference to the defilement of the land as the direct result of Israel's actions, has much greater force.

Jeremiah 2 also introduces some of the key metaphors that will be used extensively in ch. 3.[24] The first of these is the metaphor of marriage describing the relationship between YHWH and Israel (2.2). While the very citation of a law related to marriage and divorce (3.1) raises the issue of behavior within a marital relationship, the idea of a marital relationship itself has already been introduced in 2.2: 'I remember the devotion (חֶסֶד) of your youth, your love as a bride, how you followed me in the wilderness, in a land not sown'. The second central metaphor, that of Israel as adulterous wife or harlot, is introduced in 2.20. After a series of images showing how Israel has been unfaithful to YHWH, v. 20 explicitly connects Israel's behavior to gender and sexuality through the metaphor of harlotry: 'On every high hill and under every green tree you sprawled and played

23. Walter Brueggemann, 'Israel's Sense of Place in Jeremiah', in J.J. Jackson and M. Kessler (eds.), *Rhetorical Criticism: Essays in Honor of James Muilenberg* (Pittsburgh: Pickwick Press, 1974), pp. 149-65 (152).

24. For a good description of the gender issues at play in Jer. 2, see Angela Bauer, *Gender in the Book of Jeremiah: A Feminist-Literary Reading* (New York: Peter Lang, 1999), pp. 16-43.

the whore (זנה)'. The combined picture the imagery of Jeremiah 2 presents is that of God, as the husband of Israel, competing against rivals for his wife's allegiance.

In addition to introducing the primary metaphors with which Jer. 3.1–4.4 will play, ch. 2 introduces the behaviors (and their underlying discourses) against which the text inveighs. The two primary behaviors are worship of foreign gods (vv. 4-13, 20-28) and making foreign alliances (vv. 14-19, 29-37). A third, related to the other two and cutting across discussions of both, is the lack of social justice on the part of Israel's leaders (vv. 33-34). Although this third behavior receives less emphasis than the first two, it is nonetheless important for a full understanding of 3.1–4.4. The issues of justice (משׁפט) and righteousness (צדקה) appear again in 4.1-4, and will be explored in more detail in the discussion of those verses. The negative consequences of all three activities fall primarily into two spheres, economic (lack of profit or prosperity) and political (destruction), although the cosmic sphere is also represented in Jer. 3.3, in which drought is the result of political and social behavior.[25]

Still another connection between Jeremiah 2 and 3.1–4.4 is a general rhetorical strategy introduced in ch. 2 which pits 'natural' against 'unnatural' behavior. John Barton discusses the ways 'Prophetic rhetoric is designed…to make the contingencies of human history look like divine necessities'.[26] As Barton rightly points out, it was a common view in the ancient Near East that the gods controlled prosperity or destruction of nations.[27] He argues, however, that the prophets' unique contribution was in presenting a coherent and persuasive theological justification of political events, which then implicated peoples' behavior. In other words, the prophets' art lay in being able to portray the people's sins as leading 'inevitably, even obviously, to the disaster which they are sure (on quite other grounds) will fall on the nation'.[28] He discusses four strategies which the prophets used to accomplish this objective, one of which is especially relevant for Jeremiah, that of portraying the people's behavior as offending the natural order. Barton says of Jeremiah that 'The tendency in his

25. Cf. 4.23-28, which depict a systematic reversal of creation as a result of the people's actions.

26. John Barton, 'History and Rhetoric in the Prophets', in Martin Warner (ed.), *The Bible as Rhetoric: Studies in Biblical Persuasion and Credibility* (London: Routledge, 1990), p. 52.

27. Barton, 'History and Rhetoric', p. 56.

28. Barton, 'History and Rhetoric', p. 58.

day to worship gods other than Y<small>HWH</small>, which we now know was not
widely felt to be wrong in pre-exilic Judah, *he* presents as a ludicrous
breach of every natural sense of loyalty, even as an offense against common sense...'[29]

I fully agree with Barton's assessment of the prophets in general and of
Jeremiah in particular. As already mentioned, the rhetoric of Jeremiah 2 is
directed primarily against two major behaviors, worship of other gods
(2.9-13) and making foreign alliances (2.18). In 2.10-12 the author appeals
to what is natural or 'common-sense' in asking whether any other nation
would exchange their gods for what are not gods. Verse 28 cuts to the heart
of the matter: 'Where are your gods that you made for yourself? Let them
rise up, if they can save you, in your time of trouble; for you have as many
gods as you have towns, O Judah.' The implication is that it is unnatural
and absurd to worship these gods 'that are not gods', for such 'gods' have
no power.

In a similar manner, 2.18-19 implies that political alliances are not only
ineffective, but are actually infidelity to Y<small>HWH</small>. Following directly on the
assertion that Y<small>HWH</small> is the only source of living water is a section dealing
with foreign interventions in Israel. The climax of this section is 2.18-19:
'Why do you go to Egypt to drink the waters of the Nile? Or why do you
go to Assyria to drink the waters of the Euphrates?... Know and see that it
is evil and bitter for you to forsake Y<small>HWH</small> your God.' By implication,
drinking the waters of the Nile or the Euphrates is no substitute for the
spring of living water. Therefore, as with the argument against worship of
foreign gods, underlying this rhetoric is the idea that the way in which
Israel has gone about making foreign alliances is unnatural or absurd, and
that, moreover, such alliances constitute infidelity to Y<small>HWH</small>. Verses 36-37
conclude with the ineffectiveness of foreign alliances to bring the people
prosperity or security: 'you shall be put to shame by Egypt as you were
put to shame by Assyria...for Y<small>HWH</small> has rejected those in whom you trust,
and you will not prosper through them'. The only true alliance is with
Y<small>HWH</small>, and it is only this 'natural' alliance that has the power to save and
protect.

The third issue, social justice/injustice, receives like treatment; in v. 34
the accusation includes allusions to justice issues: 'on your skirts is found
the lifeblood of the innocent poor; you did not find them [the innocent
poor] breaking in'. While it would be a natural expectation for the poor to

29. Barton, 'History and Rhetoric', p. 59. Some of the passages he cites occur in
Jeremiah 2 (i.e. vv. 11, 32). He also cites 5.20-23; 8.7; 18.14.

'break in', it is the political and religious leadership who have actually acted as thieves. The metaphor of a thief is used directly in relation to the political and religious leaders in v. 26: 'As a thief is put to shame when caught, so shall the house of Israel be put to shame, they, their kings, their officials, their priests, and their prophets'. Here, as in the above examples, the actions of Israel in relation to the poor are portrayed as going against God's order;[30] even though the poor constituted no threat, the leaders of Israel have acted unjustly in relation to them.

In each of the above cases, the audience's behavior is seen to be offending the 'natural order'. While Barton does mention a few of the comparisons discussed above, he mentions neither the marital/sexual imagery in Jeremiah, nor the integral connection of the rhetoric of 2.1–4.4 with gender. Yet, when one looks closely at the text, the principal vehicle used to discuss the opposing discourses is gendered imagery. Moreover, the power of using sexual imagery in particular, as these chapters do, is that the conventions governing gender and sexuality are almost always taken as a given in any culture—as natural. Accordingly, I will take Barton's argument one step further and apply it specifically to the gendered imagery in 3.1–4.4. To anticipate the discussion below, just as the other metaphors in ch. 2 portray the people's behavior as offending the natural order, I will argue that the gendered imagery itself functions in much the same way, and that this natural/unnatural opposition is one of the factors at the root of the ways in which the gendered imagery changes in 3.1–4.4.

A final connection between Jeremiah 2 and 3.1–4.4, linked both to the natural/unnatural opposition and to the gendered imagery of 3.1–4.4, is overstepped boundaries. While God identifies Israel in the wilderness as a faithful wife in 2.2, Israel's behavior has crossed over the line in 2.5: 'What wrong did your ancestors find in me that they went far from me and went after worthless things (הַהֶבֶל)...' The rest of the chapter takes up the issue of the 'worthless things'. Overstepped marital boundaries are evoked for the first time in v. 20: 'On every high hill and under every green tree you sprawled and played the whore'. This imagery is coupled with other images of overstepped boundaries: 'long ago you broke your yoke and burst your bonds' (v. 20). The images of broken boundaries multiply in the rest of the chapter: the choice vine planted by YHWH that has become wild (v. 21); the wild ass in heat whose unrestrained lust emphasizes the lack of sexual boundaries (v. 24); the thief who will be shamed when caught

---

30. Cf. Deut. 24.14-15, 17-22. See also Deut. 10.17-19.

(v. 26); and the promiscuous woman who has something to teach the prostitute: 'How well you direct your way to seek love, so that you even teach wicked women your ways' (v. 33).[31] It is precisely this image of Israel as the wife who has overstepped the boundaries which is exploited in 3.1–4.4.[32]

In addition to the above connections between Jeremiah 2 and 3.1–4.4, there is also a common issue of the gender of the identifications of Jerusalem and Israel. John Schmitt[33] would have it that the feminine language in ch. 2 refers to Jerusalem (cf. 2.1), while the masculine language refers to Israel (who according to him is always referred to as masculine).[34] Schmitt claims 'that the editors purposively structured the passage, identifying the figures with their respective gender and number in the beginning and elsewhere as necessary'.[35] He goes on to say, 'The effect the editors intended is lost if the care they took with the grammar is not observed. Israel is clearly masculine singular in every grammatical form referring to Israel in this chapter of Jeremiah'.[36] Although I agree that the grammatical terms directly connected with 'Israel' in ch. 2 are masculine, this claim alone does not justify a differentiation in terms of imagery. To argue that the text refers to Israel every time the masculine is used in ch. 2, while the text refers to Jerusalem every time the feminine is used, is to miss the rhetorical effect of the language. The shifts themselves indicate that

31. The NRSV reads 'lovers' for אהבה ('How well you direct your course to seek lovers!') while I translate 'love'. Nowhere else in the Hebrew Bible does אהבה refer to objects of love (i.e. lovers). Moreover, the parallelism here argues for a meaning referring to sexual practices, not sexual partners.

32. The female 'you' of the discourse is differentiated from the 'wicked women' (i.e. prostitutes, who are conceived of as wicked and are treated as outcasts in patriarchal society, but who are nevertheless an accepted part of the social structure, illustrating the double standard inherent in patriarchy). The differentiation emphasizes the status of the 'you' as wife. See Phyllis Bird, '"To Play the Harlot": An Inquiry into an Old Testament Metaphor', in Peggy L. Day (ed.), *Gender and Difference in Ancient Israel* (Minneapolis: Fortress Press, 1989), pp. 75-94. Gale Yee has discussed the double standard inherent in patriarchy in 'Spreading Your Legs to Anyone Who Passed: The Pornography of Ezekiel 16' (unpublished paper presented at the 1990 Annual Meeting of the SBL in New Orleans), p. 20.

33. John J. Schmitt, 'The Gender of Ancient Israel', *JSOT* 26 (1983), pp. 115-25, and 'Israel and Zion—Two Gendered Images: Biblical Speech Traditions and their Contemporary Neglect', *Horizons* 18.1 (1991), pp. 18-32.

34. See especially, Schmitt, 'Gender', p. 122, and 'Israel and Zion', pp. 22-23.

35. Schmitt, 'Gender', p. 122.

36. Schmitt, 'Gender', p. 122.

Jerusalem and Israel are parallel (as they are implicitly in 2.1-3), that they are both names for the same entity, whether one calls that entity 'the people', 'Jerusalem' or 'Israel'.[37] Once this pairing has occurred in the reader's mind, 'Israel' shares in the 'feminine' language of vv. 16-25 and 32-37, just as 'Jerusalem' shares in the 'masculine' language of vv. 4-15 and 26-31.

The clearest instance of such a parallel is in the switch to feminine imagery and address in 2.17, where there is no corresponding shift in name (neither Israel nor Jerusalem are connected directly with this imagery here). This pairing would lead the reader to equate *both* Jerusalem and the house of Israel (as representatives of the same political and religious entity, including all the inhabitants of the country) with a promiscuous wife. In fact, such slippage in gender categories may be deliberate given the ironic accusation that the leaders have even mixed up the gender of the gods they worship (cf. v. 27).

A more serious problem occurs with reference to 'Turning Back Israel' (משבה ישראל) in Jer. 3.6-11. Arguing from the premise that reading Israel as feminine here 'would offend against the proposed universal rule that the noun Israel is masculine and its adjectives are masculine',[38] Schmitt suggests that the terms 'Apostasy' (משבה) and 'The Faithless One' (בגודה) originally referred to cities, and that 'they were both later identified with the northern and southern kingdom'.[39] Such an assertion, however, fails to deal with the text as it now appears. Moreover, his argumentation itself is circular and Schmitt gives no evidence for an 'original' reference to cities in this text. This case alone (perhaps along with 2 Sam. 17.21 and 24.9, which pair a feminine verb with 'Israel', two cases which he dismisses as 'errors' based on the fact that 1 Chron. 21.5 changes the latter to masculine),[40] indicate the necessity of a re-examination of the claim that 'Israel is never addressed in the Bible in feminine forms'.[41] While in principle I agree with Schmitt's argument for the necessity of the need for adherence to the gender of translation,[42] his particular emphasis on Israel in the prophets is consistently overstated.

37. See my discussion and conclusions regarding the identification of 'Israel' above for further evidence for this stance.
38. Schmitt, 'Gender', p. 122.
39. Schmitt, 'Gender', p. 123.
40. Schmitt, 'Israel and Zion', p. 19 n. 5.
41. Schmitt, 'Israel and Zion', p. 20.
42. Cf. Schmitt, 'Gender', pp. 123-25, and 'Israel and Zion', pp. 26-28.

As one can see from the above discussion, Jeremiah 2 introduces all three rhetorical strategies used extensively in 3.1–4.4. The legal disputation in ch. 2 sets up the citation of the law which is the primary instance of intertextuality in 3.1–4.4. The metaphors themselves set up the marital imagery through which Israel's relationship to YHWH will be played out in much of ch. 3. Finally, as will be shown, the ways in which gender is used to construct the text of 3.1–4.4 reinforce and extend the natural/unnatural comparisons and the concept of overstepped boundaries contained in ch. 2; these comparisons and images are in turn keys to understanding the changes in gendered imagery in 3.1–4.4.

3. *Structure*

Having discussed the context of Jer. 3.1–4.4 and its integral connections with the preceding chapter, it remains to give an overview of its structure. Jeremiah 3.1-5, with the citation of the law and the metaphorical basis for the following appeals, is the springboard for the entire mosaic unit. The writer announces judgment by way of applying a legal citation to the metaphorical relationship between YHWH and Israel and then overturns the law to show the radical nature of YHWH's yearning for and commitment to Israel. Jeremiah 3.6-10(11) sets the stage for this rhetorical overturning. The climax, the reversal, is reached in vv. 12-13, and is followed by an appeal to return (vv. 14-18). Verse 18 concludes with a picture of the ideal: a united kingdom gathered together along with all the other nations to YHWH's name in Jerusalem. Jeremiah 3.19–4.4 then presents a second appeal, to some extent mirroring, but also extending, that of 3.1-18. Verses 19-20 begin by restating the issue raised in 3.1-5. The text then moves into a dialogue/liturgy of repentance (vv. 21-25). In a sense this dialogue 'specifies the reader'.[43] As G. Clifford puts it:

> if the author believes that his readers can be changed and made wiser by the
> meaning of his work, then one of the most effective ways for him to
> demonstrate this is to show his heroes transformed by their experience of
> the action upon which the meaning depends.[44]

43. The phrase is that of Harry P. Nasuti, in 'Identity, Identification, and Imitation: The Narrative Hermeneutics of Biblical Law', *Journal of Law and Religion* 4 (1986), pp. 9-23. His work will be discussed in detail in Chapter 1.

44. G. Clifford, *Transformations of Allegory* (London: Routledge & Kegan Paul, 1974), p. 29.

The dialogue between YHWH and the people is just such a demonstration—the people are imaged as returning through a liturgy placed in their own mouths. This portrayal of transformation then serves as the foundation for the conditions of return (4.1-4). Thus this section as a whole (3.19–4.4) reveals what is needed to bring the ideal situation depicted in 3.14-18 within the realm of reality.

Since the shifts in address conform roughly to the overall structure of the passage, and since these shifts are important for the subsequent discussion, it will also be helpful to chart them here:

3.1-5:	2nd fem. sing.
3.6-11:	3rd fem. sing.
3.12-13:	2nd fem. sing.
3.14-18:	2nd masc. plur.
3.19-20:	2nd fem. sing.
3.21-25; 4.1-4:	2nd masc. plur.

Jeremiah 3.1a begins with a legal citation in third-person language: 'If a man divorces his wife…', but in v. 1b moves immediately into accusation using second feminine singular address ('But you [fem. sing.] have played the whore…'). This form of address continues until v. 6, where 'Turning Back' Israel and 'Treachery' Judah are discussed in third person feminine language. After the third person portrayal of the sisters in vv. 6-11, v. 12 contains an appeal directed to 'Turning Back' Israel using the feminine singular form of address. This form of address continues through v. 13. Verses 14-18, the ideal picture of what repentance would mean, introduce second masculine plural address for the first time in the chapter. Here, in keeping with the vision of a historical future, the text is addressed to the actual primary audience of the entire piece, the men of Israel.

The second half of Jer. 3.1–4.4 mirrors the first, with the exception of the discussion of Israel and Judah in third person. Verses 19-20, which restate the situation of 3.1-5, return to second feminine singular address. The remainder of the chapter, and 4.1-4, which, following an appeal to return (2nd masc. plur.), focuses on repentance and the conditions of that repentance, contains exclusively the second masculine plural form of address. The change of address represents a dramatic metaphorical shift: the people of Israel are sons to God the father/patriarch.

In light of the above discussion, the basic structure of Jer. 3.1–4.4 (including the shifts in address) may be sketched as follows:

I. 3.1-18
   A. 3.1-5: Indictment against Judah
      1. v. 1: Legal citation and rhetorical questions (2nd fem. sing.)
      2. vv. 2-5: Indictment
   B. 3.6-13: Development of the Indictment against Judah
      1. vv. 6-10: Comparison of Judah and Israel (3rd fem. sing.)
      2. v. 11: Basis for appeal to north
      3. vv. 12-13: Appeal to the north (2nd fem. sing.)
   C. 3.14-18: The Ideal Results (2nd masc. plur.)
      1. v. 14: Return to Zion
      2. v. 15: Installation of proper leaders
      3. vv. 16-17: Restoration of land and cult
      4. v. 18: Reunification of Israel and Judah

II. 3.19–4.4
   A. 3.19-20: Restatement of 3.1-5
      1. v. 19: YHWH's restatement of the situation of 3.1-5 (2nd fem. sing.)
      2. v. 20: Indictment
   B. 3.21-25: Dialogue/Liturgy of Repentance (2nd masc. plur.)
      1. v. 21: Cry of the people
      2. v. 22a: YHWH's invitation
      3. vv. 22b-25: People's response
   C. 4.1-4: The Conditions for Return
      1. vv. 1-2: The required attitude
      2. vv. 3-4: The required behavior

As can be seen from the above structure, the question raised in Jer. 3.1—namely, whether YHWH can take the people back—is dealt with from a number of perspectives throughout the piece; in one way or another the remainder of the passage deals with this question, as do the rhetorical strategies used to persuade the audience that the change of behavior advocated through the specific answer is crucial to Israel's future.

4. Plan

This study will discuss each section of Jer. 3.1–4.4 in turn. The first two chapters will examine 3.1-5, the focal piece of the extended unit. In both chapters, 3.1-5 will be discussed primarily through the lens of the rhetoric of intertextuality. Chapter 1 will look at these verses in terms of intertextuality as allusion, and will rely principally on the work of three theorists—Mikhail Bakhtin, Julia Kristeva and Jonathan Culler—while Chapter 2 will address these verses through intertextuality as discourse (a broader rhetorical discussion of intertextuality). Intertextuality as allusion deals with the ways in which past texts and traditions are re-shaped and re-used in a new context. Yet some intertexts are not as identifiable as direct allusions, but are actually whole discourses. As rhetoric, the text of 3.1–4.4 engages whole discourses, especially discourses on gender. The dynamic of both forms of intertextuality may be characterized as dialogical. As dialogue, intertextuality does not simply deal with linear tracing of allusions, but deals with a multitude of ways in which texts, traditions, conventions and discourses interact with one another. Since this aspect of intertextuality is an important part of any communication, but more specifically, is integral to the rhetoric of 3.1–4.4, it will be the foundation for the discussion of intertextuality as a whole in the second chapter.

Chapter 3 will begin with a fully developed theoretical section on metaphor. Because I have adopted and used an approach to metaphor which has not yet enjoyed much use in biblical circles, this section is necessary to articulate and defend a functional approach to metaphor. Such an approach views metaphorical meaning as residing in its function within a given text, as opposed to approaches which define metaphor either too narrowly (e.g. as a mere substitution of one thing for another, as a comparison between a literal and figurative meaning, or as a filter through which we see the world) or too broadly (e.g. as being the only way in which we perceive the world). The theoretical basis for the discussion will be the works of David E. Cooper, Donald Davidson and Wayne Booth. This chapter will also argue for a more comprehensive way of dealing with extended metaphors (often dismissed as mere 'allegories'), which will have its direct application in a detailed analysis of the extended metaphor of 3.6-11.

Also in Chapter 3, I will address the intertextual play of Jer. 3.6-11 with Deut. 24.1-4. In addition, picking up on on the idea that Jer. 3.1–4.4 contains several 'voices' in dialogue with each other, I will address the ramifications of such *intra*textuality by reading 3.6-13 as a reinterpretation and extension of 3.1-5. Finally, I will explore intertextuality with culture in these verses, looking particularly at the use of gender conventions as a vital part of the rhetoric of the section. Thus, in this chapter I will be looking at both inter/intratextuality and metaphor as rhetorical devices, again focusing on the roles of author, text and reader in the production of meaning, as well as the ways in which metaphor 'constitutes selves and societies'.[45]

---

45. Wayne C. Booth, 'Metaphor as Rhetoric; The Problem of Evaluation', in Sheldon Sacks (ed.), *On Metaphor* (Chicago: University of Chicago Press, 1978), pp. 47-70 (61).

The climax of the piece occurs in vv. 12-13, in which God overturns the law cited in v. 1 in terms of divine–human relations. This will be the subject of the fourth chapter; as with the previous chapter, it will be structured around intertextuality, metaphor and gender as interweaving rhetorical strategies.

The topic of the fifth chapter will be a discourse analysis of Jer. 3.14-18, revealing the ways in which it enters into dialogue with davidic and Zion theology, and showing how the section fits into the larger rhetorical structure of the unit. In addition, the shift from feminine direct address to masculine direct address will be discussed in terms of its necessity in the overall picture the prophet is developing. Implications of this shift for male and female readers of this text will also be explored.

Jeremiah 3.19-20 opens the second half of the mosaic comprising 3.1–4.4, and will be the focus of the sixth chapter; here I will show how 3.1-5 is restated and reframed in yet other gendered terms (an unusual father–daughter image, and the final switch to masculine imagery). Verses 21-25, the subject of the seventh chapter, will be read through the lens of the rhetoric of gender, dealing specifically with the male–male relational metaphors in the section. Various works of feminist scholarship have influenced these chapters and will find their place in the discussion of these verses.

I will draw all three rhetorical strategies together in the eighth chapter, dealing with the final section of the unit, Jer. 4.1-4. Here I will demonstrate that while intertextuality and metaphor are primary vehicles of persuasion in this text, it is gender which actually constructs the text. Gender, in fact, provides the frame, the warp and woof, and many of the threads of the woven tapestry which comprises 3.1–4.4. A final chapter will draw implications of this analysis for further research.

Chapter 1

INTERTEXTUALITY AS ALLUSION:
A FIRST READING OF JEREMIAH 3.1-5

No text is an island.
—Peter D. Miscall

In order to do justice to both types of intertextuality found in Jer. 3.1-5, in this chapter and the next I will do two 'readings' of the section, one focused on Deut. 24.1-4 as an intertext, and the second having cultural discourse of gender as its intertext. Reading the text in two ways is in keeping with Mikhail Bakhtin's insight that there is never only one way to read a text. Multiple readings may stand side by side. My conviction is that the two readings will complement each other, the second extending and refining the first.

My primary interlocutor for this chapter is Bakhtin, who developed the idea that one text is always engaged in some way, or plays with another text. A second interlocutor will be Julia Kristeva, especially in her early work. In this chapter, I will first introduce the notions of dialogism and interplay between texts and voices as Bakhtin develops them. Then I will examine the primary intertext with which Jer. 3.1-5 plays: Deut. 24.1-4. Finally, I will pull all the threads together in an intertextual reading of Jer. 3.1-5 in light of these earlier sections.

1. *Intertextuality and Mikhail Bakhtin*

The prophets are the patrons, *par excellance*, of intertextuality. The text of Jeremiah in particular seems to be filled with plays on earlier traditions, cultural conventions and direct citations of previous texts. Jeremiah 3.1–4.4 is a primary example. This passage fully illustrates Bakhtin's insight that dialogism, or interplay between texts, is 'a property of *any* discourse'.[1] As

---

1.   Mikhail Bakhtin, 'Discourse in the Novel', in *The Dialogic Imagination* (ed. Michael Holquist, trans. Caryl Emerson and Michael Holquist; Austin: University of Texas Press, 1981), pp. 259-422 (276).

he indicates, language is a site of struggle, an 'agitated and tension-filled environment'[2] which takes place between the author and the author's worldview (her/his historical, political, social background) and that of the reader and the reader's worldview. It is through the multi-faceted dialogue which ensues that meaning is produced. He also argues that, as in living communication, every written utterance is directed toward a listener and anticipates an answer.[3] For the reader of the biblical text, this means that (at least) two readers are at play in the production of meaning: the implied reader, or anticipated audience from the author's own historical/political context, and the contemporary reader/interpreter. He insists, then, on the central importance of the listener and the listener's engagement in dialogue with the text. Although the attempt to reconstruct the implied reader or anticipated audience is often circular, there are usually clues within the text itself as to who that audience is, clues which allow a dialogue between the implied audience and the text. Such clues in Jer. 3.1-5, for example, include the citation of a law in v. 1 and the quoted audience speeches in vv. 4-5. Due to the varieties of dialogue that may ensue, Bakhtin's work emphasizes varieties of interpretation. Thus, there is no *one* possible interpretation of any text, but rather, each reader's historical/political/social situation will determine how one approaches and enters into dialogue with a particular text.[4]

---

2. Bakhtin, 'Discourse', p. 276. He says that 'no living word relates to its object in a *singular* way: between the word and its object, between the word and the speaking subject, there exists an elastic environment of other alien words about the same object, the same theme... It is precisely in the process of living interaction with this specific environment that the word may be individualized and given stylistic shape.

Indeed, any concrete discourse (utterance) finds the object at which it was directed already as it were overlain with qualifications, open to dispute, charged with value, already enveloped in an obscuring mist—or on the contrary, by the "light" of alien words that have already been spoken about it. It is entangled, shot through with shared thoughts, points of view, alien value judgments and accents. The word, directed toward its object, enters a dialogically agitated and tension-filled environment of alien words, value judgments and accents, weaves in and out of complex interrelationships, merges with some, recoils from others, intersects with yet a third group...' (p. 276).

3. Cf. Bakhtin, 'Discourse', pp. 280-82.

4. This idea appears in various forms throughout Bakhtin's work. Perhaps the clearest articulation is in 'Forms of Time and Chronotope in the Novel', in *Dialogic Imagination*, pp. 84-258. Bakhtin writes, 'The work and the world represented in it enter the real world and enrich it, and the real world enters the work and its world as part of the process of its creation, as well as part of its subsequent life, in a continual renewing of the work through the creative perception of listeners and readers. Of

The roles of both author and reader (or speaker and listener) in the dialogue are articulated most clearly by V.N. Vološinov, a contemporary of Bakhtin's, and a member of the literary circle in which Bakhtin developed his ideas. He describes the roles of the author and the listener in the production of meaning as reciprocal. In his view, which elucidates that of Bakhtin, the word or utterance is a bridge, with its two pillars being the speaker and the listener: 'A word is a bridge thrown between myself and another. If one end of the bridge depends on me, then the other depends on my addressee. A word is territory shared by both addresser and addressee, by the speaker and his interlocutor.'[5]

Nowhere is this idea clearer than in Jer. 3.1-5. Jeremiah 3.1 begins with the citation of a law, a law which is also found in Deut. 24.1-4. Here the citation is posed as a rhetorical question:

> 'If a man divorces his wife and she goes from him and becomes another man's wife, can he return to her? Would not such a land be greatly polluted? You have played the whore with many lovers; and yet would you return to me?' says the Lord. (Jer. 3.1)

Jeremiah 3.1 is the pivot of the entire piece; it not only introduces the primary intertext (the law) around which the rest of the chapter will play, it also incorporates within itself elements of dialogue. The use of rhetorical questions specifies a particular audience, one which will answer these questions in a particular way. The continued use of such rhetorical questions throughout the first five verses of ch. 3 functions to create for the present-day reader an ancient dialogue between the prophet and the people; it also has the effect of drawing the contemporary reader into that dialogue. This first set of rhetorical questions also initiates an interplay with cultural conventions having to do with proper gender roles and female sexuality. Jeremiah 3.1 introduces the root metaphor of Israel as wife to God as husband, the strategy of direct address (to a primarily male audience as women, using the second feminine singular form of address), and the play between gender and boundaries. Thus, within the first verse of the

course this process of exchange is itself chronotopic: it occurs first and foremost in the historically developing social world, but without ever losing contact with changing historical space' ('Chronotope', p. 254; see also p. 253). The same sort of idea comes through in 'Discourse' as well (cf. pp. 293, 421). Gary Saul Morson and Caryl Emerson's work also contains a cogent discussion of this aspect of Bakhtin's work (*Mikhail Bakhtin: The Creation of a Prosaics*, pp. 428-29).

5.   V.N. Vološinov, *Marxism and the Philosophy of Language* (trans. L. Mateja and I.R. Titunik; Cambridge, MA: Harvard University Press, 1973), p. 86.

passage both intertextuality of texts and intertextuality of culture are to be found. Moreover, they are interwoven through the remainder of the text.

As mentioned above, Jer. 3.1 is the focal point of the mosaic unit comprising 3.1–4.4. The deuteronomic legal corpus contains a law with many similarities to the citation in Jeremiah, namely, Deut. 24.1-4. Karl Heinrich Graf was the first to notice the relationship between Jer. 3.1 and Deut. 24.1-4.[6] C.F. Keil also mentions this relationship as well as the connection in both texts between the offense depicted in the two texts and its consequences for the land.[7] Since that time there has been ongoing debate regarding the nature of the relationship between the two texts.[8] My own

6.   Graf, *Der Prophet Jeremia*, p. 51. He also begins the debate over the divergent Hebrew and Greek texts. This is one of the many issues in Jeremiah scholarship over which much ink has been spilled. The Septuagint text (G) of Jeremiah is much shorter than the MT, giving rise to the question of priority. The debaters have tended to fall into two camps: (1) those who see the MT as prior and view G as a shortened version of the MT (so Graf, pp. xliv-li); and (2) those who claim that G is prior and view the MT as being expansionistic. More recently it has been argued that there was an early divergence of the G and MT texts, leading to two separate traditions. J. Gerald Janzen (*Studies in the Text of Jeremiah* [HSM, 6; Cambridge, MA: Harvard University Press, 1973], pp. 127-35), for example, has argued for such an early divergence, contending that G has a more accurate Vorlage while the MT represents a recensionist tradition. Sven Soderlund's newer work offers an incisive critique of Janzen's position (*The Greek Text of Jeremiah: A Revised Hypothesis* [JSOTSup, 47; Sheffield: JSOT Press, 1985], pp. 247-48), argues for at least two textual traditions in Jeremiah, and offers a thorough overview of scholarship on the issue.

To return to Jer. 3, however, Graf, in keeping with his view of the priority of the MT, argues on the basis of the connection of Jer. 3.1 with Deut. 24.1-4 that the Septuagint version is incorrect (p. 52). In this regard, he attributes lack of knowledge of the original Hebrew to the translator of the Septuagint (pp. lii-lvi).

7.   Keil, *The Prophecies of Jeremiah*, I, p. 59. This debate began as early as Duhm, who thinks it highly improbable that Jer. 3 and Deut. 24.1-4 had any connection. Wilhelm Erbt, in a publication a year later, citing the numerous parallels between Deut. 24.1-4 and Jer. 3.1, disagrees with Duhm (*Jeremia und seine Zeit: die Geschichte der letzten fünfzig Jahre des vorexilischen Juda* [Göttingen: Vandenhoeck & Ruprecht, 1902], p. 237). The debate has been taken up more recently by J.D. Martin, 'The Forensic Background to Jeremiah III 1', *VT* 19 (1969), pp. 82-92; Henri Cazelles, 'Jeremiah and Deuteronomy', in Leo G. Perdue and Brian W. Kovacs (eds.), *A Prophet to the Nations: Essays in Jeremiah Studies* (Winona Lake, IN: Eisenbrauns, 1984), pp. 89-112; and T.R. Hobbs, 'Jeremiah 3.1-5 and Deuteronomy 24.1-4', *ZAW* 86 (1974), pp. 23-29.

8.   The majority view is that 3.1 is dependent on the law in Deut. 24.1-4. See, e.g., John Bright, *Jeremiah* (AB, 21; Garden City, NY: Doubleday, 1965), p. 23; Cazelles, 'Jeremiah and Deuteronomy', p. 102; Holladay, *Jeremiah 1*, p. 112; J.A. Thompson,

stance is closest to that of J.D. Martin, who argues that whether Jeremiah was dependent on Deut. 24.1-4 or whether he uses an older tradition 'must remain an open question'.[9] Intriguingly, he suggests that if the people had indeed recently heard the law in Deut. 24.1-4 (assuming it was part of the Book of the Law found in 621) with its connection with defilement of land, then the Jeremiah passage would have been all the more effective.[10] Although it is not possible to decide with certainty the question of dependence, one can posit a shared tradition as the background to both. That is the position taken here.

Both Deut. 24.1-4 and Jer. 3.1 take up a law that was presumably well known; but they present that law in differing contexts. Whereas in Jer. 3.1 the law is phrased as a rhetorical question, in Deuteronomy 24 it is included in a legal code. The overarching context of Deuteronomy 24 reveals underlying issues similar to those of Jer. 3.1, issues which are, however, addressed quite differently in Jeremiah 3.[11] It is important for a deeper understanding of 3.1–4.4, therefore, to discuss the law as it occurs in Deuteronomy.

Before doing so, however, it is necessary to look at two aspects of Bakhtin's work which will have a significant impact on how I approach

The Book of Jeremiah (NICOT; Grand Rapids: Eerdmans, 1980), p. 190. The basis for this stance is similarity of vocabulary, although some notable differences are acknowledged (e.g. the use of חנף [Jer. 3.1] instead of טמא or טמא [Deut. 24.1-4]). A more balanced view is represented by Hyatt: 'the similarity of expression in both passages (cf. especially Jer. 3.1b and Deut. 24.1) is close enough to make it probable that Jeremiah knew the passage' (J. Philip Hyatt, 'Jeremiah and Deuteronomy', in Leo G. Perdue and Brian W. Kovacs [eds.], *A Prophet to the Nations: Essays in Jeremiah Studies* [Winona Lake, IN: Eisenbrauns, 1984], pp. 113-27 [120]). He adds, however, that 'Jeremiah is speaking primarily from a moral standpoint and Deuteronomy from a cultic legal standpoint' (p. 120). Another common view is to posit a dependence of Jer. 3.1 on Deut. 24.1-4 but also to state that the Deut. 24 text goes back to an ancient law. See, e.g., Rudolph, *Jeremia*, p. 21.

9. Martin, 'Forensic Background', p. 90.

10. Martin, 'Forensic Background', p. 120.

11. The similarities between the issues dealt with in Deuteronomy and Jeremiah are not so surprising given their shared historical context. Here I adopt the position of Nicholson as modified by Seitz, that there is a close connection between the final form of Jeremiah and the deuteronomistic school. See E.W. Nicholson, *Preaching to the Exiles: A Study of the Prose Tradition in the Book of Jeremiah* (Oxford: Basil Blackwell, 1970), pp. 116-35; and Christopher R. Seitz, *Theology in Conflict: Reactions to the Exile in the Book of Jeremiah* (BZAW, 176; Berlin: W. de Gruyter, 1989), pp. 222-35, as well as the discussion of Jer. 3.6-11 in Chapter 3.

Deut. 24.1-4 in relation to Jer. 3.1-5, namely, context and value. First, Bakhtin argues that 'Discourse lives, as it were, on the boundary between its own context and another, alien, context'.[12] A central aspect of any study of intertextuality, then, will be the interaction between the contexts. Mary Orr puts this idea succinctly:

> Bakhtin's emphasis is on the polyphony of utterance, its position in community, the values implicit in its speech act and historical context. Yet the individuality of the text within its culture and genre is paramount and can be gauged evaluatively... Consequently, it is the context(s) of an intertext which is important for Bakhtin...[13]

Orr's comments also address another issue central to the Bakhtin circle[14] which will also be prominent in the discussion of Deut. 24.1-4 and Jer. 3.1-5, that of value. Due to its dialogical nature, no text is neutral, but embodies and presents a certain socio-historical view. In Pavel Medvedev's formulation,

> Every concrete utterance is a social act... Not only the meaning of the utterance but also the very fact of its performance is of historical and social significance, as, in general, is the fact of its realization in the here and now, in given circumstances, at a certain historical moment, under the conditions of the given social situation.[15]

Likewise, the reader brings a particular socio-historical background to his/her reading of a text. Both of these enter into the dialogue in the produc-

---

12. Bakhtin, 'Discourse', pp. 284, 293-94. The word 'alien' here does not necessarily mean something at odds with the author's thought, but simply means something outside or beyond the author's words themselves. An 'alien' context may indeed be complementary or similar to that of the author. The quote of Orr also addresses the issue of 'alien' contexts.

13. Orr, *Claude Simon*, pp. 80-81.

14. There is ongoing debate regarding the authorship of several works of those who worked in the 'Bakhtin circle'. For example, *The Formal Method in Literary Scholarship: A Critical Introduction to Sociological Poetics* (trans. Albert J. Wehrle; The Goucher College Series; Baltimore: Johns Hopkins University Press, 1978) has been attributed alternatively to Pavel Medvedev, to Bakhtin himself, and to both. Recently, Morson and Emerson have argued persuasively that this book is to be attributed to Medvedev alone, whose work was nevertheless greatly influenced by Bakhtin. They suggest instead that there was a dialogical relationship between Bakhtin's writings and those of the 'Bakhtin circle'. See Morson and Emerson's *Mikhail Bakhtin: The Creation of a Prosaics*, pp. 101-19.

15. Medvedev and Bakhtin(?), *The Formal Method*, p. 120. Cf. Bakhtin, 'Discourse', pp. 293-94.

tion of meaning.[16] The following discussion of Deut. 24.1-4 will give close attention to the twin issues of context and value. For the purposes of this discussion, Deut. 24.1-4 functions as 'already read'.[17]

2. *Deuteronomy 24.1-4*

In its present context, Deut. 24.1-4 stands in a collection of laws covering a wide variety of topics and issues (Deut. 12–26). Moreover, it is set in a wider paranetic context,[18] that of Moses' address and exhortation to the Israelites about to enter the land promised to the patriarchs/matriarchs. This promise connects Deuteronomy to the larger narrative context of Genesis–2 Kings. The broader narrative context is not only implicit but is also made explicit in that, in his address, Moses connects the giving of these laws to the experience of the exodus. Thus, the deuteronomic law is embedded in narrative.

Harry P. Nasuti discusses the importance of the narrative context of all biblical law, suggesting that biblical law is embedded within narrative for a reason: it retards the action of the 'story' and forces the reader to ask not only questions relating to behavior, but also questions regarding identity— Who am I? How am I related to this story? What does this story say about who I should be? His formulation for the function of law within narrative is 'the law specifies the reader';[19] that is, the law specifies the identity and behavior of one who is a proper member of Israelite society.

According to Nasuti, those laws which include identity formulae, for example, those which include the phrase 'for you were sojourners in the land of Egypt' or 'you shall remember you were a slave in Egypt', refer to God's past actions in order to ground present behavior and identity.[20] He says regarding these ordinances:

> The command to remember one's previous status is not, or, at the very least, not only, a means of urging compliance with the laws concerning the

---

16. Cf. Medvedev and Bakhtin(?), *Formal Method*, p. 120.

17. The phrase is taken from Roland Barthes, who says of intertextuality that 'the quotations of which a text is made are anonymous, untraceable, and nevertheless *already read*' ('De l'oeuvre au texte', *Revue d'esthétique* 23 [1971], pp. 225-32 [229]).

18. Cf. Gerhard von Rad, *Deuteronomy: A Commentary* (trans. Dorothea Barton; OTL; Philadelphia: Westminster Press, 1966), pp. 22-23.

19. Nasuti, 'Identity, Identification, and Imitation', p. 12.

20. See Nasuti, 'Identity, Identification, and Imitation', p. 12. The biblical references he gives for the sojourner formula are: Exod. 22.20; 23.9; Lev. 19.34; Deut. 10.19; 23.8; and for the slave formula: Deut. 5.15; 15.15; 16.12; 24.18, 22.

disadvantaged classes of Israelite society. Rather, one's actions towards
these classes are a part of preserving the proper memory of who one is.[21]

But these laws are present not merely to preserve past identity; they also
have practical implications for the present and future: 'On the practical
level, the laws specify that Israel must *act* in such a way as to preserve its
identity as Israel. Since certain *actions* make this identity impossible, these
are ruled out by the laws. In other words, they also function as a safeguard
of Israel's identity.'[22] Thus proper behavior and preservation or safe-
guarding of identity are integrally connected. As Nasuti concludes: 'The
identity of the reader has a decisive effect on the act of interpretation, and
the laws specify both an identity and the praxis by which such an identity
is constituted and maintained'.[23] As I will argue, the connection between
the law and both identity and behavior is not only important for Deut.
24.1-4, but also for Jer. 3.1–4.4.

Whereas Nasuti's argument regarding the laws as constituting and maintaining identity is helpful, he has missed two areas that are important for
my larger discussion. Although he discusses the importance of the narrative context, he does not deal with it specifically as paranesis,[24] nor does
he mention a further important connection made in Deuteronomy, namely,
the link between behavior and the land. Taking the paranetic context first,
the book of Deuteronomy is framed as Moses' last address to a new generation poised on the threshold between Egypt and the land. The framework relates the collection of laws of chs. 12–26, set in the middle of
Moses's speech, both to the past experience of the Exodus and to a present
renewal of covenant and thereby a preservation of future identity. A
choice is set before the Israelites prior to their entry into the land. If they
pledge to teach their children (Deut. 6.20-25) so that the children in their
turn may respond, then they will have life and dwell in the land. If they
choose otherwise, then there will be famine, death and loss of land.[25] The

---

21. Nasuti, 'Identity, Identification, and Imitation', p. 14.
22. Nasuti, 'Identity, Identification, and Imitation', p. 16 (my emphasis).
23. Nasuti, 'Identity, Identification, and Imitation', p. 19.
24. Paranesis is usually defined as hortatory or homiletical speech.
25. Cf. the covenant blessings and curses in Deut. 28. Although he does not emphasize the connection with the land, Michael Fishbane's discussion of Deut. 6.20-25
places a similar stress on past–present–future. He writes (*Text and Texture: Close
Readings of Selected Biblical Texts* [New York: Schocken Books, 1979], p. 80), 'for
Dt 6.20-25, the exodus event and the covenantal laws are the central religious realities
which transformed the sons of Israel–Jacob into the people of Israel... [Moses] thus
anticipates the future and the responsibility to guide succeeding generations towards

land is thus integrally connected to the relationship between YHWH and YHWH's people. Behavior, identity and land are likewise bound together. Moses is the exemplary leader, prophet,[26] and founder of Israel's faith. As such, his commands are to be obeyed. Deuteronomy 6.20-25 bridges the gap between him and the present audience. The intent is to teach *this* generation how to follow YHWH. It places *this* generation (whichever generation it may be) in the context of the covenantal relationship with YHWH and presupposes that the exodus and Sinai are taken on as part of their history.[27] These laws govern the identity of each generation. As Brevard S. Childs says, Moses' new interpretation of the law given at Sinai 'seeks to actualize the traditions of the past for the new generation in such a way as to evoke a response of the will in a fresh commitment to the covenant'.[28]

Although Deut. 24.1-4 does not have an identity formula, it is one of the laws set in the above narrative context. Therefore it, too, has as its background these notions integrating behavior, identity and land. The importance of these ideas as background not only to Deuteronomy as a whole, but to Deut. 24.1-4 in particular as a law governed by these ideas, will become clearer in the analysis of Jer. 3.1-5, which deals with these concepts as issues at stake in the ongoing relationship between YHWH and Israel.

The form of the legal prescription of Deut. 24.1-4 is casuistic. The first three verses set up the situation beginning with the traditional כי...אם. The hypothetical situation ('if...') is as follows: first, a man marries a woman and, for a reason connected with sexuality[29] divorces her. She then

participation in the legacy of the communal past'. For a similar, more comprehensive discussion of the command to teach each new generation in Deut. 6.20-25 than I have presented here, see pp. 79-83. Fishbane also makes a similar connection between the present law and the exodus; see pp. 121-25.

26. Cf. Deut. 18.9-22.

27. Hobbs, 'Jeremiah 3.1-5 and Deuteronomy 24.1-4', pp. 23-29, also connects the deuteronomic law with Sinai: 'for Deuteronomy the law is no longer a general family law, but has become part of a larger whole, the Sinai legislation' (p. 27).

28. Brevard S. Childs, *Introduction to the Old Testament as Scripture* (Philadelphia: Fortress Press, 1979), p. 312.

29. The term ערות דבר is problematic. R.P. Merendino conveniently gets rid of the difficulty by making the term secondary (*Das Deuteronomisches Gesetz* [Bonn: Peter Hanstein Verlag, 1969], p. 297). His explanation for the addition is that the redactor perhaps inferred the root שנא from v. 3a, and paraphrased the ערות דבר to match v. 3a (p. 297). He treats the second problematic term, חטא, similarly (p. 299). However, this proposal does not take into account the form in which the text now appears. The only

goes out and becomes the wife of another man.[30] Next, one of two things occur: (1) the second man 'hates' her and divorces her as well; or (2) he dies. Verse 4 then provides the prohibition: the first husband may not return to her and marry her. Three theological reasons are given: (1) she is defiled (pual טמא); (2) it is an abomination before YHWH; and (3) 'you shall not cause the land to sin' (hiphil חטא).

The use of the hiphil of חטא with 'land' as a direct object in Deut. 24.4 is unique in the Hebrew Bible. The hiphil form occurs elsewhere almost exclusively in 1 and 2 Kings with either Israel or Judah as direct object.[31] In these instances it is usually a king who caused Israel or Judah to sin. The only other uses of the hiphil occur in Isa. 29.21 and Qoh. 5.5, in both cases meaning to bring someone (Isa. 29.21) or something (Qoh. 5.5) into condemnation or punishment. The latter seem to be the closest parallels to the way חטא is used in Deut. 24.4. Given the close connection between the fertility of and possession of the land and proper human behavior (i.e. keeping God's laws) in Deuteronomy,[32] that is, the integral connection between behavior and the land I established above, it is likely that the consequence of not keeping these laws would be the condemnation or

other place in the Old Testament where this term is used is Deut. 23.15, where the meaning is equally in dispute. Elsewhere, ערוה is usually used of a woman and most often refers to a woman's nakedness; cf. Lev. 18.10; 20.17; Lam. 1.8; Ezek. 16.37. In the latter two contexts, the term ערוה is used in reference to Jerusalem and also has connotation of shame and/or shameful punishment (by exposure of her genitalia). Given this connection, it does seem clear that the use of ערות דבר has something to do with sexuality, but we still have no clue as to its legal meaning. Ancient Near Eastern sources will not help at this point since there are no parallels to this law. The only source which comes close is an Islamic law. See R. Yaron, 'The Restoration of Marriage', *JJS* 17 (1966), pp. 1-11 (4), for the citation. There are some major differences between the Islamic law and the deuteronomic law, however, and there is some question as to whether it is itself dependent (or an exegetical comment—another case of intertextuality?) on Deut. 24.1-4. Thus we are left with later interpretations. The term caused a debate in the early rabbinic schools, with the school of Shammai taking a narrow view (the woman had committed some sexual offense) and the school of Hillel taking a much broader view (the man could divorce her for almost any reason). Cf. *m. Git.* 9.9-10. Since then, even in modern scholarship, there have been proponents of both views. Thus, with regard to legal meaning, the term is murky. For the purposes of this study no further clarification is needed, for it is the *metaphorical* application of this law in Jer. 3.1–4.4 which is of real significance, and there the context makes clear that the ground for divorce is overstepping of sexual bounds.

30. The point of view here is exclusively male.

31. Cf. 1 Kgs 14.16; 15.26, 30, 34; 2 Kgs 3.3; 10.29, 31, etc.

32. Cf. the covenantal blessings and curses in Deut. 27–28.

punishment of the land as well as the people. Such a construction would moreover connect closely with the laws governing sexual relations in Leviticus 18 (v. 28 warns the people to keep YHWH's statutes 'lest the land vomit you out when you defile [טמא] it').[33] Gordon J. Wenham has argued helpfully in a similar manner for an integral connection between Deut. 24.1-4 and the incest laws in Leviticus 18 and 20. While I do not agree with his position regarding the legal meaning of Deut. 24.1-4,[34] he has established its connection to Leviticus 18 and 20 through common terminology, particularly the notions of defilement, abomination of the land, and the fact that both deal with sexual offenses.

Building on Wenham's insight, a closer look at Leviticus 18 reveals that vv. 1-5 and 24-30 frame a section of laws governing sexual relationships. Verses 1-5 remind the people of their identity—they shall not do as the Egyptians did and as the Canaanites do; rather, they are to follow God's ordinances and statutes because the statutes give life and it is YHWH who gives them. The latter part of the frame, vv. 24-30, cautions the people against defiling (טמא) themselves by such actions, labels the actions abominations (תועבות) and warns that if they do these things the land will 'vomit' them out. The reason given here is that the former inhabitants defiled the land in just such a way and the land 'vomited' them out. The

33. Von Rad also notes 'the realistic conception that unchastity defiles the land'. He cites the following references: Lev. 18.25, 28; 19.29; Num. 5.3; Hos. 4.3; Jer. 3.2, 9 (*Deuteronomy*, p. 150).

34. G.J. Wenham ('The Restoration of Marriage Reconsidered', *JJS* 30 [1979], pp. 36-40 [39]) proposes that 'running through these laws is the principle that a wife's nakedness is her husband's and *vice versa* (cf. Lev. 18.7, 14, 16; 20.11, 20; Deut. 23.1; 27.20)'. Deut. 23.1, however, does not fit. Perhaps he means Deut. 23.15. Elaborating on this theme he suggests that 'nakedness' links the generations, and that this notion in turn 'is analogous to our view of blood relationship' (p. 39). His explanation is as follows: 'spouses stand in the same relationship to each other as parents do to their children. In the words of Gen 2.24 "they become one flesh". Marriage thus creates both vertical blood-relationships in the form of children and horizontal "blood"-relationships between spouses… The wife who marries into a family becomes an integral and permanent part of that family in the same way that children born into the family do' (p. 39). Unfortunately, this case cannot be established. It is highly unlikely, however, that when one type of relationship bond (marriage) is severed, another, which only takes place through the marriage itself (a 'blood'[in quotes!]-relationship), is kept intact. Moreover, as Carolyn Pressler has indicated in her analysis of Wenham's argument, Wenham's solution does not deal adequately with vv. 2-3, but rather makes them 'irrelevant' (*The View of Women Found in the Deuteronomic Family Laws* [BZAW, 216; Berlin: W. de Gruyter, 1993], p. 52).

laws in Lev. 20.7-21 are followed by a similar exhortation (vv. 22-26).[35] Like the deuteronomic laws, the levitical laws make the same integral connections between behavior, identity and land. Furthermore, both groups of laws share the same intention: to ground relationships in the past (exodus) and to preserve identity for the future (the land).

Even with such a link established, however, the legal meaning of Deut. 24.1-4 remains in question, and the ground is hotly contested. Currently there are three major schools of thought concerning the legal meaning of Deut. 24.1-4.[36] The first view holds that it reflects 'the desire to prevent hasty divorce';[37] the second that the law is connected with prohibitions against adultery;[38] and the third that the law reflects '"natural repulsion" against such a reunion'.[39] A lone fourth opinion is that of Raymond West-brook, who argues that the law has nothing to do with sexual taboos, but is economic in scope.[40] The group with the majority of adherents is the

---

35. Deut. 27.20-23 presents prohibitions similar to those in Lev. 18 and 20. In Deut. 27, however, they are part of a series of curses. Nevertheless, their broader con-text is much the same. The people are to obey God's commands and statutes because they are the people of God (27.9). If they follow God's ways they will experience blessing; if they do not follow, they will experience the covenantal curses, including loss of land (Deut. 28).

36. Calum M. Carmichael tries to connect this law with Gen. 12.20 (*Law and Narrative in the Bible* [Ithaca, NY: Cornell University Press, 1985], pp. 255-57, and *The Law of Deuteronomy* [Ithaca, NY: Cornell University Press, 1974], pp. 203-207). See Wenham, 'The Restoration of Marriage Reconsidered', p. 37, for a good critique.

37. Yaron, 'The Restoration of Marriage', p. 5.

38. Cf. Yair Zakovitch, 'The Woman's Rights in the Biblical Law of Divorce', *JLA* 4 (1981), pp. 28-64 (29, 32).

39. The phrase is Yaron's ('The Restoration of Marriage', p. 5). He proposes that the law of Deut. 24.1-4 should be connected specifically with incest in its broadest sense. According to him, this law is 'designed to protect the family and to isolate, or insulate, existing socially approved relationships from the disruptive influences of sexual tension' (p. 8). In other words, the remarriage creates a kinship problem—one of incest. While I disagree that incest is the root issue here, his suggestion that kinship is an issue is insightful and will be discussed further below.

40. Raymond Westbrook ('The Prohibition on Restoration of Marriage in Deuter-onomy 24.1-4', in Sara Japhet [ed.], *Studies in Bible* [Scripta Hierosolymitana, 31; Jerusalem: Magnes Press, 1986], pp. 387-405 [404]) suggests that the law is based on 'what in modern law would be called estoppel', which he defines as 'the rule whereby a person who has profited by asserting a particular set of facts cannot profit a second time by conceding that the facts were otherwise'. Although no mention is made of any financial terms with regard to either of the marriages in Deut. 24.1-4, he suggests the following scenario: 'The first husband has divorced his wife on the grounds of her

second, particularly because of the way Jeremiah takes up the law. None of the above suggestions accounts for every aspect of Deut. 24.1-4, however. I suggest that the link between Deut. 24.1-4 and Leviticus 18 and 20 provides a helpful clue.

With regard to the levitical laws, Danna Nolan Fewell and David M. Gunn have argued convincingly that there is a systemic need tying these laws together, specifically the need to preserve a clear hierarchy and lineage. They note that *males* are the subject of the law, not females (*contra* Wenham), and propose that three principles underlie these laws: (1) that 'nakedness' is the property of men; (2) that the foundation on which society is built is father–son hierarchy, that women's place in the hierarchy is dependent on their relationship to men (i.e. either the daughter of X or the wife of Y) and that 'The children of proscribed relations would create havoc with the hierarchy';[41] and (3) that 'By owning women's nakedness in the context of a well-defined male-dominated hierarchy, men can control the means of production (e.g. through inheritance) and the propagation of a man's line/name/identity...'[42] Thus the reason *these*

"indecency" and therefore escaped the normal financial consequences—he paid her no divorce-money and most probably kept her dowry. The woman nonetheless managed to find another husband, and that marriage has ended in circumstances which leave her well provided for... Now that she is a wealthy widow or divorcée, the first husband forgets his original objections and seeks to remarry her'. The law of estoppel seeks to prevent just such 'a flagrant case of unjust enrichment' (p. 404). There are several problems with this interpretation: (1) the law does not mention financial terms in any way; (2) the intentions and reasons for the divorces/remarriage are left ambiguous; (3) there is no indication in the text that this is a more profitable match for the first husband; (4) there are parallels between this law and the laws carrying sexual taboos in Leviticus for which this explanation does not account; and (5) his parallel is Old Babylonian marriage law (see pp. 392-401). Westbrook simply assumes that such marriage law applied in Israel, but it is not clear that such an assumption is warranted given the paucity of evidence. Pressler's independent critique agrees in substantial measure with my own, and goes further by discussing each aspect of Westbrook's interpretation. See Pressler, *The View of Women*, pp. 53-59. Based on the differences between the laws, Westbrook also argues against any connection whatsoever between Deut. 24.1-4 and Jer. 3.1 ('Prohibition', p. 405 n. 66). I disagree; it seems to me that his real (and unexpressed) reason for rejecting any connection is his desire to base the deuteronomic law in economics rather than sexual taboo.

41. Danna Nolan Fewell and David M. Gunn, *Gender, Power, and Promise: The Subject of the Bible's First Story* (Nashville: Abingdon Press, 1993), p. 103.

42. Fewell and Gunn, *Gender, Power, and Promise*, p. 103. See pp. 102-104 for the complete discussion.

particular relationships are grouped together has to do with patriarchal lineage and paternity.

Although the law in Deut. 24.1-4 is somewhat more complicated, I see the same issues at stake. If a man remarries his wife after she has already been in another marriage, the second marriage becomes an oddity—it does not fit the need for clear lines and the maintenance of clear hierarchy. The remarriage tampers with clear structures in several possible ways. First, it has been argued that by remarrying the woman, the first husband makes her an adulterer, which puts the entire second marriage in the category of adultery. As Patrick Miller puts it, 'It is most likely that the potential remarriage was seen as allowing the possibility for a kind of legal adultery... The second marriage, while legal, would end up being a violation of the relationship to her first husband when the two were remarried.'[43] Another way in which structures may be confused concerns the issue of paternity: the identity of any offspring from either the first or the second marriage could come into question.[44] Another potential problem arises from the fact that a sexual matter (ערות דבר, v. 1) is the reason for the first divorce (and, presumably, the 'nakedness' at stake is that of the woman since the first husband divorces her). If 'nakedness' is the criterion for the first divorce, perhaps the husband's own status in the hierarchy/ lineage would be compromised if he remarried her. Although the paucity of evidence prohibits any definite conclusion, each of the possibilities raised indicates that in some way the patriarchal structures are compromised by this law.[45] Thus, it is likely that by forbidding a remarriage, this

43. Patrick Miller, *Deuteronomy* (Interpretation; Louisville, KY: John Knox Press, 1990), p. 164. See also Peter C. Craigie, *The Book of Deuteronomy* (NICOT; Grand Rapids: Eerdmans, 1976), pp. 304-306, and Pressler, *The View of Women*, pp. 60-61.

44. At stake here would be the status of sons of the second marriage *vis-à-vis* sons from the first or remarriage. What status do the sons from the second marriage have? Whose line do they represent? This problem becomes even clearer if there are no sons from the first or remarriage. Even more problematic is the question of adultery raised above. If the second marriage is viewed as adultery, then the status of any offspring from that marriage would be called into question in any event.

45. See also, Pressler, *The View of Women*, pp. 61-62, who has argued independently for just such an understanding of the law. Using as a springboard the work of Tikva Frymer-Kensky ('Pollution, Purification, and Purgation', in C. Meyers and M. O'Connor [eds.], *The Word of the Lord Shall Go Forth: Essays in Honor of David Noel Freedman* [Winona Lake, IN: Eisenbrauns, 1983], pp. 399-414) and Mary Douglas (*Purity and Danger: An Analysis of Concepts of Pollution and Taboo* [New York: Praeger, 1966]), Pressler holds that 'the boundaries of the family and thus the integrity of a man's lineage are threatened by crisscrossing relationships. Sexual

law prevents any possible confusing of hierarchy, lineage, property lines and paternity.

Returning to the host text, Jer. 3.1–4.4 will pick up all of the themes present in Deut. 24.1-4: marriage, the connections between identity, behavior and the land; and the notion that the broken marriage bond cannot be restored. What makes Jer. 3.1–4.4 so startling is its dialogue with these aspects and its upsetting of the apple cart, so to speak, by offering a restoration of the divine–human bond.

3. *Jeremiah 3.1-5*

While the entire chapter plays on the law in Deut. 24.1-4, Jer. 3.1-5 constitute the most direct intertextuality between the law, the issues underlying the deuteronomic text, and Jer. 3.1–4.4. Here, as noted before, is the citation of the law that appears in legal form (that is, in the midst of a law code) in Deuteronomy. Yet the context in which the citation is placed differs from Deut. 24.1-4. Likewise the form is different.

Jeremiah 3.1-5 reads:

> [1]'If a man divorces his wife and she goes from him and becomes another man's wife, can he return to her? Would not such a land be greatly polluted? You have played the whore with many lovers; and yet would you return to me?' says the Lord.
> [2]'Lift up your eyes on the bare heights and see: Where have you not been lain with? You have sat along the roads for them, like an Arab in the desert, and you have polluted the land with your harlotry and with your evil.'
> [3]Therefore the copious showers have been withheld, and the spring rain has not come. But you have a harlot's brow. You refuse to be ashamed.
> [4]Have you not just now[46] called to me, 'My father, you are the husband of my youth?'
> [5]'Will he remain angry forever; will he keep [anger] continually?'[47] Behold you have spoken, but you have done all the evil you could'.[48]

relations, whether legal or not, which bind a woman to first one man, then to a second, then again to the first confuse the boundaries which define the (patrilineal) family' (*The View of Women*, p. 61).

46. Cf. BDB, p. 774.

47. The two questions attributed to the people in vv. 4-5a are punctuated as separate questions because of the switch from second to third person. These questions may represent two speakers or simply two quotations of the people from two different contexts. Here, however, they are connected to present a comprehensive picture of the audience's viewpoint.

48. Literally, 'you did evil things for you were able'.

The form of Jer. 3.1-5 has been the subject of considerable debate, with various scholars calling it a 'didactic question' (thus positing a wisdom background),[49] a 'juridical parable'[50] and, most recently, a 'disputation'.[51] With its primary proponent, Burke O. Long, I adopt the latter designation. On the basis of other similar uses in Jeremiah itself,[52] in which one or more rhetorical questions are followed by an indictment, Long says, 'these texts…convey a clear adversarial intent. The rhetorical questions are not didactic. They do not instruct. They rather lay a rhetorical basis for indictment.'[53] His designation of 'disputation' for 3.1-5 'conveys…the subtle interplay of content, form, and intention'.[54] Thus, rather than a law embedded in a law code as in Deut. 24.1-4, the legal citation in Jer. 3.1-5 serves a different purpose and form: it provides the legal basis for YHWH's dispute with Israel.

The basis for the designation 'disputation' is provided by three cases outside of Jeremiah which have a very similar form: each case is set up beginning with the term הן plus the imperfect, followed by a question. They are Hag. 2.10-14, Lev. 10.18 and Exod. 8.22.[55] Long says:

> all three cases have to do with dispute; all three texts have the *hen* clause stating the situation, usually a legal or cultic one, which is the subject in question. And Hag 2.12…is part of a larger rhetorical basis for indictment (Hag 2.14). Hence, the use of *hen* in Jer 3.1, can be understood as being modeled after similar usages in disputes over points of law, but now turned, as in Haggai, to the service of highlighting a basic failing in Israel's dealings with Yahweh.[56]

Taking Long's position a step further, I suggest that the legal connections of these three parallels fit with the disputation background of Jeremiah 2, as well as the content of 3.1-5. Jeremiah 3.1 is indeed a citation of a law which is then applied metaphorically to the relationship between YHWH and Israel as a basis for indictment. Moreover, I see yet another parallel

---

49. Hobbs, 'Jeremiah 3.1-5 and Deuteronomy 24.1-4', pp. 23-29.

50. U. Simon, 'The Poor Man's Ewe Lamb', *Bib* 48 (1967), pp. 207-42.

51. Burke O. Long, 'The Stylistic Components of Jer 3.1-5', *ZAW* 88 (1976), pp. 376-90. This article also has an excellent critique of the former two positions.

52. Cf. 2.11-12, 32; 13.23; also 8.4-5; 18.14-15 (Long, 'Stylistic Components', p. 387).

53. Long, 'Stylistic Components', p. 387.

54. Long, 'Stylistic Components', p. 388.

55. Long, 'Stylistic Components', pp. 388-89.

56. Long, 'Stylistic Components', p. 389.

between Jer. 3.1-5 and Haggai 2 in particular: both introduce a legal situation with לֵאמֹר (cf. Hag. 2.11).[57] Thus, the legal situation in each is accentuated by a term marking what follows as a citation.[58]

If לֵאמֹר does indeed function as a citation marker, then the quality of *représentation*, a term used by Orr in her discussion of 'the *dramatic* qualities of intertextuality',[59] is also present here. Drawing an analogy between drama and intertextuality, Orr argues:

> In the study of intertextuality, drama is the paradigm of the totally quoted form. Past utterance receives a new body in which it is a voice or collection of voices... By extension, the intertext, as recognizably different speech-act, speaks and shows its otherness by being placed in literal or meta-phorical speech-marks, made present by its staging in the new discursive space... Language is...perceived in embodied form on the stage. The actor remakes the play by voicing the given words with his/her *own* accentuation and hence interpretation. Comparable to this is the writer's reusage of an intertext, which 'speaks' in a new way because of its different context. In addition, just as the actor uses his/her memory to reconstruct the lines, the reader does the same to build up the text in his/her mind and form it as a whole.[60]

Her analogy illustrates again the importance of context and the reader in producing meaning. Of more importance, however, the analogy itself may be applied fruitfully to prophetic literature. Like drama, prophetic literature is often a 'paradigm of the totally quoted form'. For example, in much of Jer. 3.1–4.4 the prophet (corresponding to the actor) is quoting the words of YHWH 'with his/her *own* accentuation and hence interpretation'. Another way in which the prophet in prophetic texts often fulfills the same role as the actor in drama is through quoting and interpreting previous tradition in a new context. Orr's term for this dynamic in drama is *représentation*: 'Not only is the intertext made present within the new structure: it

---

57. Hag. 2.11 is the citation of a legal inquiry, while Jer. 3.1 cites a specific law.

58. If לֵאמֹר merely marks the text of Jer. 3.1 as a legal citation, a satisfactory explanation has been found for the 'truncated introductory formula', long debated in Jeremiah scholarship. In short, rather than being part of an original introduction, לֵאמֹר marks this text off as a legal citation.

59. Orr, *Claude Simon*, p. 36.

60. Orr, *Claude Simon*, pp. 36-37. Bakhtin makes a similar assessment of all language: 'language...lies on the border between oneself and the other. The word in language is half someone else's. It becomes "one's own" only when the speaker populates it with his own intention, his own accent, when he appropriates the word, adapting it to his own semantic and expressive intention' ('Discourse', p. 293).

is visible in its new "performance"'.[61] To apply this concept to Jer. 3.1, the marker, לאמר, flags what immediately follows as a citation dealing with the law, which in turn *re*-presents the original (legal) context in the present one. In other words, the intertext, the law, is visible as such in its present context.

In addition to being a basis for indictment, the form of Jer. 3.1-5 serves another purpose: the use of rhetorical questions instead of prescriptive language (as in Deut. 24.1-4), has the effect of actively engaging the audience. Such questions draw the audience/reader into dialogue.[62] Moreover, this dialogue is intertextual in nature. Jonathan Culler's work on intertextuality is particularly helpful in this regard. He states that rhetorical questions 'explicitly assert their intertextual nature, not just because they seem to request an answer and hence designate themselves as incomplete, but because the presuppositions carried by their questions imply a prior discourse'.[63] In Jer. 3.1, the prescriptive language of a law is transformed into a rhetorical question. The law is thus a prior discourse, one that is visible (re-presented), presupposed and reinterpreted in a new context.

Verse 1a is the hook. The writer draws the audience in with a seemingly innocent question about a law which is presumably well known. The question draws forth the expected response, 'Of course the husband may not return to the wife again; of course the land would be defiled'. Having hooked the audience, the writer, through metaphorical analogy, thrusts the point home: Israel is not just an adulterous wife; Israel has become a prostitute going out and seeking her lovers. By posing the law as a rhetorical question, the writer, by presuming the audience's agreement, has enticed the people to indict themselves.[64] The first rhetorical question, with its analogous metaphorical description of Israel, picks up the issue of identity: the audience is identified collectively as an adulterous wife because of

61. Orr, *Claude Simon*, p. 58.

62. Bakhtin says of rhetorical genres that 'for the most part these are intensely dialogized forms' ('Discourse', p. 354).

63. Jonathan Culler, 'Presupposition and Intertextuality', *The Pursuit of Signs: Semiotics, Literature, Deconstruction* (rev. repr.; Ithaca, NY: Cornell University Press, 1981), pp. 100-18 (113-14).

64. Allan Graffy ('The Literary Genre of Isa 5, 1-7', *Bib* 60 [1979], pp. 400-409), has also noticed this aspect. He connects Jer. 3.1-5 with Isa. 5.1-7; 2 Sam. 12.1-7a; 14.1-20; 1 Kgs 20.35-42. Basing his discussion on that of U. Simon, he designates these as 'self-condemnation parables'. He says, 'with this designation attention can be focused on the basic technique common to all: leading the unsuspecting hearer to pass judgment on his own offenses' (p. 408).

their behavior. Yet in Jer. 3.1 the audience has overstepped in ways far beyond the situation expressed by the law—they 'have played the harlot with many lovers'. To use Kristeva's terms, this text 'absorbs' the law, but 'transforms' it, both formally (rhetorical question) and functionally (the law is used to indict the people).

Kristeva's contribution to this study of intertextuality in Jer. 3.1-5 is her early writing building on Bakhtin's work in dialogism, specifically, her idea that that language has 'subversive political effects';[65] that is, it upholds some values and behaviors while distorting or repressing others. Any intertext, maintains Kristeva, is not swallowed whole, but is changed. In her view, 'Bakhtin considers writing as a reading of the anterior literary corpus and the text as an absorption of and a reply to another text'.[66] However, for Kristeva a text does not merely absorb another: when a text enters into dialogue with another text, such a dialogue 'transgresses'; it implies 'an idea of rupture (of opposition and analogy) as a modality of transformation'.[67] Absorption, transgression, and transformation describe the interaction between the host text and an intertext. As such, they can incorporate a number of ideas, including structure, form, content and context.[68] I argue that these notions of absorption, transgression and transformation are important for determining and describing the types of interactions between Jer. 3.1–4.4 and its intertexts.

In Jer. 3.1, although the law is in one sense absorbed, the prophet also transgresses the law cited in this verse in several ways. First, Jack R. Lundbom rightly likens the use of the law in 3.1-5 to talmudic argumentation:

> the argument contains in addition [to analogy] an inference *a minori ad maius*, or to use talmudic terminology, a *kal vechomer*. The man cannot return

65. See Toril Moi's Introduction to *The Kristeva Reader* (ed. Toril Moi; New York: Columbia University Press, 1986), p. 35.

66. Julia Kristeva, 'Word, Dialogue and Novel', in *The Kristeva Reader*, pp. 34-61 (39).

67. Kristeva, 'Word, Word, Dialogue and Novel', p. 58. Earlier in the essay she describes transgression as 'the practice of a signifying structure in relation or opposition to another structure' (p. 36).

68. Thaïs Morgan states, 'Kristeva's most valuable contribution to the debate on intertextuality is the idea that an intertextual citation is never innocent or direct, but always transformed, distorted, displaced, condensed, or edited in some way in order to suit the speaking subject's value system' ('Space of Intertextuality', in Patrick O'Donnell and Robert Con Davis [eds.], *Intertextuality and Contemporary American Fiction* [Baltimore: The Johns Hopkins University Press, 1989], pp. 239-79 [260]).

to his former wife because she has known (or been known) by *one* other man; in Jeremiah's argument Israel has had *many* lovers (רעים רבים).[69]

In the relations between YHWH and Israel, there has been no second marriage (with one man); rather, the wife has committed harlotry (with many lovers).[70] What she has done goes far beyond the situation presented in the legal citation. Moreover, there is no divorce mentioned in vv. 1b-5. The link between a law concerning divorce and the idea of return, however, indicates that the notion of divorce plays a part in this text. At the very least, divorce in the metaphorical relationship between YHWH and Israel is being threatened if it has not already occurred. The ambiguity may be due to the two possible rhetorical situations. If we accept that vv. 1-5 are early and from the hand of Jeremiah himself, then divorce is a future possibility—that is, the implication of the link between the law and Israel's present actions is that those actions will lead to an irrevocable divorce. If, however, we view these verses from the perspective of the final form (i.e. from an exilic perspective), then divorce in the form of exile has already occurred both to Judah and to the former Northern Kingdom, and the issue at stake is the possibility of a renewed relationship between YHWH and Israel. That divorce is indeed an issue at stake in the rhetoric of the whole of the piece is indicated by Jer. 3.6-11, where the historical exile of the Northern Kingdom is depicted metaphorically as YHWH's divorce of 'Turning Back Israel'.

A third transgression of the law cited in Jer. 3.1, is the final clause of the verse: ושוב אלי נאם־יהוה.[71] Rather than the husband returning to the

69. Jack R. Lundbom, *Jeremiah: A Study in Ancient Hebrew Rhetoric* (Missoula, MT: Scholars Press, 1975), p. 38.

70. Pressler puts it this way: 'The contrast is between a legal second marriage (which is nonetheless polluting) and harlotry (how much more polluting!)' (*The View of Women*, p. 59).

71. The reference to the wife's return here may be an allusion to Hos. 2.9, where, also using a husband–wife metaphor, YHWH indicates that Israel will seek to return (שוב) to her first husband once she is punished, and, ultimately, YHWH takes her back (vv. 14-22). There are no other verbal connections between Hos. 2 and Jer. 3.1–4.4, however, and the rhetoric of Hos. 2 is also quite different: in Hos. 2 there is a period of punishment (vv. 12-15), an indication that Israel did not know that it was YHWH who had given her all the good things in her life (v. 10), and a portrayal of YHWH creating an unconditional covenant with her (vv. 14-22 [20-22]). As the following analysis will show, in Jer. 3.1–4.4 the nature of both the present and future relationship of Israel and YHWH and the rhetorical flow in Jer. 3.1–4.4 diverge greatly from Hos. 2. Rudolph argues that both Jer. 3.1–4.4 and Deut. 24.1-4 are dependent on Hosea (*Jeremia*, p. 15).

wife, as in the law, here the wife seeks to return to the husband. The real issue, as indicated by the rest of 3.1–4.4, however, is whether YHWH will turn again to take Israel back.

The root שוב ('to return'), is introduced here for the first time in this text. This term is central both to the citation of the law and to Jer. 3.1–4.4 as a whole. Indeed, it is a central term for the entire book. William L. Holladay, who has written the definitive study of the various connotations of the root שוב in the Hebrew Bible and in Jeremiah in particular, argues that 'Jeremiah plays with *šûbh* in two ways: first, by juxtaposing the two contradictory meanings of the verb, and second, by exploiting to the limit the related noun *mešûbhâ* and the adjectives'.[72] Jeremiah 3.1 presents an example of the first type of wordplay, while 3.6-11 uses the second type of wordplay. In 3.1-5, the citation of the law is transgressed by the reversal in v. 1 (i.e. it is the wife who wishes to return to the husband), yet the issue raised by the law (i.e. a husband returning to his wife) is absorbed in the larger rhetorical context of the chapter.

The rhetorical questions of vv. 1-5 also revolve around the root שוב. The formulation of the legal citation as a question raises the issue of whether the hypothetical husband may return (שוב) to his wife (v. 1a). In v. 1b, in the context of the marital/harlotry metaphor, the wife raises the question of return again. A second connotation of the root is also present in these verses: through the cultic connections of the marital metaphor, the root שוב may also refer to repentance. However, vv. 3-4 make it clear that repentance is not what Israel has offered YHWH. Indeed they have refused to accept any accusations of wrongdoing. Assuming innocence, they have

---

Most recent commentators assert that, to use John Bright's terms, 'Similarities to Hosea...are striking. Not only is the dominant theme (the adulterous wife) borrowed from that great prophet of Northern Israel, there are verbal similarities...' (*Jeremiah*, p. 26; cf. Robert Carroll, *Jeremiah* [OTL; Philadelphia: Westminster Press, 1986], pp. 142-43; Thompson, *Jeremiah*, pp. 189, 191). The 'verbal similarities' which are mentioned, however, arise in connection with Jer. 3.22 (Hos. 14.1, 4) and Jer. 4.3 (Hos. 10.12), and, moreover, have nothing to do with the metaphor of adultery present in Hos. 2. An adequate treatment of the relationship between these two texts would go beyond the scope of the present study. Because the verbal connections are so few, and because the situations described in the two texts are so different, this study will not discuss Hos. 2 as an intertext. Nevertheless, such an exploration would be a fruitful subject for further study.

72. William J. Holladay, *The Root Šûbh in the Old Testament: With Particular Reference to its Usages in Covenantal Contexts* (Leiden: E.J. Brill, 1958), p. 153. For his larger argument, see pp. 128-39, 152-53.

called on YHWH for help. The assumed innocence raises the issue of true as opposed to false 'turning', which is here portrayed in the metaphorical context of the husband–wife relationship. The question of true or false turning also connects with the issue of covenant; by analogy with the marital metaphor, שוב acts on the metaphorical level to refer to covenant renewal as well.[73] Both the term שוב in its many connotations, and, more particularly, the ideas of true or false 'turning'/repentance, will be common threads running through the rest of the chapter.

In addition to the intertextual implications of ושוב אלי נאם יהוה, the phrase also contains semantic ambiguity; it may be construed either as a statement or as a question.[74] As a question, it is a sarcastic utterance: 'you have done all this and yet you would return to me?!' As a statement, it foreshadows the appeals of the rest of the chapter: 'Israel cannot legally expect a restoration with her god, but divine grace can provide hope where it is least to be expected'.[75] Michael Fishbane argues that the ambiguity should remain, since 'it is around this twisted cord that the legal–religious paradox of Jeremiah's aggadic rhetoric is spun'.[76] I would add that the

73. As Holladay notes, 'Jeremiah had in mind no such category as "covenantal *šûbh*"... Yet so saturated was Jeremiah's consciousness with the issues of Yahweh and Israel that the verb became largely a vehicle for the expression of these issues' (*The Root Šûbh*, p. 152).

74. So also Michael Fishbane, *Biblical Interpretation in Ancient Israel* (Oxford: Oxford University Press, 1985), p. 310.

75. Fishbane, *Biblical Interpretation*, p. 310.

76. Fishbane, *Biblical Interpretation*, p. 310. His analysis of Jer. 3.1-5 has been helpful in that it has provided the springboard and frame for some of my early thoughts on the passage, particularly in terms of intertextuality. His book, *Biblical Interpretation in Ancient Israel*, focuses on what he calls 'inner biblical exegesis', which Gail R. O'Day characterizes as the 'textual-exegetical dimension' of scripture in general ('Jeremiah 9.22-23 and 1 Corinthians 1.26-31: A Study in Intertextuality', *JBL* 109 [1990], pp. 259-67 [259]). However, there are three major differences between his approach and my own. First, because of his concentration on inner biblical exegesis, Fishbane's analysis is confined to the connections between Deut. 24.1-4 and Jer. 3.1-5, and the ways in which Jer. 3.1-5 reinterprets the text of Deut. 24.1-4. My own work looks at the ways in which the metaphors raised by the quotation of the law, also included in Deut. 24.1-4, form a rhetorical argument extending throughout the chapter. Second, while Fishbane differentiates his work from traditio-historical criticism (pp. 6-9), he nevertheless approaches the biblical text from a historical point of view which does not take into account either the reader's role or the role of the contemporary context of the reader in the production of meaning. The third and most critical difference, however, is that he does not deal with the ways in which traditions are both

very ambiguity of this statement serves another rhetorical function as well: like the rhetorical questions, it keeps the reader actively engaged and draws her/him on.

Verses 2-5 extend the indictment of v. 1. While the connection between behavior and land is already flagged in the second rhetorical question of v. 1 ('Would not such a land be greatly polluted?'), v. 2 illustrates the heinousness of the crime and emphasizes the link between wife Israel's actions and the land: 'you have polluted the land with your promiscuity and your evil'. Although the root, חָנַף ('to pollute'), is used in relation to the land in both of these verses, according to Deut. 24.4 the effect of the proposed remarriage on the land is characterized by a different term, the hiphil of חָטָא. There the remarriage would 'cause the land to sin'.[77] While the terms are different, the idea is similar. The idea of 'causing the land to sin' connects the law with overstepped boundaries, as does 'polluting' the land.[78] Yet while it is the man who causes the land to sin in the deuteronomic law,[79] in Jer. 3.1-2 it is the wife who 'pollutes' the land by her sexual actions.[80] This discrepancy is consistent with the idea that it is the wife who seeks to return according to Jer. 3.1. In addition, if Carolyn Pressler's and Miller's interpretation of the law in Deut. 24.1-4 stands (i.e. that a remarriage would make the woman an adulterer because of her second

absorbed and, more crucially, transformed in their new context. In other words, while he does discuss the new meaning that the use of tradition creates, he does not deal with the ongoing play of meanings between the tradition and the new text. Fishbane's work is nevertheless evocative and provocative for my own intertextual study. For his complete discussion of Jer. 3.1-5, see *Biblical Interpretation*, pp. 307-11, and 'Torah and Tradition', in Douglas A. Knight (ed.), *Tradition and Theology in the Old Testament* (Philadelphia: Fortress Press, 1977), pp. 275-300 (285-88).

77. See my discussion of this term in the section on Deut. 24.1-4, above.

78. So also Pressler. She rightly argues that, due to the 'considerable semantic overlap between חָטָא and טָמֵא (cf. Lam 1.8-9; Ez 37.23; Isa 64.4-5…)', the distinction between the two terms 'should not be overdrawn' (*The View of Women*, p. 50). As she puts it, 'Sin leads to defilement; the very land itself may be polluted by the sin of its inhabitants' (p. 50 n. 20). In the same note, see also her argument for such an interpretation on the basis of 'the close resemblance between Deut 24.4c and Deut 21.23', the latter of which uses the verb טָמֵא in reference to the land.

79. Since the law is addressed to men, and it is the man who is prohibited from remarrying, it must also be the man who causes the land to sin (cf. Pressler, *The View of Women*, p. 62).

80. Frymer-Kensky argues that there are three categories which pollute both people and the land: murder, sexual abomination, and idolatry ('Pollution, Purification, and Purgation', p. 408).

marriage),[81] then the agency of defilement is essentially the same in both Deut. 24.1-4 and Jer. 3.1 as well—adultery.

Verse 3 spells out the consequences of the pollution in terms of its threat to the land: drought, which brings to mind the covenant curses in Deuteronomy 28, where transgression of the law results in famine and drought. Thus, the lines of connection between behavior and the land, illustrated in the foregoing discussion of Deut. 24.1-4 and its context, are drawn in this context as well. Here, I extend Walter Brueggemann's assertion regarding Jer. 2.7 to 3.3 as well, namely, that 3.3 'illustrates the integral connection between the people's action and what happens to the land'.[82] Just as with Deut. 24.1-4, the boundaries of human relations affect the center of the people's identity—the land. This connection with the land will also remain important throughout the following sections.

Verses 3b and 4 are connected together, the rhetoric of both suggesting that the covenantal curses have started to take place, yet even this has not caused Israel to be humbled. On the contrary, wife Israel has brazenly called on God for help as if she had done nothing wrong: 'But you have a harlot's brow. You refuse to be ashamed. Have you not just now called to me, "My father, you are the husband of my youth"?'

In v. 4, 'my father' (אָבִי) appears to be an odd term to use with respect to one's husband.[83] The term invokes a father–daughter metaphor (God as father and Israel as daughter), which disrupts the husband–wife metaphor used in the remainder of vv. 1-5. There may be several reasons for such a use. Considering the rest of the quotation of the people, 'you are the husband of my youth', perhaps the term is one of deference used between a young woman and an older man. Such a term thus emphasizes the difference in power and status between Israel and YHWH.[84] The usage of אָבִי in v. 4 is also proleptic: the term creates a slippage between the husband–

---

81. See the complete discussion in the section on Deut. 24.1-4, above.

82. Brueggemann, 'Israel's Sense of Place in Jeremiah', p. 152.

83. Many commentators omit the term as a gloss because, to quote Holladay, 'there is no parallel in the Old Testament for "my father" as a wife's designation for her husband' (*Jeremiah 1*, p. 115). See Rudolph, who argues that the term is displaced from v. 19 (*Jeremia*, pp. 21-22; note that he also argues that v. 19 is the continuation of vv. 1-5).

84. The term אָב is frequently used of the head of household or clan (cf. Gen. 24.10; 38.11; 41.51; 46.31; Lev. 22.13; Num. 18.1, 2; Josh. 2.12, 18; 6.25). It is also used as a term of respect and honor, particularly with regard to someone in a prominent social position within the community: See, e.g., 1 Kgs 5.13 (applied to one's master); Judg. 17.10; 18.19 (applied to priest); 2 Kgs 2.12; 6.21; 13.14 (applied to prophet).

wife metaphor, which dominates vv. 1-5, and a father–daughter metaphor, which is introduced in 3.19 ('I thought how I would set you [fem. sing.] among the sons, and give you a pleasant land, the most beautiful heritage of all the nations. And I thought you would call me "my father" [אָבִי], and would not turn from following me').[85] This term foreshadows v. 19 in two ways: (1) it heralds the father-daughter metaphor taken up in v. 19; and (2) it anticipates a similar slippage which is evident in vv. 19-20 (the analogy between a woman's faithlessness to her lover and Israel's faithlessness to YHWH both fits the father–daughter situation in vv. 19-20 and reinvokes the husband–wife situation in vv. 1-13).[86] In addition, by placing the words 'my father' together with a plea to return at the beginning of the piece, the poignancy and irony of YHWH's thoughts in v. 19 are highlighted (YHWH's hopes were dashed—to anticipate the discussion below, rather than behaving as a daughter should [i.e. having no sexual relations whatsoever],[87] Israel acted as if she had no sexual restraints [v. 20]).

Verse 5b implies that Israel's show of repentance (שׁוּב) is just that, a show. Although the syntax in v. 5b is not clear (the waw may have either an adversative or conjunctive function), it makes more sense with an adversative waw: 'Look, you have spoken (i.e. these words asking for my help), *but* you have done all the evil you could'. This construal not only connects v. 5b directly to vv. 4-5a, but it also brings out the play on the root רעה. This root is used in v. 1 to designate lovers—'you have played the harlot with many lovers (רֵעִים)'—while in vv. 2 and 5 it denotes evil—v. 2 accuses Israel of polluting the land with their evil (וּבְרָעָתֵךְ), and v. 5 makes clear the connection between many lovers and 'all the evil (הָרָעוֹת)' that one could do.[88]

Verses 4 and 5 also explicitly indicate previous dialogue between the prophet (YHWH) and the implied audience through two quotations of audience speech within the speech of the prophet (YHWH). In vv. 4-5, in the midst of YHWH's speech to Israel, YHWH asks, 'Have you not just now called to me, "My father, you are the husband of my youth"?' (v. 4) and '"Will he remain angry forever; will he keep [anger] forever"?'(v. 5a).

85. Translation issues in this verse will be discussed in Chapter 6.

86. For further discussion of this idea, see the section on vv. 19-20 in Chapter 6.

87. See the discussion of the father's control of his daughter's sexuality in ancient Israel in Chapter 6.

88. The use of the root רעה also foreshadows another meaning for the root taken up in v. 15: the good shepherds (רֹעִים, from רעה I) which YHWH will place over Israel. In effect, the shepherds replace the lovers (רֵעִים, from רעה II) of v. 1.

Here the prophet quotes YHWH quoting (a) previous supplication(s) on the part of Israel.

Culler defines prior discourse as 'a text or set of attitudes prior to the poem itself'.[89] These quotations indeed presuppose a discourse prior to the poem—one in which, presumably, Israel has found itself in trouble and has called on YHWH for help. Culler says further, 'the problem of interpreting the poem becomes that of deciding what attitude the poem takes to the prior discourse which it designates as presupposed'.[90] While I would not confine interpretation of intertextuality to deciding its attitude toward prior discourse (my definition is much broader, including many possible interactions between a text and other discourse[s]), his statement nonetheless indicates an important component of intertextual interpretation. In the case of vv. 4-5, there are clues both to the prior discourse and to the attitude taken both within the text of Jer. 3.1-5 itself and in the larger context of ch. 2.

The quotations of the people in 3.4b-5 represent one of two possible situations. They may be words which the people have directed to the prophet himself in response to his prophecies. More likely, however, since they are quoted by YHWH in the rhetoric of vv. 1-5, they reflect a cultic situation in which the people are praying to God. The quotation of v. 5a, in particular, reflects an understanding of YHWH's character in keeping with Ps. 103.8-9, where the people appeal to YHWH as a God who is 'compassionate and gracious…long forbearing and of abundant loving-kindness. He will not contend without end, nor rage forever.' Fishbane has argued persuasively that Ps. 103.8-9 is itself a liturgical echo of Exod. 34.6-7.[91] Analogously, Jer. 3.4b-5a may represent some liturgical language incorporated into the context of YHWH's indictment of Israel. While such language does indicate prior discourse between YHWH and the people, the discourse itself is transgressed through recontextualization. That is, by placing a liturgical response within the marriage metaphor (and *after* the indictment of the people), the response itself appears to mean something quite different than it does within liturgy. Rather than an innocent appeal in the context of worship, the people's words to YHWH in this context are portrayed as a request for YHWH to act illegally. Moreover, YHWH's answer in v. 5b—'Behold, you have spoken, but you have done all the evil

---

89. Culler, 'Presupposition', p. 114.

90. Culler, 'Presupposition', p. 114.

91. Fishbane, *Biblical Interpretation*, pp. 335-37, 348-49. I will return to his discussion in the consideration of intertextuality in Jer. 3.12.

you could'—illustrates the manipulative and double-faced nature of Israel's request: at the same time Israel was using its relationship with YHWH as 'father' and 'husband of their youth' to get YHWH to act without anger, they were doing evil. Thus, Israel's words and actions are portrayed as being incongruent and hypocritical.

In an article entitled, 'Jeremiah 2 and the Problem of "Audience Reaction"', Thomas Overholt suggests:

> on the basis of his experience Jeremiah may have selected from, altered, even created 'audience reactions' to serve as foils for his indictment of the people...the quotations may in fact represent the general type of reaction Jeremiah experienced from some segment of his audience, but investigation indicates that they are not untampered with.[92]

With this statement Overholt indicates two concepts: (1) the quotations themselves indicate the attitude of the writer to the prior discourse; and (2) they function dialogically and rhetorically in that they are used by the writer for a certain purpose. Overholt notes that 'the prophet's quotations of other persons' speech occur exclusively in the accusation...[and they] uniformly present the people in a bad light'.[93]

This idea may be fruitfully applied to Jeremiah 3 as well. Doing so further illuminates the dynamic at work in 3.4-5. Although he does not use the term intertextuality or discuss the quotations in terms of dialogue, Overholt nonetheless indicates that such quotations function in these terms. His observation ties in neatly both with Culler's discussion of the importance of presupposition and with the idea of transgression in intertextuality. In my view, the writer uses the quotations as a basis for indictment and to contrast the words and the behavior of the people. This interpretation lends force to the translation of v. 5 for which I argued above. The words of the people are thus not taken over wholesale, but are interpreted—transgressed—to highlight their manipulative, evil behavior.

92. Thomas Overholt, 'Jeremiah 2 and the Problem of "Audience Reaction"', *CBQ* 41 (1979), pp. 262-73 (263). See his insightful discussion of Hans Walter Wolff's extended essay on quotation in prophetic speech, 'Das Zitat im Prophetenspruch', in his *Gesammelte Studien zum Alten Testament* (Munich: Chr. Kaiser Verlag, 2nd edn, 1973 [1964]), pp. 36-129; as well as W.J. Horwitz, 'Audience Reaction to Jeremiah', *CBQ* 32 (1970), pp. 555-64.

93. Overholt, 'Jeremiah 2', p. 266. This is where I disagree with Overholt. As will be established below with regard to the quotation of the people's speech in 3.21-25, quotation is not always used in accusation. There the citation is hopeful rather than accusatory (i.e. vv. 21-25 present not what the people actually said, but what YHWH hopes they will say).

Also without mentioning the term intertextuality, Brueggemann makes a link between quoted audience speech and rhetorical questions similar to that of Overholt, and develops the link further in essentially intertextual terms. Brueggemann suggests that 'Jeremiah uses the rhetorical question to restate a traditional, generally accepted presupposition which he then challenges or by which he offers a different cause for a visible effect'.[94] Citing Jer. 3.5 as one of his examples, he says, 'each of these question pairs can have only a single answer and the poet and his listeners would surely agree'.[95] He adds, 'in each case he turns the consensus to make a new point'.[96] Brueggemann's statements illustrate how presupposition and intertextuality work together. In v. 1, the citation of the law contains the 'generally accepted presupposition', which is then turned into accusation via a rhetorical question directed to the audience. The remaining rhetorical questions of 3.1-5 reinforce the accusation and forcefully state[97] that the people are guilty and deserve punishment.

Yet these quotations of audience speech not only reveal the author's/ God's attitude toward the audience, they also reveal the intention of the audience, and indicate the audience's participation in the ongoing dialogue. Although the author retains control of audience speech (it is framed within the context of YHWH's indictment of the people), the quotation nevertheless indicates an ongoing dialogue between YHWH and the people. This particular type of 'double-voiced' speech is an example of Bakhtin's category of 'varidirectional passive doublevoiced words' which, like his example, parody, 'introduces into that discourse a semantic intention that is directly opposed to the original one'.[98] Jeremiah 3.4-5 incorporates a bit of liturgical language, which, in a liturgical context is an appeal to God, but in this context is instead used to accuse the audience of improper behavior. The extended analysis of 3.1–4.4 will also show that this opposing semantic voice is in view and is a dialogue partner throughout the text of Jer. 3.1–4.4 (e.g. in 3.12-13, 21-25).

To extend the discussion briefly to 3.1–4.4 as a whole, the multiple voices in 3.1–4.4 reveal a text which is characterized by dialogism. More-

94. Walter Brueggemann, 'Jeremiah's Use of Rhetorical Questions', *JBL* 92 (1973), pp. 358-74 (359).

95. Brueggemann, 'Rhetorical Questions', p. 359.

96. Brueggemann, 'Rhetorical Questions', p. 360.

97. Overholt's definition of rhetorical questions is, 'questions which function as forceful statements' ('Jeremiah 2', p. 266).

98. Mikhail Bakhtin, *Problems of Dostoevsky's Poetics* (ed. and trans. Caryl Emerson; Minneapolis: University of Minnesota Press, 1984), p.193.

over, these multiple voices are most visible through the use of quotation in the piece. The people are quoted by YHWH (cf. 3.4-5), future words are put in the people's mouths (cf. 3.21-25), and at one point there is dialogue between YHWH and the prophet who usually speaks for YHWH (3.6-11). Through the strategy of quotation, various voices are heard or portrayed throughout the piece, each one adding to the argument of the whole, but each also interacting with the other voices in the text. Moreover, as we have seen, both Jer. 3.1-5 and its intertext (Deut. 24.1-4) convey similar but yet different uses of the same law, neither of which is value-neutral.[99]

The implied reader of Jer. 3.1-5 is a pre-exilic Judahite audience (cf. 2.2) living some time before the events of the 590s and 580s BCE. The audience is drawn in through the use of the legal citation and rhetorical questions of v. 1. The presupposition of the law is an appeal to outside authority, which in turn lends the speaker authority to accuse the audience. Further, the use of quoted audience speech makes the ongoing dialogue between the prophet/YHWH and the audience visible by introducing an opposing voice which, nevertheless, is manipulated and controlled by the prophet/YHWH. The quotations are chosen and used in such a way as to place the audience in an even more damning position. The socio-historical view being presented by the prophet is one in which the audience has strayed from God yet calls on God for help when trouble looms. The final statement in v. 5 highlighting the people's two-faced approach to YHWH reinforces the sarcastic question uttered by YHWH at the end of v. 1: 'and yet you would return to me?!'

To sum up the discussion of intertextuality in Jer. 3.1-5 in this chapter, the legal citation of 3.1 has been seen to be a powerful persuasive tool. The presupposition of the law is an appeal to outside authority, which in turn lends the speaker authority to accuse the audience. The form that the citation takes, a disputation through a series of rhetorical questions, high-lights the interplay between this text and the intertext, Deut. 24.1-4. The background of covenantal curses is evoked in vv. 2-5, as is the connection between proper behavior and the land. The quotations of audience speech

99. Bakhtin argues that due to its dialogical nature, no text is neutral, but embodies and presents a certain socio-historical view. In Medvedev's formulation, 'Every concrete utterance is a social act... Not only the meaning of the utterance but also the very fact of its performance is of historical and social significance, as, in general, is the fact of its realization in the here and now, in given circumstances, at a certain historical moment, under the conditions of the given social situation' (Medvedev and Bakhtin[?], *The Formal Method*, p. 120; cf. Bakhtin, 'Discourse', pp. 293-94).

indicate prior discourse between the people and the prophet (YHWH) and illustrate the ongoing dialogue between YHWH and the people. Moreover, the use of rhetorical questions draws the audience/reader in to participate in the dialogue. In the switch from a legal context to rhetorical questions, the law is absorbed, re-presented and transformed into an instrument both of dialogue and of accusation. With one blow, Jer. 3.1-5 shatters Israel's security. As my analysis of the remainder of the piece will attempt to show, its security is shattered on a number of levels. Verses 6-11 of ch. 3 indicate some of those levels, and, in addition, continue the interplay with the law of Deut. 24.1-4, culminating in the actual transgression of the law in vv. 12-13. Before discussing 3.6-11 and 12-13, however, it is necessary to look at yet another form of intertextuality in 3.1-5, intertextuality of culture, as evoked through the metaphors and gender issues in 3.1-5.

Chapter 2

GENDER CONSTRUCTION AND INTERTEXTUALITY OF CULTURE:
A SECOND READING OF JEREMIAH 3.1-5

> Although it may be impossible, in the end, to escape the hegemony of patri-
> archal structures, none the less, by unveiling the prejudices at work in our
> cultural artefacts, we impugn the universality of the man-made models pro-
> vided to us, and allow for the possibility of sidestepping and subverting
> their power.
>
> —Nelly Furman

Jeremiah 3.1-5 plays as much upon conventions of gender as it does on the
legal citation in v. 1. My second reading will address this type of intertextuality directly. Mikhail Bakhtin's work provides a necessary foundation for this reading of the text as well. As noted above, one of his crucial
insights is that language is a site of struggle, and it is through dialogue that
meaning is produced. Because language is always a locus of struggle,
boundaries are central to Bakhtin's thought. He argues that 'Discourse
lives, as it were, on the boundary between its own context and another,
alien, context'.[1] The rhetoric of Jer. 3.1–4.4 itself is also concerned with
boundaries within a range of contexts (including legal, religious, political
and sexual contexts).

Moreover, Bakhtin's idea of an utterance as a social act realized in a
specific social/political/historical situation paves the way for the notion of
dialogue to be extended beyond literary texts to the cultural conventions
with which a text plays. Often, social conventions and/or ideals will come
into dialogue within any given text. The interchange that ensues is frequently one between an authoritative (or centripetal) voice, and marginal

---

1. Mikhail Bakhtin, 'Discourse in the Novel', in *The Dialogic Imagination*,
pp. 284, 293-94. The word 'alien' here does not necessarily mean something at odds
with the author's thought, but simply means something outside or beyond the author's
words themselves. An 'alien' context may indeed be complementary or similar to that
of the author.

(or centrifugal) voices.[2] Bakhtin's dialogical approach further highlights the ways in which the multiple voices in a text represent various power structures. The voices incorporated in a text will both 'reflect and refract'[3] the structures of power in a society.[4] We will see these dynamics at work not just in Jer. 3.1-5, but in the entire passage.

2.   Cf. Bakhtin, 'Discourse', p. 270. Bakhtin's work has been severely criticized by feminists because it does not deal with gender differences. For example, his concept of dialogism in the novel is applied exclusively to novels written by men. Moreover, in his discussion of marginal voices, he omits the female voice as a possible voice from the margins. The Introduction to Dale M. Bauer and Susan Jaret McKinstry (eds.), *Feminism, Bakhtin, and the Dialogic* (Albany: SUNY, 1991), pp. 1-6, offers a more thorough critique. Nevertheless, Bakhtin's work has been adapted and used as a basis for a 'feminist dialogics'. Bauer and McKinstry argue that 'Bakhtin's theories of the social nature of the utterance…provide a critical language that allows us to pinpoint and foreground the moments when the patriarchal work and the persuasive resistance to it come into conflict. By highlighting these contradictions, a feminist dialogics produces occasions for the disruption and critique of dominant and oppressive ideologies. The conflict of discourses in a novel, the inevitable polyvocality of a genre that reproduces language as a web of communications between narrator and narratee, speaker and listener, character and character, and even (implied) author and (implied) reader, does reveal the dominant discourse… At the same time, however, the novel's polyvocality can indicate potential resistances to oppressive conventions in interpretive or discourse communities—such as an individual character's response to that social dictate, or a disapproving narrative tone' (pp. 3-4). While their comments are directed specifically toward the novel as a genre, they may be applied just as well to the text of Jer. 3.1–4.4. By looking at the ways in which gender is used in the piece, both the dominant discourse and various marginal discourses of gender and other cultural ideals will be brought to the fore.

3.   The metaphor of reflection and refraction of societal power differentials is that of Josephine Donovan, 'Style and Power', in Bauer and McKinstry (eds.), *Feminism, Bakhtin, and the Dialogic*, pp. 85-94 (85).

4.   Attention to this dynamic is of particular applicability to the text of Jer. 3.1–4.4, where issues of power in all realms of society (politics, religion, sexuality and familial relationships, and nature) are central to the rhetoric of the piece as a whole. We must, however, add a note of caution with regard to critique and appropriation of gender values in any text. Deborah Jacobs argues for the importance of avoiding the overlaying of a twentieth-century conception of gender and women's place in the rhetoric of the text. Rather than asking some variation of the question, 'Where am I in this text?', she suggests that feminists should be asking questions related to the specific historical construction of gender at work in a specific text: 'to ask *why* a body is staged in a certain way at a certain time; to ask how a sign is used rather than what it might mean…' ('Critical Imperialism and Renaissance Drama: The Case of The Roaring Girl', in Bauer and McKinstry [eds.], *Feminism, Bakhtin, and the Dialogic*, pp. 73-84

Verse 1 not only introduces the legal quotation with which 3.1-5 plays, but also introduces intertextuality with culture. By invoking a law dealing with *sexuality*, the prophet invokes powerful cultural ideas and stereotypes. By invoking a *law* which to an extent defines gendered relationships, the prophet insists on a specific reading of gender with which he assumes his audience will agree. Verse 1 also contains the first instance of metaphor in 3.1–4.4. After a citation of a law regarding marital relationships, the prophet takes the rhetoric to the metaphorical level by the direct address to Israel as wife, '"You (fem. sing.) have played the whore with many lovers; and yet you would return to me?" says the Lord'. In this verse a legal boundary is invoked along with sexual boundaries in phrasing the question of repentance. Just as the citations of audience speech introduce an opposing voice as described above, the metaphor itself also introduces opposing characters, placing the (male) audience in opposition to God, this time as promiscuous wives in relation to God the husband. Jeremiah 3.1-5 thus begins by merging images of gender and overstepped boundaries. As wife, the audience is accused of overstepping a primary boundary constructing the marriage bond, that of sexual fidelity. That alone would be enough to sever the marital relationship, but Israel has gone beyond even that boundary, as v. 2 depicts.

Verse 2 deepens and extends the metaphor, illustrating the extreme nature of the promiscuity: 'Lift up your eyes on the bare heights and see: Where have you not been lain with? You have sat along the roads for them, like an Arab in the desert, and you have polluted the land with your harlotry and with your evil.' This is no ordinary promiscuity. Wife Israel is portrayed as insatiable, willing to practice her trade of prostitution anywhere. Even worse, Israel's behavior is pictured as predatory, targeting and accosting anyone who passes. In sexual terms, the extension of Israel's behavior from adultery to prostitution-like actions also deepens and extends their transgression. They are not just guilty of adultery, but of adultery taken to the extreme.

Here metaphor and gender are being used analogically. As an analogue for the religious and political relationship between the deity and the

[76]). She argues persuasively that such questions will perhaps reveal far more about gender identities and constructions over the centuries, perhaps even some great discontinuities, which may enable the imagination of a different future for women. In addition to asking questions regarding the structures of power as represented in the literary devices and style of the piece, this study adopts Jacobs' questions when looking at the role of gender in the rhetoric of Jer. 3.1–4.4.

people, the metaphorical marital relationship highlights the importance and inviolability of the boundary of fidelity. Just as a marital relationship is severed beyond the possibility of recovery by the wife's acts of sexual infidelity,[5] so Israel's religious and political infidelities have severed the divine–human relationship.

The preoccupation of this text with overstepped boundaries is well-served by the metaphor chosen to represent this transgression. The metaphor of woman as unfaithful wife, or harlot, assumes a society where women are defined in terms of their relation to men (e.g. wife, mother, daughter). Men have legal and social jurisdiction over women, and are thus the central members of society. More particularly for our purposes, they have authority over women's sexuality. Women, on the other hand, represent the boundaries, or limits of society. Those women who act within the sexual confines of their roles (as defined by males), represent the inner boundary of society, while those overstepping the sexual confines (in particular, prostitutes) represent the outer boundaries.[6] In patriarchal society, women who choose to have sex for money (or have to do so in order to survive) are marginalized, representing the outer boundaries of society. More dangerous, however, is a *wife's* infidelity, for it calls into question the very issues of control and paternity that the patriarchal system protects. In such a society, an unfaithful wife is in a dangerously autonomous position.[7] The image of Jer. 3.1-2, that of the unfaithful wife who

5.   Indeed, the deuteronomic law code specifies that the party or parties guilty of adultery shall die (Deut. 22.22-27). In her discussion of the deuteronomic laws regarding adultery (Deut. 22.13-29), Pressler indicates that these laws 'recognize the rights of the father to exclusive disposal of his daughter's sexuality and especially the rights of the husband to exclusive possession of his wife's sexuality. The wife has no such reciprocal claim' (*The View of Women*, p. 42).

6.   Cf. Toril Moi, *Sexual/Textual Politics: Feminist Literary Theory* (London/New York: Routledge), pp. 163-67. She writes regarding these boundaries: 'Women seen as the limit of the symbolic order will...share in the disconcerting properties of *all* frontiers: they will be neither inside nor outside, neither known nor unknown'. She says further, 'It is this position that has enabled male culture sometimes to vilify women as representing darkness and chaos, to view them as Lilith or the Whore of Babylon, and sometimes to elevate them as the representatives of a higher and purer nature, to venerate them as Virgins and Mothers of God. In the first instance the borderline is seen as part of the chaotic wilderness outside, and in the second it is seen as an inherent part of the inside: the part that protects and shields the symbolic order from the imaginary chaos' (p. 167).

7.   These issues come up in another guise in the Wisdom Literature, particularly in Proverbs, where the Strange Woman is pictured as luring young men in order to seduce

has gone to the extreme of acting like a prostitute, therefore, is the ideal way to represent overstepped limits of society. It is this danger that is played upon in the images of overstepped boundaries or limits, particularly sexual limits, in these verses. Also visible here is an authoritative (male) voice (the prophet) asserting domination over a marginal (female) voice (those who would continue current political and religious practice).

It is important to note here that the alternation of masculine and feminine forms of address in Jer. 3.1–4.4 signifies that the metaphors do not refer literally to sexual cultic practice, but rather, that promiscuity is a general metaphor for non-allegiance to YHWH.[8] Instead of viewing the metaphors of promiscuity as arising out of sexual cultic practice, as have many previous scholars, I propose, in line with exegetes such as Phyllis A. Bird and Claudia V. Camp,[9] that the background of the metaphors is to be found in cultural conventions surrounding the relations between genders. In a patriarchal world, where the males are the full members of society, the primary audience for this passage is male. In patriarchal marriage, the wife's sexuality is controlled by and reserved for her husband alone. This state of affairs is pictured as the natural, the 'common-sense' way things ought to be. And it is the use of 'common sense' or natural arguments which makes this rhetoric so powerful.

them (see especially Prov. 7). Claudia Camp, says of this image: 'the professional prostitute does have a place in a patriarchal world, even if it is a liminal one... Far more dangerous is the woman who exists within the boundaries of male-controlled sexuality, but who decides for herself to opt out of them. Such is the wife *šît zônâ* in Proverbs 7' ('What's So Strange about the Strange Woman?', in David Jobling, Peggy L. Day and Gerald T. Sheppard [eds.], *The Bible and the Politics of Exegesis: Essays in Honor of Norman K. Gottwald on His Sixty-Fifth Birthday* [Cleveland: Pilgrim Press, 1991], pp. 17-31 [28]). For the full argument, see Camp, 'What's So Strange?', pp. 22-31. I argue that it is this same danger which is played on in the marital metaphors of Jer. 3.1–4.4, where Israel is imaged as the wife who has stepped out of 'the boundaries of male-controlled sexuality'.

8.   This supports Phyllis A. Bird's conclusion that the term זונה 'has, in itself no cultic connotations' ('"To Play the Harlot"', p. 88), that is, the term itself, contra much of previous scholarship, has no relationship to supposed Canaanite ritual prostitution. For a full discussion of the term and its connotations, see the entire article. For further discussion of the lack of connection between the image of the harlot and actual sexual promiscuity in the Hebrew Scriptures, see Camp, 'What's So Strange?', esp. pp. 20, 28-29.

9.   See the preceding footnote. It is surprising that in an otherwise sophisticated reading of Jer. 3, that Angela Bauer adopts the traditional 'fertility cults' view of this imagery (*Gender in the Book of Jeremiah*, p. 53).

With the rhetorical questions of vv. 1b-2, the perspective has shifted from an unidentified subject ('a man') to the audience as subject ('you' [fem. sing.]). Taken together with the first questions in 3.1 ('Behold a man divorced his wife and she went from him and she married another man. Can he return to her again? Has not that land become indeed polluted?') the rhetorical questions here function in a similar fashion to Nathan's re-counting of the parable of the ewe lamb in 2 Samuel 12. The first question of Jer. 3.1 arouses the immediate and expected response that of course the first husband could not return to her. The second question brings to mind the issue of the connection of behavior and the land, eliciting the implied response that of course the land would be polluted. Note that the reference to 'that land' in v. 1b, may also metaphorically refer to the woman herself. In the broader context, the woman is metaphorically land to be ploughed, sown, harvested, etc.[10]

Having hooked the audience by eliciting the expected response, the prophet next puts the audience in a similar position to David listening to Nathan's story. Where Nathan says to David, 'you are the man', the prophet is saying: you (the Israelite community) are a predatory and insatiable harlot. Suddenly the law, which in its legal form applied generally to human marriage, is applied specifically to the metaphorical relationship between YHWH as husband and Israel as wife. Because the picture is metaphorical, it is immediate.

Verse 3 shows that the actions have a cosmic effect as well: 'Therefore the showers have been withheld and the spring rains have not come, yet you have a harlot's brow; you refuse to be ashamed'. Here creation and sexuality are symbolically linked. In 3.3a, YHWH's control over nature is indicated in the withholding of divine rains from the land. The danger associated with overstepped sexual boundaries is made even more explicit by evoking the danger of chaos in the connection between infidelity and infertility of the land.[11] Just as in the patriarchal social fabric the woman

---

10. Cf. Carol Delaney, *The Seed and the Soil: Gender and Cosmology in Turkish Village Society* (Berkeley: University of California Press, 1991). Although her study deals with a specific Islamic Turkish village, she argues that women as soil/land and men as seed are governing metaphors in all three monotheistic religions (Judaism, Christianity and Islam), and that the roots of such metaphors reach into early antiquity (see esp. pp. 14-40). This idea and its ramifications in Jer. 3.1-5 will be discussed in detail later in the present chapter.

11. Above, in connection with the intertextuality between Jer. 3.1-5 and Deuteronomy, it was noted that promiscuity had negative effects on the land in that the people's actions would result either in blessing or in cursing for the land. In the prophets,

who oversteps the boundaries is punished either by legal means (divorce, public humiliation) or by social means (ostracism), so in 3.3a the land is punished because of Israel's misbehavior. In the prophet's imaging, her behavior leads to a disruption of the cosmic order.[12]

Verse 3.3b returns to and extends the marital metaphor of vv. 1-2: 'But you have the brow of a harlot; you refuse to be ashamed'. It is Israel's promiscuous behavior which has directly caused such infertility. Moreover, faced with the consequences of their behavior, the people still have not changed their ways. The problematic phrase, 'you have a harlot's brow', is unparalleled in the Old Testament. However, it seems to be roughly similar in meaning to the following phrase, 'you refuse to be ashamed'.[13] The connotations of stubbornness, haughtiness, refusal to acknowledge culpability, brazenness, or any combination of the four, are evoked through the two phrases. In addition to extending the metaphor itself, as with the direct address and metaphorical language of vv. 1-2, couching the accusation in metaphorical terms and using direct address adds to the immediacy of the accusation: 'you *have* a harlot's brow'. The audience, once again, is *identified* as a harlot.[14] Moreover, through this juxtaposition of the withholding of divine fertility with the reminder that the sexuality of Israel is unbridled and unrepented, YHWH's claim to power over fertility in the natural world (ideal of creation) reinforces his

beginning with Hosea, this theme is taken over and described in relational rather than exclusively covenantal terms. T. Drorah Setel argues with regard to Hosea (esp. ch. 2) that, 'his underlying concern is to contrast Yahweh's positive (male) fidelity with Israel's negative (female) harlotry. In so doing, he introduces the themes of the degradation of females and their identification with the land and denies their positive role in human reproduction and nurturance' ('Prophets and Pornography: Female Sexual Imagery in Hosea', in Letty M. Russell [ed.], *Feminist Biblical Interpretation* [Philadelphia: Westminster Press, 1985], pp. 86-95 [93]). As we shall see, similar issues underlie the use of metaphors of harlotry in Jeremiah.

12. The extreme of this disruption, a depiction of the un-making of creation, occurs in Jer. 4.23-26.

13. Cf. Prov. 30.20.

14. Renita Weems goes even further, arguing that this imagery does what the animal imagery of Jer. 2 cannot—it identifies the woman as 'culpable, accountable, and responsible for her behavior' (*Battered Love: Marriage, Sex, and Violence in the Hebrew Prophets* [Overtures to Biblical Theology; Minneapolis: Fortress Press, 1995], p. 55). Weems' treatment of Jeremiah, while having much in common with my own treatment (and written about the same time as my article on Jer. 3.1–4.4), is quite brief. For my critique of her conclusions, see my article, 'Multiple Exposures: Body Rhetoric and Gender Characterization in Ezekiel 16', *JFSR* 14 (1998), pp. 5-18.

claim to jurisdiction over sexuality in the metaphorical marriage relationship (ideal of gender).

This juxtaposition between the natural and gender ideals plays on a certain view of YHWH's relationship with the land, of the integral connection between human fertility and fertility of the land, and on a certain view of gender relations. First, regarding YHWH's relationship with the land, YHWH is, like most ancient Near Eastern male deities,[15] associated with rain and the fertility that rain brings.[16] Yet YHWH's role in the Bible differs radically from those of ancient Near Eastern male deities. In ancient Near Eastern societies, the male god procreates with a female goddess. Thus, fertility is ensured through the actions of a male and female god(dess). In the biblical text, however, there is no female counterpart to YHWH. Therefore, to anticipate the discussion below, YHWH alone must have the power to control all fertility.

The second relationship, the intimate connection between human fertility and fertility of the land, has already been alluded to above: sexual behavior and the land are linked in Deut. 24.1-4, in the laws of Leviticus 18 and 20, and in Jer. 3.1-5. Deuteronomy provides another example: the blessings which come from proper worship include fertility of land and people, while the curses which come from disobedience include drought and barrenness.[17]

---

15. Frymer-Kensky argues that 'Rain is always considered a male power within Near Eastern polytheism; agricultural fertility is thought to result from the collective activity of male and female deities acting in concert (or consort)… As YHWH appropriates each of these powers, the image of divine mastery emerges, with all its consequences for the conceptualization of nature and humanity' (*In the Wake of the Goddesses: Women, Culture, and the Biblical Transformation of Pagan Myth* [New York: Free Press, 1992], p. 89).

16. For YHWH's giving or withholding of rains, see, e.g., Lev. 26.4; Deut. 11.14; 28.12, 24; 1 Kgs 8.35-36; 2 Chron. 6.26-27; 7.13; Job 5.10; 28.26. YHWH's power over rain and fertility is mentioned frequently in Jeremiah as well (cf. 5.24; 10.11, 13; 14.1-10; 51.15-16). Among the other prophets, Hos. 6.3 portrays God's coming to the people in response to their returning as 'like the showers, like the spring rains that water the earth'. The connections between the people's return and God's coming as rain is particularly evocative in connection with Jeremiah, where God removes himself (and his rains) in response to the people's infidelity.

17. Cf. Deut. 11.10-17 and ch. 28. See also similar ideas in the Psalms which speak of YHWH's just and righteous reign, which will result in prosperity and fertility (rain) both for the people and for the land (cf. Ps. 68.9-10). Likewise, in the passages dealing with the rule of the righteous king, fertility both for land and people are linked, and they come ultimately from the hand of God (cf. Ps. 72.6, 16; Isa. 11; 32.9-20).

Third, this juxtaposition between the natural and gender ideals plays on a certain view of relations between genders. Uncontrolled women are here portrayed as representing the danger of chaos.[18] Moreover, the logical outcome of the threat women pose to society is also depicted: women's sexual autonomy threatens the very structures upon which patriarchal society is built, and such behavior will lead to chaos (both in society and nature). The idea that this behavior offends the natural order suggests that the behavior itself is 'unnatural'. Verse 3b also extends the play on over-stepped boundaries. Just as with the many oppositions between 'natural' and 'unnatural' ways of doing things set up in ch. 2,[19] 3.3 contains an implied opposition between promiscuous behavior ('unnatural') and fidel-ity ('natural'). The metaphorical connection between promiscuous behavior and chaos plays on this distinction. And the fact that the distinction is im-plicit rather than explicit renders it more power. The audience is presumed to agree with this view of sexual and marital relations as the 'common-sense' way things are to be. The application of an existing 'natural' ideal, namely, that YHWH has control over nature, is thus used rhetorically to reinforce the ('common-sense') gender ideal. The mutual reinforcement of these ideals adds to the power of the rhetoric of Jer. 3.1-5.

Another aspect of the language in 3.1-5 which deals with gender and intertextuality of culture is the connection between the wife's (Israel's) behavior and the land. As I have argued elsewhere,[20] underlying this

18. According to Moi, 'if patriarchy sees women as occupying a marginal position within the symbolic order, then it can construe them as the *limit* or borderline of that order. From a phallocentric point of view, women will then come to represent the necessary frontier between man and chaos; but because of their very marginality they will also always seem to recede into and merge with the chaos of the outside' (*Sexual/ Textual Politics*, p. 167). In biblical studies, the issues of ambiguity, limits and fron-tiers have been dealt with in reference to the female imagery in Proverbs in two articles, one by Claudia V. Camp ('Wise and Strange: An Interpretation of the Female Imagery in Proverbs in Light of Trickster Mythology', *Semeia* 42 [Atlanta: Scholars Press, 1988], pp. 14-36) and the other by Carol A. Newsom ('Woman and the Dis-course of Patriarchal Wisdom: A Study of Proverbs 1–9', in Day [ed.], *Gender and Difference in Ancient Israel*, pp. 142-60). While Camp uses anthropological theory, Newsom comes to some similar conclusions using socio-linguistic theory.

19. See the discussion of these oppositions and their connection with the categories 'natural' vs. 'unnatural' in the 'Context' section in the Introduction.

20. In my 'The Root of the Matter: Seedy Reflections on Jeremiah 3.1–4.4', a paper presented at the 2000 Annual Meeting of the Society of Biblical Literature in Nash-ville, TN.

connection is a root metaphor of seed and soil, with men representing the seed and women representing the soil.[21] Basing my discussion of the biblical text on the anthropological work of Carol Delaney,[22] who has shown how the concept of seed and soil as gendered terms, specifically as terms related to procreation, structure the theological, political and social structure of Islamic Turkish village society, I analyzed the ways in which this idea carried over into the gender rhetoric of 3.1–4.4, specifically answering the question of why sexual activity was said to pollute the land.

In the citation of the law, and the rhetorical questions with which Jer. 3.1 begins, polluting sexual behavior is linked with pollution of the land. The overstepping of sexual boundaries is one of three types of actions which pollute the land, the other two being apostasy and bloodguilt, according to Carolyn Pressler.[23] But why sexual impurity? Why do sexual actions have an effect on the *literal* soil of ancient Israel?

As noted in my discussion of the law as found in Deuteronomy in the first chapter, the problem with remarriage is that it makes the second marriage a sort of adultery, and legally sanctioned adultery. As Pressler has shown, the deuteronomic view of adultery (Deut. 22.13-29) is that it violates 'the husband's rights to exclusive possession of his wife's sexual-

21. A.R. Pete Diamond and Kathleen M. O'Connor argue that the root metaphor for Jer. 2–3 (4.2) is actually the marriage metaphor ('Unfaithful Passions: Coding Women Coding Men in Jeremiah 2–3 [4.2]', *BibInt* 4 [1996], pp. 288-310 [292]). In contrast, I see the seed/soil metaphor to be at the root of even the marriage imagery as it is presented in these chapters.

22. Delaney, *The Seed and the Soil*. While one must be cautious in adapting and applying anthropological research to biblical texts from a much earlier culture to which we no longer have direct access, there are several aspects of her study which nevertheless make it suggestive for biblical studies, including the Islamic context which does not separate politics and religion as our own culture does (while Turkey itself is a secular state, Islam permeates all aspects of this village's culture). See Delaney's discussion of the centrality of Islam to the village which she studied, especially pp. 18-21 and 283-323. For a discussion of some of the tensions between the village's Islamic center and the secular Turkish state, see especially pp. 221-25, 283-385). That Delaney herself sometimes goes too far in globalizing her theory has been aptly addressed by Frymer-Kensky her article, 'Virginity in the Bible', in Victor H. Matthews, Bernard M. Levinson and Tikva Frymer-Kensky (eds.), *Gender and Law in the Hebrew Bible and the Ancient Near East* (JSOTSup, 262; Sheffield: Sheffield Academic Press, 1998), pp. 79-96 (82). Nevertheless, with caution, her work is helpful for addressing issues in Jer. 3.1–4.4 and may also be helpful in elucidating some basic concepts/metaphors that underlie the gender constructions of the Hebrew Bible.

23. Pressler, *The View of Women*, p. 51.

ity'.[24] Two issues are at stake; the husband's authority and 'his need to be certain that his children are his own'.[25]

Pressler adds that 'Frymer-Kensky's work on sexuality and pollution suggests a possible way of understanding the matter'.[26] If Mary Douglas is right in arguing that purity beliefs are a way to set in place and maintain proper boundaries in society,[27] and Tikva Frymer-Kensky is correct that sexual relations can blur the line between families and thus break down needed boundaries between family and family, or even break down boundaries at the clan and tribal levels,[28] then, in Pressler's terms, 'sexual relations, whether legal or not, which bind a woman first to one man, then to a second, then again to the first, confuse the boundaries which define the (patrilineal) family'.[29] Pressler's conclusion is convincing, namely, that what this law does is limit the husband's authority over the woman 'for the sake of the purity of the community and to support the patrilineal family structure'.[30]

What I am suggesting is that these arguments be taken a step further. I posit that underlying the whole of this law may be the seed and soil metaphor. The remarriage causes a confusion of both seed and soil. In Jer. 3.1, the problem is magnified. If a remarriage after a second husband causes such confusion, how much more does the adultery/prostitution of wife Israel? Whose seed is this? Whose soil is this? If woman as soil is a root metaphor, then the connections between a woman's overstepping of sexual boundaries and pollution of the land becomes clear. A woman's adultery or prostitution means there is a mixture of seed in her.[31] Symbolically

24. Pressler, *The View of Women*, p. 61.

25. Pressler, *The View of Women*, p. 61.

26. Pressler, *The View of Women*, p. 61.

27. Douglas, *Purity and Danger*.

28. Tikva Frymer-Kensky, 'Law and Philosophy: The Case of Sex in the Bible', *Semeia* 45 (1989), pp. 89-102, and 'Pollution, Purification, and Purgation in Biblical Israel, in Meyers and O'Connor (eds.), *The Word of the Lord Shall Go Forth*, pp. 399-414.

29. Pressler, *The View of Women*, p. 61.

30. Pressler, *The View of Women*, p. 62.

31. Delaney writes that semen (seed) leaves 'an indelible imprint inside the woman, one that no amount of washing can erase' (*The Seed and the Soil*, p. 41). The man, however, only becomes temporarily defiled, until he performs his ritual ablution (which is required after any sexual intercourse). Given how women who are raped (Dinah and Tamar) or otherwise defiled are treated in the biblical texts, and given how the laws on sexual impurity in Leviticus and Deuteronomy are framed (see particularly

then, the land also has a mixture of seed (cf. Lev. 19.19 and Deut. 22.9, which prohibit sowing two kinds of seed in the same field). Both the woman and the land become polluted.

If a woman oversteps sexual boundaries, she threatens the very fabric of society. First, her actions threaten the patriarchal family unit: no longer is the field/woman pure; any child is seen as mixed seed rather than purely that of the woman's husband. A woman's infidelity also blurs the lines according to which society is structured. If the core unit of society, that of the family, is compromised, the effects extend to all of society. It rocks the foundations of society, so to speak. This is one of the reasons why women's sexuality is controlled in patriarchal societies.[32] It is this idea that is manifest in v. 2. The wanton sexuality of which Israel is accused in v. 2a is linked directly with pollution of the land in v. 2b. The text reads, 'Lift up your eyes on the bare heights and see: where have you not been lain with? By the roads you have sat waiting for them like an Arab in the desert. You have polluted the land with your whorings and your evils.' The metaphor itself extends the scope of the pollution. If the metaphorical woman is Israel, and her husband is God, then Israel's actions affect all of God's land, that is, all of the territory of Israel (cf. Deut. 32.8-9).[33] This idea in turn, makes sense of v. 3, where Israel's behavior has consequences in the realm of nature. In this verse we have the logical conclusion to the idea that the seed and soil theory of procreation underlies the structure of all of society. The root metaphor which ties all these ideas together is the

Pressler, *The View of Women*, for a thorough discussion of the latter), this idea may be at the root of how women and men are imaged in the biblical texts.

32. Here, Delaney's discussion of the ways in which the seed and soil metaphor structures society is helpful. She talks about the village society as being constructed in concentric circles, with the innermost being the nuclear family, moving out by stages to the village, and even extending to how the Turkish nation is structured rhetorically. In so doing, she makes a good case for the root of this structure being the seed and soil theory of procreation. In each circle, the woman, home, village, nation, or world is symbolically female, and needs to be enclosed and protected, while the political and leadership structures function to enclose and protect, and are symbolically male (*The Seed and the Soil*, pp. 198-200). A thorough study of how such a theory might make sense of what we know of ancient Israelite society as imaged by the prophets is beyond the scope of this book. However, the diagram and idea are very suggestive in terms of how the text of Jer. 3.1–4.4 develops, which is my primary purpose here.

33. To use the image of Delaney, the territory of Israel is the outer ring of the concentric circles, with God as the one protecting and enclosing it. In other words, God is the one with power and authority over it, who represents it to others.

seed/soil metaphor. In both the creation and the gender ideals, the seed is represented by the male deity, God (as rain and as husband), while the soil is represented by woman (as the ground which is planted and as the wife).[34]

There is yet another link between the images of Jer. 3.3 and the law cited in Jer. 3.1 which the idea of a root metaphor of soil and seed elucidates. At stake in both the rain imagery of v. 3a and the accusations against the people in vv. 1-2 are issues of power and identity.[35] With regard to creation, the issue is: Who has the power over fertility in creation—YHWH or other gods—and, therefore, whose issue (crop) is the result of that fertility? With regard to the accusations in v. 1, the problem is similar: Who has the power over human fertility? How can a pure line of descent be ensured? The only way a pure line of descent can be ensured is through a woman's sexual fidelity to her husband.[36] For paternity to be certain, the husband must retain control over a wife's sexuality.[37] In the case of Jer.

34. Not only does this metaphor reveal how women's actions pollute the land, but, as will be shown in subsequent chapters, the metaphor provides some clues to the shifts in imagery the text of Jer. 3.1–4.4.

35. Coming back to Delaney's discussion of how the Turkish Islamic village society is structured in concentric circles (see nn. 32 and 33), her further argument that, viewed three-dimensionally, the concentric cirlces are actually cones, with the apex of each cone representing a power structure, applies here. All the heads of the power structures are male. At the apex of the largest, all-encompassing cone is God. See her diagram on p. 199 and the discussion surrounding that diagram on pp. 198-200.

36. Pressler concludes her study of the deuteronomic laws concerning women, including Deut. 24.1-4, with a discussion of the purpose of such laws. She holds that these laws in large part are concerned to preserve order, integrity and continuity within the family system. Moreover, the way in which both order and integrity are preserved are primarily through 'male control over female sexuality' (*The View of Women*, p. 97). With regard to integrity, she argues that one of the concerns is to maintain the paternal line: 'if lineage is defined in terms of the father, then he must be certain that the children are his own. The woman has the potential to adulterate his lineage. The biological integrity of his family depends upon his exclusive possession of his wife's (or wives') sexuality' (p. 99).

37. J. Cheryl Exum, in an exploration of the gender ideology of the patriarchal narratives, makes a compelling argument for similar concerns being central to the patriarchal narratives of Genesis. She says, 'concern with the issue of the proper lineage of the chosen people…lies at the heart of the patriarchal narratives' (*Fragmented Women: Feminist [Sub]versions of Biblical Narratives* (JSOTSup, 163; Sheffield: JSOT Press, 1993], p. 104). She discusses the ways in which 'Genesis offers 'ancestral' justification to two key biblical concepts: Israel's claim to be the chosen people

3.1-5, when paternity cannot be established the land is polluted, and the consequence is the withholding of YHWH's fertility (drought/no rains). The images of 3.3 illustrate not only the interweaving of women's fertility and the fertility of the land, but also YHWH's ultimate control over all procreation and fertility. Here the ideal of creation is used to reinforce a legal ideal, and together they reinforce a gender ideal. The complex inter-weaving of these ideals in turn shows YHWH's claim of control over every aspect of life, both creation (non-human) and culture (human), including both legal and gender relations. Moreover, their combination gives greater force to the rhetoric, revealing just how dangerous Israel's religious behavior has been to the very structures of society and fabric of creation.

In Jer. 3.3, the complex interaction of the ideals of gender (sexual fidelity on the part of women), creation (YHWH as grantor or withholder of fertility) and the law (incorporating both gender and creation) is mutually reinforcing. Moreover, the ways in which they play upon each other, both implicitly and explicitly, are exceptionally powerful rhetorically. It is gender, however, which unites these ideals, and which in turn gives the rhetoric its force. It is precisely the marginality of women, their place at the boundaries of patriarchal society, which makes the imagery work so well. The main offense of Israel, the wife/harlot, is that her sexuality is uncontrolled (she lies in wait 'Like an Arab in the desert'), and, further, that it is not controlled by YHWH, her husband/father (2.1-22; 3.19-20). Male fear over the consequences of that lack of control becomes an underlying force adding to the potency of the metaphors. With regard to relations with other nations, for example, just as sexual promiscuity posed a danger to the very fabric of Israelite society, so did (according to the prophet) the various foreign alliances in which Israel involved itself. The power of this imagery lies in the fact that its roots are embedded in the patriarchal social system of Israel—it is 'common sense'—as well as that the listeners to which it is addressed (who, as noted before, are implicitly men) would have a stake in maintaining the social structures on which the metaphors were based.

---

and its claim to the land of Canaan. Abraham (= Israel) is singled out by God as the recipient of the promise that his descendants will inherit the land of Canaan. As this promise will be passed from generation to generation, the crucial question becomes, how is a pure line of descent to be maintained?' (p. 107). For her extended argument, see pp. 107-20. The preoccupation of the remainder of Jer. 3.1–4.4 with sexual matters, including the allusions to the patriarchal promise and the patriarchal sign, circum-cision, indicate that the two issues so central to Genesis are also central here.

Verses 4 and 5 continue to address many of the issues already raised above. Couched in terms of quoted audience speech followed by YHWH's response, vv. 4-5 accuse the audience as a harlot, but describe its behavior as deceptive/treacherous. Following the accusation of v. 3b indicating their unwillingness to accept responsibility for their behavior, vv. 4-5a capture a hint of disbelief in the two questions, 'Have you not just now called to me, "My father, you are the husband of my youth?"' (v. 4); and '"Will he remain angry forever; will he keep [anger] continually?"' (v. 5a). The contrast between whom Israel is imitating (a harlot who refuses to be ashamed) and the relationships Israel claims with YHWH (YHWH as father, as husband of her youth) could not be greater. In vv. 4-5a, the people have called on God for help as if nothing were wrong. The metaphorical language assumes a loving, marital relationship. The promiscuous wife has had the temerity to remind God of their past intimate relationship. In these verses the metaphorical language provides not just immediacy, but again carries forward in pictorial terms the extremes to which Israel has gone. In v. 5b, YHWH emphasizes the duplicitous nature of their words: 'Behold you have spoken, but you have done all the evil you could'.

The emphasis on incongruence between behavior and words, as well as the accusation of treachery,[38] also plays upon the images of overstepped boundaries, which have already been discussed with relation to vv. 1-2. The image of overstepped boundaries binds v. 3 with the legal rhetoric of v. 1, thus returning the reader (and the audience) to the legal and relational issues at stake in the chapter as a whole. As with vv. 1-3, it is cultural conventions of female gender which provide the grounds for accusation and unite the metaphors and ideas of vv. 4-5, adding force to the rhetoric of the entire section (vv. 1-5). Thus, like the previous verses, the rhetoric of vv. 4-5 gains its power by its interweaving of several ideas already introduced, but with an additional issue, that of the incongruence between

---

38. While deception can be a positive vehicle for women to claim power in a patriarchal society (cf. J. Cheryl Exum and Johanna W.H. Bos [eds.], *Reasoning with the Foxes: Female Wit in a World of Male Power* [Semeia, 42; Atlanta: Scholars Press, 1988]), it nevertheless reflects poorly on the character of women themselves. As Exum says, this portrayal is one lever used by patriarchy to claim the need to control women and women's actions. Cf. her discussion in *Fragmented Women*, pp. 133, 139, and especially p. 133 n. 68, where she says, 'gender plays an important role in the way character traits are evaluated; consider only how differently our society evaluates ambition or competition on the part of men and the part of women' (cf. also Fuchs' article, also in *Semeia* 42, '"For I Have the Way of Women": Deception, Gender, and Ideology in Biblical Narrative', pp. 68-83).

words and behavior. The same incongruence will resurface in 3.6-11 and 19-20.

A final rhetorical strategy which plays on conventions of gender is the rhetorical strategy of addressing the male audience with the feminine form of address; it is one of the primary strategies in which gender and metaphor work most closely together both in Jer. 3.1–4.4 as a whole, and more specifically in 3.1-5.[39] Moreover, this strategy foregrounds a theme we have already seen running through the gender rhetoric of vv. 1-5, the theme of identification.

In Jer. 3.1-5, the feminine direct address begins with the rhetorical question addressed to the audience: 'but you (fem. sing.) have played the harlot with many lovers…', and continues with every direct address in the remainder of these verses. In each case, the audience is not only identified as the promiscuous wife, but, taken cumulatively, the effect of the rhetoric is to pressure the audience into such self-identification. In v. 1, the very phrasing of the question presumes that the audience will identify themselves as acting promiscuously. Verse 2 asks the audience to look at its own behavior, implying that once Israel 'looks up on the bare heights' it will not be able to deny such behavior. In v. 3, the audience is accused of unwillingness to acknowledge wrongdoing in the face of drought, one of the pieces of evidence that it is engaged in wrongdoing: 'you have a harlot's brow; you refuse to be ashamed'. Verses 4-5 extend the rhetoric further, indicating both the people's resistance to and the continuing pressure for that identification. This final accusation addresses the incongruence between the audience's words and behavior by directing the accusation *to* them as the promiscuous wife/harlot of the previous verses. Verses 4-5a represent a false self-identification, followed by an appeal to YHWH based on that identification, and v. 5b exposes the falsity with one stroke.

In Jer. 3.1-5, the prophet, who speaks for God, quotes God as 'I' and addresses the audience as 'you' (fem. sing.). The strategy of direct address asks men (i.e. the primarily male audience) both to identify themselves as the promiscuous woman and to resist that identification. As husbands (present, past or future), the 'natural' identification, and thus, the subtle pressure, is to identify with the male voice, the righteous husband—God. Yet the address forces them first to identify themselves as the promiscuous wife. In short, this section uses direct address to identify the audience as a

---

39. This strategy is also used in the majority of the other texts mentioned above which use images of harlotry.

harlot, to expose their own false self-identification, and to pressure them into a change of behavior as a way of changing their identity. As Diamond and O'Connor observe, 'Besides shaming men...Jeremiah's metaphor cautions men about women in a rhetoric of fear'.[40]

This technique of direct address compounds the effect of the rhetoric. On one level, the use of direct address operates to grab the attention, particularly of a primarily male audience. On another level, the direct address in particular would be offensive to a male audience (e.g. only women can be harlots). The use of metaphor and direct address allow no distancing, no denying. Israel stands accused and condemned.

As we have seen, the use of the marriage metaphor in these verses is very powerful rhetorically. Indeed, this metaphor is perhaps the one image that can draw together all the different ideas and ideals with which the prophet plays. When a text uses categories of 'natural' or 'commonsense' ideas to present its case, those very categories often indicate that a subtext is present as well. This is especially true of rhetoric constructed in terms of gender and sexuality. Judith Butler, a well-known theorist of gender, argues, based on the work of Foucault, that sexuality is 'an artifical concept which effectively extends and disguises the power relations responsible for its genesis'.[41] In using gendered language to construct the rhetoric of Jer. 3.1–4.4, the prophet also reinforces certain gender and sexual ideals, ideals that are harmful to women who read this text. Taken to its full conclusion, this imagery, as I argue elsewhere,[42] is dangerous both for men and for women. In what follows, I will lay out some of the problems that this imagery poses particularly for women.

Through the strategy of direct address, as noted above, this rhetoric reconceptualizes a primarily male audience as female, and, through the rhetoric, exerts pressure for them to change their behavior and reidentify

---

40. Diamond and O'Connor, 'Unfaithful Passions', p. 309. O'Connor adds to this idea in her later reading, saying that 'the metaphor tricks [the male readers], for they discover that they are the wanton, treacherous female, doubly shamed by being identified as a woman and as a whore' (Kathleen M. O'Connor, 'The Tears of God and Divine Character in Jeremiah 2–9', in Tod Linafelt and Timothy K. Beal [eds.], *God in the Fray: A Tribute to Walter Brueggemann* [Minneapolis: Fortress Press, 1998], pp. 172-88 [175]).

41. Judith Butler, *Gender Trouble: Feminism and the Subversion of Identity* (New York: Routledge, 1990), p. 92.

42. See my 'Multiple Exposures', pp. 5-18, and 'An Abusive God? Identity and Power/Gender and Violence in Ezekiel 23', in A.K.M. Adam (ed.), *Postmodern Interpretations of the Bible—A Reader* (St Louis: Chalice Press, 2001), pp. 129-51.

themselves as men. Butler suggests that any construction of identity goes beyond the construction itself:

> Paradoxically, the reconceptualization of an identity has an *effect*; that is, as *produced* and *generated*, it opens up possibilities of 'agency' that are insidiously foreclosed by positions that take identity categories as foundational and fixed. Construction is not opposed to agency; it is the necessary scene of agency, the very terms in which agency is articulated and becomes culturally intelligible.[43]

One of the effects of the gender construction in Jer. 3.1-5 is that it opens up the possibility for men to take on a different, and, as I will argue in future chapters, more comfortable gender identity. We will see how that new identity is specifically constructed, and why that identity is more comfortable in the discussion of 3.21–4.4.

The effect on women, however, is much different. In Jer. 3.1-5 (and continuing through the whole of the piece, the rhetoric actually marginalizes women, and the marginalization takes place on several levels. First, as shown above, the imagery works *because* it views women as marginal to society. Yet it goes further than that. It also reinforces that marginalization. In her article dealing with discourse and female imagery in Proverbs 1–9, Carol Newsom notes that any symbolic thinking which uses a specific group of people cannot simply be symbolic—it also has implications for the behavior of that group of people.[44] This is especially true in a patriarchal text that uses symbolic language referring to women. When it is only males in a given society who enter into public discourse,[45] one does not

43. Butler, *Gender Trouble*, p. 147.
44. Newsom, 'Woman and Patriarchal Wisdom', p. 155.
45. Discourse is a synonym for rhetoric; it is defined by Emile Benveniste, an influential linguist, as any use of language, written or verbal, which assumes a speaker and a hearer, in which the speaker intends to influence the hearer. He argues further that language, discourse and subjectivity are inseparable (*Problems in General Linguistics* [trans. Mary Elizabeth Meek; Coral Gables: University of Miami Press, 1971], pp. 208-209). Bruce Lincoln sees discourse as working both ideologically and affectively. He writes, 'it is through these paired instrumentalities—ideological persuasion and sentiment evocation—that discourse holds the capacity to shape and reshape society itself' (*Discourse and the Construction of Society*, pp. 8-9). Discourse, moreover, acts to cause the hearer to re-draw boundaries. Lincoln discusses such boundaries in terms of social borders, which he defines as 'those imaginary lines that distinguish one group of persons from another' (p. 9). I am suggesting that the discourse of Jer. 3.1-5, and more broadly, of 3.1–4.4, works by re-drawing certain political and religious borders, at the same time reinforcing and prescribing certain borders of behavior at the

notice such implications. Once, however, women enter into public discourse by acting as speaking subjects (rather than being merely the objects of discourse), the symbolic language becomes confused. When a woman reads this text she 'cannot occupy the same symbolic relation to herself that she does to a man'.[46]

As a subordinate social group, women have a different relationship to language.[47] When a woman is subjected to and becomes the subject of this discourse, something different happens. Although the discourse is disguised as neutral (the devoted wife is the 'natural' order of things, sexually promiscuous women have transgressed the 'natural' boundaries), the rhetoric acts ideologically to exert pressure on the woman to be a faithful wife, mother and/or daughter, the only positive roles allotted to her within the boundaries created by patriarchy. The consequences for women who overstep the boundaries are the same as they were for the male audience: drought (or, in this case, lack of fertility or barrenness). When this metaphor is folded back into literal talk about women and men, and/or male/female relationships, particularly marriage, women could, and at some level will take the language as being literal and addressed to them.[48] In other words, as J. Cheryl Exum puts it, women are constrained to 'read these texts against our own interests'.[49]

This imagery, moreover, uses a binary opposition which is also often seen as 'natural' both in the ancient world and in our society, female vs. male. Women are marginal, while men are central; women are confined to certain very narrowly defined social roles, while men do the defining. This state of affairs is particularly evident in the metaphor itself. God is sym-

gender level. That is, in re-drawing boundaries of proper political and religious behavior, the prophet also re-draws the boundaries for proper male and female behavior.

46. Newsom, 'Woman and Patriarchal Wisdom', p. 155.

47. Moi, *Sexual/Textual Politics*, p. 154.

48. I have seen this phenomenon at work for both men and women in my teaching. Some women have shared with me privately that when they read this text, they thought that, even though they had never led sexually promiscuous lives, this text nevertheless told them *they* were bad. On the other hand, when I taught a Sunday school class on this text in a large upper-class urban church in Atlanta, the men in the class said 'you women better watch out'. They too tended to flatten out the metaphor and see this text as applying to real twentieth-century men and women, and depicting women in a negative manner.

49. J. Cheryl Exum, 'Prophetic Pornography', in her *Plotted, Shot, and Painted: Cultural Representations of Biblical Women* (JSOTSup, 215; Gender, Culture, Theory, 3; Sheffield: Sheffield Academic Press, 1996), pp. 100-28 (103).

bolically identified with men in this metaphor. Conversely, God is *not* symbolically identified with women. Therefore power is also symbolically identifed with men and not women. Imaging God as husband re-inforces male domination and patriarchal prescription of proper female roles.[50] While male agency is opened up in this text, female agency is foreclosed. As adulterous wife, Israel is viewed as an 'erotically charged chaos agent'.[51] Her very sexuality is something that is out of control. Again, since language is never simply symbolic, the way men and women are portrayed in this text will both reflect and prescribe gender roles in the real world. This text will have an influence on the way that real men and women read or hear this text, particularly when they read or hear it as sacred text or speech. This applies both to historical and contemporary readers and hearers.

This chapter has focused on intertextuality of culture, identifying in particular ways in which Jer. 3.1-5 both constructs and is constructed by conventions of gender. The last portion of this chapter has shown the disturbing effects of such constructions on real men and women who encounter this text. We shall see all of the ideas set forth in this chapter developed in ever more disturbing ways through the rest of the piece.

50. Cf. Exum, 'Prophetic Pornography', p. 113.

51. The term comes from a colleague from Drury College (now University), Charles M. Ess, Professor of Philosophy. He has noted that women are often imaged in this way both in ancient Near Eastern myths, for example, *The Gilgamesh Epic*, and in present-day discourse.

Chapter 3

JEREMIAH 3.6-11:
A NARRATIVE INTERPRETATION OF JEREMIAH 3.1-5

All sorts of things in the world behave like mirrors.
—Jacques Lacan

As we have already seen, Jer. 3.1-5 makes use of a marriage metaphor as a primary vehicle for describing the dynamics of YHWH's relationship to Israel. Moreover, in the previous chapter it is evident that metaphor is part and parcel of the way in which cultural ideals of gender are incorporated into the rhetoric. Because of the multiplicity of theories surrounding metaphor and its use, and the fact that I adopt a functional and social approach to metaphor which has not been addressed thoroughly in biblical circles, I will spend the first portion of this chapter delineating the theory of metaphor with which I am working, followed by a discussion of narrative metaphor, thus paving the way for my examination of Jer. 3.6-11 in the second half of the chapter. The following analysis will focus on three aspects of 3.6-11: (1) its use of metaphor; (2) its use of both intertextuality (with Deut. 24.1-4) and intratextuality (with Jer. 3.1-5); and (3) its use of conventions of gender.

1. *Metaphor as a Rhetorical Strategy in Jeremiah 3.1–4.4*

Like intertextuality, metaphor is a rhetorical strategy in the text of Jer. 3.1–4.4; that is, metaphor is used persuasively to influence the audience's attitudes and behavior. For example, a variety of relational images are used to suggest the type of relationship the people of Israel has or should have with YHWH. We have already seen the primary marital image at work in Jer. 3.1-5. Some other metaphorical images which are important for an understanding of the larger text are father–son images (seen especially in 3.21–4.4) and circumcision images (4.1-4). In addition to the use of the marital image itself, in the previous chapter we also saw how direct address both utilizes the marriage metaphor and transforms it into a rhetorical strategy. Finally, there is an extended metaphorical narrative, utilizing the image of YHWH as husband and Israel and Judah as wives who are sisters (3.6-11). An approach to metaphor that addresses the *functions* of metaphor, as well as takes into account the dialogue between author, audience and their respective contexts is required for this study. Such an approach is that of Donald Davidson[1] as modified by David E. Cooper.[2] Some relevant insights from Wayne Booth[3] will also be incorporated into the discussion. This approach is one which has gained much philosophical attention in the last few years, although it has not yet drawn much attention in biblical circles. Moreover, it is an approach which is consistent with and correspondent to the use of intertextuality as a rhetorical strategy in 3.1–4.4.

Theories of metaphor have burgeoned in the last few decades. The current debate ranges from definition to uses of metaphor. As Wayne Booth has said:

> There is a problem for students of any subject when the word for that subject expands to cover everything. And that is precisely what has happened to this word. Metaphor has by now been defined in so many ways that there is no human expression, whether in language or any other medium, that would not be metaphoric in *someone's* definition.[4]

Booth argues cogently that no one definition of metaphor will account for *all* aspects of metaphor; rather, we 'need taxonomies, not frozen single definitions'.[5] Yet, as Booth himself says:

> In spite of differences in the scope of our definitions, we all meet everyday certain statements that everyone recognizes as metaphor and calls by that name. We seem to have a kind of common-sense agreement about a fairly narrow definition, one that survives even while our theory expands the original concept beyond recognition.[6]

In practice, we all do share some common sense of what metaphor is. Thus, following theorists such as Davidson and Cooper, I will put forth the argument that a functional definition has the best chance of accounting for at least most of the aspects of metaphor.

---

1. Donald Davidson, 'What Metaphors Mean', in Sheldon Sacks (ed.), *On Metaphor* (Chicago: University of Chicago Press, 1978), pp. 29-45.
2. David E. Cooper, *Metaphor* (Oxford: Basil Blackwell, 1986).
3. Wayne Booth, 'Metaphor as Rhetoric' and 'Ten Literal "Theses"', in Sacks (ed.), *On Metaphor*, pp. 47-70 and 173-74, respectively.
4. Booth, 'Metaphor as Rhetoric', p. 48.
5. Booth, 'Ten Literal "Theses"', p. 173.
6. Booth, 'Metaphor as Rhetoric', pp. 48-49.

Metaphors bring two different words, ideas, statements, pictures, into conjunction—sometimes in a shocking or absurd manner. According to Davidson and Cooper, most metaphorical statements contain some absurdity: they are either literally false or absurdly true.[7] The resulting shock or absurdity of such yoking forces the reader to make other connections. And those connections are virtually unlimited: 'there is no limit to what a metaphor calls to our attention, and much of what we are caused to notice is not propositional in character. When we try to say what a metaphor 'means', we soon realize there is no end to what we want to mention'.[8] To use an illustration from Jer. 3.1–4.4, in the metaphorical relationship between YHWH as husband and Israel as wife the absurdity is the fact that the relationship between YHWH and the people of Israel is *not* that of husband and wife. Thus, the reader must make new connections in determining what it means to characterize the relationship between YHWH and Israel as a marriage.

Most people would agree that the image of YHWH as husband and Israel as wife is a metaphor. Yet many would hold different theories as to what defines the image as metaphor rather than something else. The traditional theory of metaphor identifies metaphor as a trope, or a play on words. Beginning with Aristotle, long acknowledged as one of the first theorists of metaphor, metaphor was seen as having two levels of meaning, a 'literal' and a 'figurative' meaning. Robert J. Fogelin, a contemporary theorist, has returned to the traditional definition: for him, 'metaphors are similes with the terms of comparison suppressed; they are elliptical similes'.[9] Such a definition confines metaphor to a specific syntactic relationship (a metaphor is a simile without the 'like'). Such a definition also confines metaphor to a comparison. Many theorists have seen these limitations as problematic, not least for the reason that many metaphors do not fit this definition.[10]

---

7.   T. Brinkley has also addressed the paradox of truth and falsity as a dynamic of metaphor. See 'On the Truth and Probity of Metaphor', in M. Johnson (ed.), *Philosophical Perspectives on Metaphor* (Minneapolis: University of Minnesota Press, 1981), pp. 136-53.

8.   Davidson, 'What Metaphors Mean', p. 44 (cf. pp. 43-45 for his critique of other theories). For a much more complete critique, see Cooper, *Metaphor*, Chapter 2.

9.   Robert J. Fogelin, *Figuratively Speaking* (New Haven: Yale University Press, 1988), p. 25.

10.   For an excellent critique of this approach, see Cooper, *Metaphor*, pp. 46-66. See also Paul Ricoeur, *The Rule of Metaphor: Multi-Disciplinary Studies of the Creation of Meaning in Language* (Toronto: University of Toronto Press, 1975), Chapter 1.

Davidson and Cooper differ from Fogelin and traditional theorists in that they do not ascribe two meanings to metaphor. Briefly stated, Davidson's thesis—and Cooper follows him in this—is that a metaphorical statement *means* no more and no less than the literal statement.[11] Instead of examining 'the meaning' of metaphor, a more fruitful avenue of exploration is an examination of the *function* of metaphors, the roles they play in discourse:

> I depend on the distinction between what words mean and what they are used to do. I think metaphor belongs exclusively to the domain of use. It is something brought off by the imaginative employment of words and sentences and depends entirely on the ordinary meanings of those words and hence on the ordinary meanings of the sentences they comprise.[12]

Thus, although we cannot identify a theory of metaphorical meaning, we can discuss what sorts of connections are made by metaphorical statements, as well as what makes metaphorical statements so powerful—how they persuade.

Returning to the metaphorical relationship between YHWH as husband and Israel as wife, as we have already seen in the previous chapter, the ordinary or literal meanings of husband and wife, as well as the conventions surrounding the husband–wife relationship, are put into play in describing the divine–human relationship. In this case, the metaphor functions analogously—the relationship between YHWH and Israel may be characterized as a husband–wife relationship in certain ways, and that characterization is used for a particular rhetorical purpose. The specific interpretation of that characterization, or, to put it another way, the meaning(s) of the metaphor, will reside in the connections made by the reader, together with the ways in which the author images or portrays this relationship. Thus, 'metaphorical meaning' is not to be differentiated from literal meaning. Moreover, it does not strictly depend on comparison, but goes much further, incorporating any number of possible connections.[13]

In addition to discussing metaphor in terms of function rather than meaning, one of the greatest strengths of Cooper's approach, which also

11. Davidson, 'What Metaphors Mean', p. 30.

12. Davidson, 'What Metaphors Mean', p. 31.

13. For a thorough discussion of this theory in relation to the more common theories of metaphor within biblical circles, such as those of Max Black, Lakoff and Johnson, or Paul Ricoeur, see the extensive discussion in my doctoral dissertation, 'Circumscribing the Prostitute: The Rhetorics of Intertextuality, Metaphor, and Gender in Jeremiah 3.1–4.4' (doctoral dissertation, Emory University, 1996), pp. 70-85.

fills a major gap in other theories, is his discussion of the social dimension of metaphor. It is in this area that he modifies and greatly expands the approach of Davidson. Building on the work of Ted Cohen,[14] Cooper discusses the ways in which metaphorical speech creates 'special' intimacy between the implied speaker and the implied reader. He defines 'special intimacy' as 'the bond which unites those who are reasonably deemed capable of hearing it—and, indeed, uttering it—with understanding'.[15] More often than not, such intimacy is greater than a shared historical context. The sort of shared context creating such intimacy is what other scholars call a shared community and/or a shared interpretive tradition.[16] And that shared community and/or tradition will in turn place certain boundaries on the possibilities of interpretation. Cooper's comments indicate a crucial link between intertextuality and metaphor—the importance of the interpretive community, and the ways in which that common community shapes interpretation.

Cooper further clarifies his view by dealing with the ways in which 'metaphorical talk can reflect and reinforce a sense of intimacy'.[17] In this regard, his assessment of the social dimension of metaphor modifies that of another influential theorist of metaphor, Paul Ricoeur, in a crucial way. Many biblical scholars follow Ricoeur in emphasizing the ability of metaphors to redescribe reality,[18] or to 'organize our view of human nature'.[19] In addition, Ricoeur stresses the necessity of the reader assenting or submitting to the metaphorical statement on some level. While agreeing that metaphors can redescribe reality, indeed, that such redescription may at times be their purpose, Cooper takes issue with the view of the necessity of assent and/or submission. He argues that, while metaphor brings about a

14. Ted Cohen, 'Metaphor and the Cultivation of Intimacy', Sacks (ed.), *On Metaphor*, pp. 1-10.

15. Cooper, *Metaphor*, p. 156.

16. Cf. Cooper, *Metaphor*, pp. 156-57. For a similar acknowledgment of the importance of community/interpretive tradition from a theological perspective, see Janet Martin Soskice, *Metaphor and Religious Language* (Oxford: Clarendon Press, 1985), pp. 148-58. It is necessary to note, however, that the theory I am using does not take up her notion of metaphorical realism.

17. Cooper, *Metaphor*, p. 176. Note, however, that he cautions that the sense of intimacy may or may not be illusory. That is, metaphorical speech may create a bond where there normally would not be one, or it may create a bond which, on balance, becomes specious. (For his complete argument, see pp. 176-78.)

18. See, e.g., Carol Newsom, 'A Maker of Metaphors—Ezekiel's Oracles Against Tyre', *Int* 38 (1984), pp. 151-64 (164).

19. Newsom, 'Maker of Metaphors', p. 152.

kind of intimacy, the intimacy constituted and assumed by metaphor can be used both for good and for evil: 'If intimacy can be illusory, it can also be genuine; and if some kinds of intimacy, through their correlative animosity to "outsiders", can be dangerous, other kinds are not'.[20] There- fore, he argues for a critique of metaphor which 'will...be a critique of its role in bolstering false senses of intimacy and unity'.[21]

Booth, whose argument in this regard is quite similar to that of Cooper, adds to the discussion by delineating ways in which metaphors constitute a critique of culture. He argues that 'The metaphors we care for most are always embedded in metaphoric structures that finally both depend on and constitute selves and societies'.[22] In other words, metaphors rely on con- ventions of society as well as influence individuals' and societies' view of reality. Returning again to the example of the metaphorical husband–wife relationship in Jer. 3.1–4.4, this metaphor depends on a structuring of society where women's and men's roles are defined in relation to each other in a certain way,[23] but it also participates in 'constituting selves and societies' by arguing for a particular view of the proper relationship between husband/wife and deity/human.

Booth's aforementioned comments allude to the speaker's role in meta- phorical utterances, which he further clarifies in relation to the hearer's engagement with the speaker later in the same article: 'The speaker has performed a task by yoking what the hearer had not yoked before, and the hearer simply cannot resist joining him; they thus perform an identical dance step, and the metaphor accomplishes at least part of its work even if the hearer then draws back and says, 'I shouldn't have allowed that!'[24] He adds a caution similar to that of Cooper, however:

20. Cooper, *Metaphor*, p. 178. The incorporation of the awareness of both the positive and negative uses of metaphor is an important corrective to Ricoeur's notion of second naiveté and the need to submit oneself to the text. Yes, metaphors do provide a different description of reality. However, it may be necessary to resist rather than to appropriate that reality or aspects of that reality. For a more detailed critique of this aspect of Ricoeur's work, cf. Kevin J. Vanhoozer's description and critique in *Biblical Narrative in the Philosophy of Paul Ricoeur: A Study in Philosophy and Theology* (Cambridge: Cambridge University Press, 1990), esp. pp. 63-65. See also, Soskice, *Metaphor and Religious Language*, pp. 86-90.

21. Cooper, *Metaphor*, p. 176.

22. Booth, 'Metaphor as Rhetoric', p. 61.

23. For example, as has been shown in the previous chapter, the metaphor depends on a societal structure in which control of women's sexuality is crucial to the mainte- nance of that structure.

24. Booth, 'Metaphor as Rhetoric', p. 52.

The question is not *whether* we will judge the character of metaphorists and the societies that produce and sustain them. We all are forced to do that all the time... To *understand* a metaphor is by its very nature to *decide* whether to join the metaphorist or reject him, and that is simultaneously to decide either to be shaped in the shape his metaphor requires or to resist.[25]

This espousal of the necessity for evaluation of the claims of metaphorical speech is Booth's greatest addition to the discussion.

In addition to advocating the necessity of evaluation, Booth's argument regarding the rhetorical use of metaphor presents a crucial link between the theory of intertextuality I have adopted and metaphor. Using 'the major philosophies' as examples of systems of thought which depend on root metaphors, he argues that

they are great precisely because they have so far survived the criticism of rival metaphors. Each view of the totality of things claims supremacy, but none has been able to annihilate the others. They all thus survive as still plausible, pending further criticism through further philosophical inquiry... In fact we find in every major philosophy not just this implicit critique of all rival metaphors but quite explicit consideration of the validity of particular metaphors.[26]

Such a view has much in common with Mikhail Bakhtin's view that both marginal and dominant voices alike are present in texts. It is also a view that has particular applicability to Jer. 3.1–4.4 in which, as will be shown in the following chapters, there is a claim to supremacy and a critique of rival metaphors, especially political and religious metaphors.

The evaluative role of the reader discussed above is of special relevance for a text such as Jer. 3.1–4.4, which seeks to present one view of reality as the proper one in opposition to others. In some cases it is more appropriate to resist the worldview, persuasive as it may seem to be. In some cases, it is more dangerous to be molded in the shape of the metaphors, than to maintain one's own shape. If metaphorical statements can be used for evil or for good, it is necessary not only to study the ways in which the rhetorical use of metaphors 'both depend on and constitute selves and societies' and redescribe reality, but also the ways in which such metaphors may be dangerous. These types of evaluative questions are addressed to the metaphors of 3.1–4.4 as well. The task of the reader of rhetorical metaphor is to assess it as it enters into dialogue with: (1) other metaphors

25. Booth, 'Metaphor as Rhetoric', p. 63.
26. Booth, 'Metaphor as Rhetoric', p. 64.

(adopting or critiquing those metaphors); and (2) the social contexts of those metaphors (both the speaker's and the hearer's context). As Cooper suggests, there is a need for 'mapping the uncharted and subtle ways in which this or that metaphor, this or that block of metaphorical talk, reflects and is reflected in the complex play of human relations'.[27] My analysis of Jer. 3.1-5 has already begun such mapping and has pointed out ways in which the metaphorical language must be read critically and with some resistance as well.

It is this kind of mapping which will be the concern in the discussion of the metaphorical speech in the rest of Jer. 3.1–4.4. In keeping with a functional approach to metaphor, the governing questions in that portion of the analysis focusing on metaphor address how the metaphors and metaphorical language function in their discursive and historical contexts, how that language functions for contemporary readers, what conventions metaphors play on or establish, and the ways in which the metaphors may break out of those conventions. In short, by paying attention to author, context(s) and reader, the focus of attention is on the ways in which metaphor is used in the rhetorical dialogue established in 3.1–4.4, as well as ways in which contemporary readers may evaluate the metaphorical rhetoric.

2. Narrative Metaphor in Jeremiah 3.6-11

In addition to the variety of metaphors used to describe the people and their relationship with YHWH in Jer. 3.1–4.4, the text of 3.6-11 contains an extended narrative metaphor, usually called an allegory. The designation allegory is misleading, however, implying as it does a one-to-one correspondence between each element and its counterpart in the real world.[28] Such an understanding of allegory fails to take into account the ways in which many, if not most allegories function as extended metaphors,[29] that

27. Cooper, *Metaphor*, p. 178.
28. See, e.g., Soskice, *Metaphor and Religious Language*, pp. 55-56; Ricoeur, *Rule of Metaphor*, pp. 60-61, 84; E. Honig, *Dark Conceit: The Making of Allegory* (Evanston: Northwestern University Press, 1959); Clifford, *Transformations of Allegory*; J. Rosenberg, *King and Kin: Political Allegory in the Hebrew Bible* (Bloomington: Indiana University Press, 1986); and James A. Durlesser, 'The Rhetoric of Allegory in the Book of Ezekiel' (unpublished doctoral dissertation, University of Pittsburgh, 1988), pp. 18-22.
29. This is Ricoeur's term (*Rule of Metaphor*, p. 243). See also K. Snodgrass, who defines allegory as 'an extended metaphor in narratory form' ('What Method Should

is, they have the same qualities of ambiguity and polyvalence that metaphor does. Like metaphor, allegory

> presupposes readers assiduous in interpreting (rather than simply following or responding to) a narrative. This emphatically does not imply that interpretation is reductive: the greatest allegories are intransigent and elusive... because they are concerned with a highly complex kind of truth, a matter of relationships and process rather than statement.[30]

If allegory is extended metaphor and concerns relationships and process rather than simple one-to-one correspondence, then what has been said of metaphor may also be said of allegory and vice versa. Like metaphor, 'the heart of allegory is a focus of multiple interpretations rather than *a* meaning'.[31] Thus, an extended metaphor such as Jer. 3.6-11 has a number of different possible interpretations, which are dependent on the reader, the content of the allegory itself, and the contexts of interpretation.

As extended *metaphor*, allegory presents a redescription of reality. As *extended* metaphor, it carries a storyline or plot. In the case of Jer. 3.6-11, the storyline corresponds to historical events. In such cases, temporality is displaced: when allegory refers to historical events it imposes a different temporality, a different frame of reference, on those events. As Paul de Man says, 'allegory is at the furthest possible remove from historiography'.[32] With regard to 3.6-11, as will be shown in the following discussion, it is in the temporal break, in the portrayal of historical events in completely different terms, that new connections are drawn between Israel and Judah, and between the histories of Israel and Judah—in short, that a new description of reality is presented.[33]

---

be Used?', in *idem*, *The Parable of the Wicked Tenants: An Inquiry into Parable Interpretation* [Tübingen: J.C.B. Mohr (Paul Siebeck), 1983], pp. 12-30 [19]).

30. Clifford, *Transformations of Allegory*, p. 10. Her comments here stress that the involvement of the reader in the production of meaning, as well as the context(s) and interpretive tradition, is as important for allegory, or extended metaphor, as it is for metaphor in its more limited forms. Honig argues similarly: 'literary text which has been assimilated in a cultural tradition requires a restructuring from every reader. This occurs when the reader gradually reflects in his own imagination the creative process embodied in the text' (*Dark Conceit*, p. 29).

31. Clifford, *Transformations of Allegory*, p. 94.

32. Paul de Man, 'Pascal's Allegory of Persuasion', in Stephen J. Greenblatt (ed.), *Allegory and Representation: Selected Papers from the English Institute, 1979–80* (Baltimore: The Johns Hopkins University Press, 1981), pp. 1-25 (1).

33. Traditional scholarship's approach to Jer. 3.6-11 has been to dismiss it either as a secondary addition or as a transparent portrayal of historical events. However

Although allegory may occur in many different settings, a recent theorist has said that 'allegory seems regularly to surface in critical or polemical atmospheres, when for political or metaphysical reasons there is something that cannot be said'.[34] Allegory is one way to recast ideas, events, and so on, which enables a writer to make a point which may not be able to be made directly given the political or social climate. To take this idea a step further, many allegories occur in the same types of situation as does prophecy: they both tend to arise in situations of conflict or crisis, when there is a need for a response of some kind to the impending crisis, when the traditional or usual way of looking at things is no longer working. It is precisely because the traditional way is not working that indeterminate language, such as metaphor and allegory, become important vehicles of persuasion. They allow for new connections to be made. They are powerful persuasive tools *because* they allow for such new interpretations. Such is the case with the allegory or extended metaphor in Jer. 3.6-11. Arising in a situation in which the traditional pattern of dealing with the world and world events is not working, this narrative places historical events in a different temporal and relational frame, enabling a critique of Judah to be made in a rhetorically powerful manner.

Methodologically, the following analysis of Jer. 3.6-11 will include the types of questions asked of the metaphorical language in general, as noted above, with added attention given to the temporal displacement and how placing a new frame of reference on historical events functions rhetorically. Thus, the metaphorical analysis of 3.6-11 will be concerned primarily with the connections between the divine–human relationship portrayed in the language itself and its connections with the historical events to which the language refers.

3. Analysis of Jeremiah 3.6-11

As we have seen above, Jer. 3.6-11 represents a shift in form and style from 3.1-5. The style shifts from poetry to prose and from direct address to third person narrative, and the form is an extended metaphor. There is a

transparent that portrayal may be, the dismissal is precipitous. It ignores the function of allegory both in the literary context and in the rhetorical context. The analysis in the following chapter will show the allegory in Jer. 3 to have an important place in the rhetoric of the entire chapter.

34. Joel Fineman, 'The Structure of Allegorical Desire', in Greenblatt (ed.), *Allegory and Representation*, pp. 26-60 (28).

further shift as well, that of perspective. In Jer. 3.6-11 the people's behavior is looked at from another angle, while addressing the same issue of the (im)possibility of return introduced by the rhetorical questions of 3.1-5. These shifts have led scholars to judge vv. 6-11 as a secondary expansion, most likely not from the hand of the prophet.[35] While that may indeed be

35. Since the time of Duhm, virtually every scholar has considered this piece to be secondary based on one or more of the following criteria: it is prose as opposed to poetry; and/or it seems to be dependent on 3.1-5 (and, according to some, on 3.12-13 as well). The major issues of debate have been: (1) to whom it is addressed (i.e. to the former northern tribes or to Judah); and (2) whether it is deuteronomistic. The dating of the section is a third issue which is integrally related to the first two. The view that Jer. 3.6-11 was originally jeremianic and addressed to the ten northern tribes during Josiah's reign goes back to aggadic sources. Aggadic tradition has it that Jeremiah went to bring back the ten tribes from the north during this time, which explains Jeremiah's silence about the josianic reforms and the fact that Josiah did not consult him regarding the changes (Arnold A. Wieder, 'Josiah and Jeremiah: Their Relationship According to Aggadic Sources', in Michael A. Fishbane and Paul R. Flohr [eds.], *Texts and Responses* [Festschrift Nahum N. Glatzer; Leiden: E.J. Brill, 1975], pp. 60-72 [62]). A majority of scholars espouse the basic view, if not the legend behind it. Cf. Volz, *Der Prophet Jeremia*, A. 15, 20; Rudolph, *Jeremia*, p. 23; and Stephen A. Kaufman, 'Rhetoric, Redaction, and Message in Jeremiah', in Jacob Neusner, Baruch A. Levine and Ernest S. Frerichs (eds.), *Judaic Perspectives on Ancient Israel* (Philadelphia: Fortress Press, 1987), pp. 63-74 (65). Two scholars have suggested a broader application of the address to the Northern Kingdom: H.W. Hertzberg, 'Jeremia und das Nordreich Israel', *ThLZ* 77 (1952), pp. 595-602, who believes that 3.19-22 was addressed to the north as well; and R. Albertz, 'Jer 2–6 und die Frühzeitverkündigung Jeremias', *ZAW* 94 (1982), pp. 20-47 (34), who believes that all of Jer. 2.4–4.2 was originally addressed to the north. A recent article argues the same: Dieter Böhler, 'Geschlechterdifferenz und Landbesitz: Strukturuntersuchungen zu Jer 2,2–4,2', in Walter Gross (ed.), *Jeremia und die 'deuteronomistische Bewegung'* (Weinheim: Beltz Athenäum, 1995), pp. 91-127.

A second issue is the relation of this text, and indeed that of the book as a whole, to Deuteronomy, the deuteronomist and the deuteronomistic school, with its attendant question of the provenance of the final form. The primary scholars in this debate are Hyatt, 'Jeremiah and Deuteronomy', and Cazelles, 'Jeremiah and Deuteronomy'; Winfried Thiel, *Die deuteronomistische Redaktion von Jeremia 1–25* (Neukirchen–Vluyn: Neukirchener Verlag, 1973); and Nicholson, *Preaching to the Exiles*. For an excellent discussion of all of these, see Siegfried Herrmann, *Jeremia: Der Prophet und das Buch* (Erträge der Forschung, 271; Darmstadt: Wissenschaftliche Buchgesellschaft, 1990), pp. 66-87.

At issue for Jer. 3.1–4.4 is the identity of the redactors of the final form. For the reasons articulated in his book, *Preaching to the Exiles*, I will adopt a modified form of Nicholson's position that the earlier jeremianic oracles were reinterpreted by a

the case, the rhetoric itself both builds on and extends that of vv. 1-5 in several ways, including the use of the marital metaphors and images of overstepped boundaries, as well as the continuation of the textual interplay with Deut. 24.1-4.

My translation of the section is as follows:

> [6]And YHWH spoke to me in the days of King Josiah: 'Have you seen what Apostasy Israel[36] did? How she went up on every high mountain and under every leafy tree and played the harlot there? [7]I thought, after she has done all this, she will return to me. But she did not return. And Treachery Judah saw her sister: [8]She[37] saw that because of all the harlotry which Apostasy Israel committed, I sent her away and I gave her a bill of divorce. But Treachery Judah, her sister, did not fear, and she also played the harlot. [9]But her harlotry was too light for her: she polluted the land and played the harlot with stone and tree. [10]But even in all this her sister, Treachery Judah, did not return to me with all her heart, but instead fraudulently', saying of YHWH. [11]And YHWH said to me, 'Apostasy Israel is more righteous than Treachery Judah'.

In vv. 6-11 the metaphorical language of sexual promiscuity is taken to a new allegorical level through the vehicle of a change in point of view. The effect is a kind of distancing. The reader takes a step back from the confrontation of direct address to view, through the eyes of the prophet, God's description of the behavior of two nations. Verses 6-11 constitute a reading of history, one with which the audience may or may not be familiar, but which, through the transparency of the narrative metaphor, they will not be able to miss.

The section is framed as a quotation of YHWH which assumes the context of a dialogue between YHWH and the prophet. The prophet is asked to

---

community close to the deuteronomistic circle for the exilic situation in Babylon. See especially, Nicholson, *Preaching to the Exiles*, pp. 116-35, for the establishment of this view, and Seitz, *Theology in Conflict*, pp. 222-35, for the modified view I adopt. Such a position emphasizes the re-use of traditions and material that occurred in the writing process of the Bible itself. Jer. 3.6-11 is one such re-use of traditions and material, as will be shown below.

36. I have translated both משבה ישראל and בגודה יהודה as names, in keeping with the form of narrative metaphor or allegory. Moreover, this translation attends to how the words are used in these verses: they are almost nicknames—denoting the predominant feature of each sister. Note, too, that the term משבה continues the play on שוב begun in vv. 1-5. To highlight that play, one could translate it 'Turning Back Israel', as I do in Chapter 1.

37. Reading with G, S, and many manuscripts, third feminine singular ('she saw') instead of the MT first common singular ('I saw').

'see' what these two sisters have done. Like vv. 1-5, vv. 6-11 are thus dialogical, but in a different way. Here the roles of the prophet and YHWH are separated. Verse 6 begins with YHWH's question to the prophet, 'Have you seen...?' Verses 6-11 contain YHWH's speech to the prophet. In a sense, in reading these words, the reader sees what the prophet has been invited to see. These verses give insight into God's motivations through the use of a rhetorical technique which George Savran describes: often 'the narrator uses the quotation as a means of characterizing the *quoter* as he speaks the quotation, at the present moment of narration'.[38] In this case, I argue that the quotation of God's words reveal God's patience and on-going care for Israel in that the judgment for improper behavior did not come immediately ('And I thought that after she did all these things, she would return to me', v. 7). The verses also function to drive home the point once again that Judah is guilty.

a. *Metaphor in Jeremiah 3.6-11*
Using the metaphor of marital promiscuity established in v. 1, the extended metaphor of 3.6-11 portrays YHWH the husband with two wives who are sisters, 'Apostasy Israel'[39] (or 'Turning Back Israel', a play on the root שוב) and 'Treachery (בגד) Judah'.[40] In v. 6 YHWH asks the prophet, 'Have you seen what Apostasy Israel did?' By implication, her behavior has been

---

38. George Savran, *Telling and Retelling: Quotation in Biblical Narrative* (Bloomington: Indiana University Press, 1989), p. 79.

39. Here is where Schmitt's insistence that the Hebrew Bible refers to 'Israel' in masculine terms alone breaks down completely. His explanation for the term משובה ישראל is 'to see Israel in apposition...as an interpretive addition... The grammar and imagery summon up cities (cf. 14b). I propose that the original referents were cities and that they were later identified with the northern and southern kingdoms' ('The Gender of Ancient Israel', pp. 122-23). Schmitt, however, gives no textual or other evidence for such a view. Moreover, his explanation goes against the rhetorical force of the section, which pits two halves of a nation (rather than two cities) against each other (Northern vs. Southern Kingdom) in order to make one an example for the other.

40. Here, for the first time in this piece, a differentiation is made between Israel and Judah, who are pictured as two sisters. As noted above, the differentiation between north and south in 3.6-11 has often been seen as an indication of historical circumstances—an appeal to people living in the former Northern Kingdom to return. The date given in 3.6a makes this an option. There is too little evidence to decide with certainty. In the overall context of 3.1–4.4, however, 3.6-13 serves a different function: the fate of the former Northern Kingdom is being set up as a negative example to the South for the purpose of showing Judah that its current behavior is leading to the same historical conclusion.

conspicuous enough for anyone to notice. Like vv. 1-5, this section plays on overstepped boundaries through the image of harlotry. Although the accusation of committing harlotry 'on every hill and under every leafy tree', is generally regarded as terminology for fertility cult worship in Jeremiah,[41] there is no evidence that this term applied specifically to Israel's participation in fertility cults. In fact, such language is best understood metaphorically: because the text as a whole deals with the relationship between God and Israel, there are religious ramifications to the language. Thus, the language of promiscuity refers to religious infidelity in general, not to fertility cult worship in particular.[42] The term 'Apostasy' as a name for Israel highlights YHWH's accusation that the people have worshipped other gods, and hence have overstepped religious boundaries. Yet the religious dimension of the language does not exhaust its possible reference. In view of Jer. 2.20, where the language of harlotry is used after a warning to Israel that turning to Assyria and Egypt cannot help them, this language may also apply to Israel's political affiliations.[43] Here the root שוב in the name given to Israel may also illustrate Israel's wavering behavior, turning first to one nation and then to another for help. In this case the language represents overstepped political boundaries. The ambiguity of the metaphorical language allows the harlotry imagery and the root שוב to apply equally to both situations.

In v. 7 YHWH the husband reports his response to the actions of his wife. Surprisingly, especially given the citation of the law in 3.1,[44] YHWH hoped that she would return (here שוב acts a metaphorical term for covenant renewal/repentance). While the possibility of repentance is not offered outright, it is by implication raised for the first time in this verse.

41. See, e.g., Bright, *Jeremiah*, p. 25.

42. See my discussion in Chapter 2, above, as well as Phyllis A. Bird's article, '"To Play the Harlot"', for a detailed discussion of this language.

43. Jer. 2.18-19 accuses Israel of forsaking YHWH by making political alliances with Assyria and Egypt, and v. 20 accuses the people of sexual promiscuity. The metaphor of adultery/promiscuity applies to religious and political infidelity alike.

44. While this section mentions an actual divorce for the first time since the legal citation (v. 8; cf. v. 1a), as in the case of vv. 1-5, vv. 6-11 portray no second marriage. Rather, as is the case with vv. 1b-2, Israel's many lovers replace such a second marriage. Yet in vv. 6-11, as in the law of v. 1a, because a divorce has taken place within the metaphorical rhetoric (v. 8), remarriage *is* at issue. The intertextual connections between the law and this section will be discussed in greater detail below. It should be noted here, however, that the above discussion has already illustrated significant ways in which this section both absorbs and transforms the law itself, and the ways in which it absorbs, extends and transforms the rhetoric of vv. 1-5.

The narrator (YHWH) continues in v. 8 by describing the consequences of 'Apostasy Israel's' behavior. Here the removal from temporality which narrative metaphor achieves allows the point to be made much more forcibly than it could have otherwise. The historical event of the end of the nation of Israel[45] is described in terms of divorce: YHWH sent Apostasy Israel away and gave her a bill of divorce. Because the Judean audience has been directly accused of harlotry in vv. 1-5, those addressed can hardly miss the implied analogy between their situation and that of Israel's barely a century earlier (particularly after the aside at the end of v. 7). The implied threat of judgment is destruction and exile. The vehicle of extended metaphor allows the prophet to use the Northern Kingdom as a case study for the Southern Kingdom. Yet the matter is not allowed to rest there.

Drawing out the metaphor to its fullest, in the remainder of v. 8 'Treachery Judah' is described as following in her sister's footsteps even though 'she saw' (v. 7b) what had happened to her sister. Thus, her crime is even worse—the clear-cut example before her did not deter her from behaving in the same way. Again, rather than leaving the audience to draw out the analogy, the point is made directly. Verse 9 portrays Judah's actions as worse than that of her sister: 'her whoring was too light for her', and 'she polluted the land and committed adultery with stone and tree'. In the narrative world, her committing of adultery 'with stone and tree' and pollution of the land are seen as cause and effect.[46] Moreover, the consequences of such behavior were concrete: Apostasy Israel's behavior resulted in actual loss of the land. Verse 10 continues with a statement to the effect that Treachery Judah did not take warning from what happened to Israel. She did not truly return; rather she merely pretended to return.[47]

45. That this refers to the defeat and exile of the nation Israel is made clear by vv. 12-13.

46. See the discussion of the connection between sexual behavior and pollution of the land in Chapter 2. What is so striking about Jeremiah is that he applies this connection to the (metaphorical) relationship between YHWH and Judah.

47. This tension between true and false turning was already noted in vv. 4-5, and will remain a theme in the rest of the chapter, especially in 3.21–4.4. James Muilenberg has also noted this tension in Jeremiah in general. He says there are 'constant tensions between the language of *mendacity* and *veracity*, between what is spurious and what is authentic, between truth and falsehood' throughout the Old Testament, but that these are most especially present in Jeremiah. He also notes that 'the tensions between apostasy and repentance, the two ways of turning', are closely related ('The Terminology of Adversity in Jeremiah', in Harry Thomas Frank and W.L. Reed [eds.], *Translating and Understanding the Old Testament: Essays in Honor of Herbert*

With v. 11 the narrator steps out of the frame of the metaphor to deliver the punch line. The new introductory formula which opens v. 11 (ויאמר יהוה אלי), sets this statement apart from the descriptive language of vv. 6-11 and indicates a shift from the view given to the prophet (and overheard by the reader) to the conclusion YHWH has drawn from the picture presented. I translate: 'And YHWH said to me, "Apostasy Israel is more righteous than Treachery Judah"'. In this verse the judge pronounces judgment.

While the story and the language used may seem to belabor the obvious, that is one of the strategies of narrative metaphor. Its very transparency makes the message crystal clear. Given the quotation of the audience's original response to YHWH's accusations of vv. 1-3 in vv. 4-5a ('Have you not just called to me: "My father, you are the husband of my youth?" "Will he remain angry forever; will he keep [anger] forever?"') perhaps such clarity is necessary for this audience. The transparency of narrative metaphor also allows for a direct application of the rhetoric of sexual promiscuity to a specific historical situation, to political events. Through the vehicle of the extended metaphor it is evident that it is not only religious behavior which is implicated, but political behavior as well.

For readers familiar with the Hebrew Bible, this allegory is indeed perhaps a little too transparent, but if we remember that much of the Hebrew Bible came into its final written form during the exile, it is not safe to assume that this reading of history would have been as self-evident to a pre-exilic or exilic reader as it is to today's reader. Placing historical events in this allegorical form may have been as startling for the original audience as the strategy of direct address. While such a surmise cannot be established, it would not do to underestimate the potential power of this rhetoric on an audience never confronted with the reading of historical events presented in 3.6-11.

Another strategy of extended metaphor which adds to the persuasive power of vv. 6-11 is that of temporal displacement. By portraying events in indirect terms, the writer is able to make connections which could not be made as forcibly in historical terms. If one of the referents of the metaphor is historical events, that is, the defeat and exile of the former Northern Kingdom (722 BCE) and the coming threat against Judah (Jer. 1.13-16; 4–6, that is, the rise of Babylon and its threat to Judah), the temporality is

Gordon May [Nashville: Abingdon Press, 1970], pp. 49-63 [43]). To my knowledge, however, because Jer. 3.1–4.4 is usually treated as a collection of not-very-well-unified sections, there has been no discussion of this tension in the piece as a whole.

different from that of the events themselves. The positioning of Israel and Judah as sisters, that is, their relationality within the smallest familial unit, relates them and their histories much more closely than the historical situation would warrant. The technique of personification thus adds to the effectiveness of the temporal displacement. Not only is Israel made an example for Judah, but also the narrative metaphor attempts to persuade sister Judah to compare her actions to those of Israel and to take note of the consequences of following the same path.

Finally, the extended metaphor cloaks radical speech. As other texts in Jeremiah show,[48] the idea that Jerusalem and the country of Judah were inviolable because YHWH had promised to protect them eternally was thriving in Jeremiah's time. This particular narrative metaphor is thus an ideal way to counter currently cherished assumptions about Judah's security in a way that is picturesque enough to claim full attention of an audience. The metaphor is the vehicle through which historical events are displaced temporally to drive home the message that the nation, as the harlot wife of YHWH, is guilty and deserving of divorce (defeat and exile). The very transparency of the metaphor makes the point so obvious that the message cannot be missed. YHWH's interpretation of history is crystal clear, and the implications for Judah are equally clear.

b. *Intertextuality in Jeremiah 3.6-11*

If narrative metaphor provides the form for the accusation of Judah in Jer. 3.6-11, then intertextuality provides the content. In some senses vv. 6-11 constitute an intertextual play with the law of Deut. 24.1-4 which is even more direct than that of Jer. 3.1-5. Here the law is revealed already to have been applied to YHWH's relationship with one portion of Israel as a whole, the former Northern Kingdom.

One way in which the intertextual play with Deut. 24.1-4 is more visible and immediate in vv. 6-11 is through direct verbal connections between the two. First, the piel of שלח ('I sent her away') is used both in v. 8 and in Deut. 24.1, 4. Second, both passages use the term ספר כריתתיה (Jer. 3.8; Deut. 24.1, 3). A third connection, the link between behavior and pollution of the land (3.9), was already noted both in the discussion of Deut. 24.1-4 and of Jer. 3.1-5. These verbal connections establish a direct allusion to the law of Deut. 24.1-4. Together with the use of legal terminology (i.e. 'sending away' [= divorcing], 'bill of divorce'), these connections establish a juridical context for these verses. While Jer. 3.1 presents the

---

48. Cf., e.g., Jer. 7, 26, 27–28.

law as a rhetorical question, these verses apply the law directly to the historical situation of Israel and Judah in terms of their metaphorical marital relationship with YHWH. Here the law is also portrayed as effective and authoritative: it has already been implemented in the case of the former Northern Kingdom (Judah sees that Israel has already been given a bill of divorce).

As already noted above, however, the law is not only absorbed, but is transgressed as well, and in ways similar to vv. 1-5. While the law concerns a remarriage after an intervening second marriage, vv. 6-11 portray no such second marriage. Rather, like vv. 1-5, the second marriage is replaced with sexual promiscuity on a grand scale ('on every high mountain and under every leafy tree'). Thus, the relation of the narrative metaphor to the law is much like that of vv. 1-5: 'an inference *a minori ad maius*, or to use talmudic terminology, a *kal vechomer*'.[49] Finally, the narrative metaphor itself transforms the law not only by applying it metaphorically to a divine–human relationship (a new form of social application), but by applying it to a historical situation (a religious and political application), as discussed above.

c. *Intratextuality in Jeremiah 3.6-11*
In addition to an intertextual relationship with Deut. 24.1-3, Jer. 3.6-11 constitutes an *intra*textual relationship with 3.1-5. As has been partially shown in the metaphorical section above, intratextually 3.6-11 both extends and sharpens the message of 3.1-5, providing a new view of reality with which the readers are asked to identify. Jeremiah 3.6-11 absorbs the marriage metaphor developed in vv. 1-5, yet at the same time transforms it. The legal citation is now applied to the political entities of Israel and Judah, each imaged as a wife of YHWH. In this transformation, the rhetoric of vv. 1-5 is built upon and given shape. While in vv. 4-5 the audience is portrayed as having not understood (or wanted to understand) the implications of the rhetoric of vv. 1-3, the transparency of the extended metaphor and the directness of its application make the audience's guilt and YHWH's judgment unmistakable. Furthermore, the very names used for Israel and Judah ('Apostasy' and 'Treachery'), embody the sort of two-facedness described in vv. 4-5. Finally, the picture of Judah's behavior presented in these verses illustrate YHWH's accusation made in v. 5, 'Behold you have spoken, but you have done all the evil you could'.

49. Lundbom, *Jeremiah*, p. 38. Lundbom, however, does not extend his discussion of the law of v. 1 to vv. 6-11.

Jeremiah 3.6-11 also transgresses vv. 1-5, however. The transgression of these verses comes in the hint that YHWH would have taken Israel back (v. 7), raising the possibility of return in a way that vv. 1-5 seem to exclude. This transgression will be built upon in vv. 12-13, which will be discussed in the next chapter.

d. *Intertextuality of Culture: Gender in Jeremiah 3.6-11*
The two rhetorical strategies viewed thus far in relation to Jer. 3.6-11, metaphor and inter/intratextuality, are bound together and made stronger through the vehicle of conventions of gender. The continued intertextual play with the law cited in v. 1 allows for a metaphorical scenario to be presented as an example of how the law has been applied. While both the scenario and the application are hypothetical in the sense that they offer a reading of history rather than a real-life case in point, their hypothetical nature allows for gender to be played on in such a way as to elucidate some new dimensions of the relationship between YHWH and the nation. These new dimensions presuppose and build on the dimensions already discussed.

Before moving to a discussion of these dimensions, however, it will be helpful to note where and how the strategies used in vv. 1-5 are played out in these verses. First, like vv. 1-5, in this section the images reveal (a) woman/en stepping over the boundaries set by patriarchy, thus escaping her/their husband's (divine) control. The verb קלל in v. 9 also plays with the theme of transgression and overstepped boundaries which has pervaded the rhetoric up to this point by highlighting the fact that Judah refused to accept any boundaries. In v. 9 issues of honor and shame are addressed indirectly, just as in v. 3, where YHWH accuses the audience of having 'a harlot's brow' and of refusing to be ashamed. Ilona Rashkow has identified the verb קלל among a group of verbs 'used to convey the violation of goals and ideals', most specifically, shame.[50] In v. 9, then, the use of the root קלל contains an implication similar to v. 3: 'it was too light for you' implies 'you refused to be ashamed', thus constituting a way in which 3.6-11 acts both intratextually with vv. 1-5 and intertextually with conventions of gender.

---

50. Ilona Rashkow, 'Daughters and Fathers in Genesis... Or, What is Wrong with this Picture?', in J. Cheryl Exum and David J.A. Clines (eds.), *The New Literary Criticism and the Hebrew Bible* (JSOTSup, 143; Sheffield: JSOT Press, 1993), pp. 250-65 (253 and n. 8).

Second, the larger danger which a promiscuous wife poses to society, as opposed to an actual prostitute who is an accepted part of patriarchal societies (albeit at the borders), is played upon in these verses. The image of two sisters, wives to the same husband, who both overstep the sexual boundaries of marriage, extends the indictment of vv. 1-5 in part by playing with the limits of control in the marital relationship. The words of YHWH to the prophet in vv. 6-8 portray a husband who cannot prevent or stop his wives' promiscuity. Verse 6 portrays the sexual promiscuity of one of those wives, Apostasy Israel. Verses 7 and 8 portray the options explored by the husband (YHWH). He can either wait and hope that the wife will come to her senses and stop the behavior ('I thought, after she has done all this, she will return to me', v. 7) or he can divorce her, thereby dissolving the bond which has threatened his honor ('because of all the harlotry which Apostasy Israel committed, I sent her away and I gave her a bill of divorce', v. 8).

The very options presented in vv. 7-8 go beyond simple limits of control, however. They also present the emotional side of the marriage relationship. It is clear from these verses that the legal option of divorce is taken only as a last resort; the very fact that the husband explored the first option (v. 7) before divorcing his wife indicates his care for her.

e. *Implications*

The extended metaphor portrayed in Jer. 3.6-11 would have a strong rhetorical impact on a predominantly male audience in several ways. First, while the portrayal of marriage in vv. 6-11 cannot be taken as a mirror for actual practice, it is likely that actual marriages reflected the possibility of lack of male control over female sexuality. A male audience would therefore be inclined to identify with YHWH's plight. The tension between love and the husband's right to control his wife's sexuality was probably also reflected in actual marital practice. This rhetoric plays on male fear of losing that control over their own wives (and daughters?, cf. vv. 19-20).

The rhetoric also magnifies the threat that loss of control presents to society. In this text, one woman's behavior is portrayed as being a snare for another woman (vv. 7-8). A more explicit reference to this dynamic occurs in Ezekiel 16 and 23 where the text actually states that the woman's public humiliation is to serve as a warning to all women.[51] Even here,

---

51. Cf. Ezek. 16.41 and 23.48. Ezek. 23 is even more explicit than ch. 16; it is also the closest parallel to Jer. 3.6-11, employing the image of two sisters, one acting more corruptly than the other, in a similar way to the Jeremiah text. An issue in scholarship

however, the language implies that the public example of the first sister should have been the means for control of the other (and, by extension, the public example of one woman should be the means of control for all women). Because this example did not work, Judah is portrayed as acting far more horribly and incomprehensibly, given the example of what happened to Israel, than sister Israel herself did.

The interweaving of the metaphorical and intertextual rhetoric, together with its plays upon cultural assumptions of gender, is very powerful. All three aspects reinforce each other, creating an effective persuasive tool. The application of a law dealing with male control over female sexuality allows for the exploration of the implications of lack of such control, thus revealing the threat of such behavior to society. The use of an extended narrative metaphor makes transparent how that threat can be applied to the nation's current religious and political actions. The use of gender allows a male audience to identify with the husband's plight. Yet by virtue of the fact that this audience in vv. 1-5 has already been identified as the promiscuous wife of v. 11, there is pressure placed on the audience to change their behavior. Thus far, however, the audience has only been given a negative example. It is in the next two verses that incentive is given: vv. 12-13 give hope that a change in behavior might enable them to avoid the original fate of Israel. To these verses we turn in the next chapter.

is whether 3.6-11 is dependent on Ezek. 16 and 23 or vice versa. Proponents of the opposing viewpoints are as follows: Ezekiel dependent on Jeremiah—Rudolph, *Jeremia*, p. 25; Jeremiah based on Ezekiel—Carroll, *Jeremiah*, p. 145; no dependence—Bright, *Jeremiah*, p. 26. See these commentaries for a complete discussion. A subject for further study would be the intertextual play between Jer. 3.6-11 and Ezek. 16 and 23.

Chapter 4

JEREMIAH 3.12-13: THE IMPOSSIBLE MADE POSSIBLE

> The purpose of 'law' is absolutely the last thing to employ in the history of
> the origin of the law: on the contrary…the cause of the origin of a thing and
> its eventual utility, its actual employment and place in a system of purposes,
> lie worlds apart; whatever exists, having somehow come into being, is again
> and again reinterpreted to new ends, taken over, transformed, and redirected.
> —Friedrich Nietzsche

Given the fact that the law set up in Jer. 3.1 and applied to the slightly different situations[1] of vv. 1-5 and vv. 6-11 prohibits a remarriage or return
of the spouse, after the pronouncement of Judah's guilt in v. 11, one expects a scathing accusation or statement of punishment directed against
Judah. But there is an unexpected twist. After all the rhetoric of judgment
in the preceding verses, the greatest surprise of the chapter, and its climax, is the overturning of the law in terms of divine–human relations in
vv. 12-13. Properly speaking, vv. 12-13 are integrally related to vv. 6-11.
However, because these verses represent both the climax and the turning
point of the piece as a whole, they will be discussed separately. Here the
law, quoted in accusation against the people, is overturned; here too, the
rhetorics of intertextuality, metaphor and gender coalesce so as to show
clearly how they apply to the religious and political behavior of the people.
This chapter will look at each of these aspects of the text in turn.

I translate:

> (12)Go and call these words to the north, and say: 'Return, Apostasy Israel',
> saying of YHWH. 'I will not be angry with you, for I am gracious', saying of
> YHWH. 'I will not maintain anger.
> (13)Only know your guilt, that you have transgressed against YHWH your
> God, and you scattered your ways to strangers under every leafy tree, and
> have not obeyed me', saying of YHWH.

---

1.   See the discussions of the transgression of the legal citation in the intertextuality sections of vv. 1-5 and vv. 6-11, above (pp. 40-41 and 87-89, respectively).

In v. 12 the dialogue shifts to the more familiar command of YHWH to the prophet to proclaim YHWH's message. This time, however, the message is addressed 'to the north', that is, to the former Northern Kingdom. The shift in addressee, coming immediately after a declaration of Judah's guilt (v. 11), leaves Judah's fate hanging in the balance, for it is only at 4.3-4 that one realizes that Judah is included in the appeals. Even more startling is the content of the message to the north. YHWH offers 'Turning Back Israel', the one whom he had divorced (v. 8), the possibility of return, the only requirement being acknowledgement of guilt. The tension created by this shift is calculated to engage the (Judean) audience's attention. While the possibility of return in general is introduced by this declaration, the verdict that Judah is more guilty than Israel in v. 11 leaves the question of the possibility of *Judah's* return wide open. One of the effects of this tension would be to keep the audience wondering if the offer directed to the north could possibly apply to them as well. This audience would have a stake in the content and requirements associated with the appeal to the north.

1. *Intertextuality in Jeremiah 3.12-13*

Intertextually, vv. 12-13 present the transgression of the previous intertexts. Whereas the law of Deut. 24.1-4 and the rhetoric of Jer. 3.1-5 allow no possibility of return, v. 12 reverses the prohibition, rhetorically overturning the law. In vv. 1-5 and 6-11 the law has been used as an 'accuser of the present', to use Walther Zimmerli's words.[2] The law, which has been shown to be effective in the past (even with regard to the metaphorical relationship between YHWH and the Northern Kingdom), has been used to show the people how they have done wrong and made clear the impossibility of return, even in the face of the people's appeals (cf. vv. 4-5). In vv. 12-13, the prophetic 'No' of vv. 1-11 is turned into a 'Yes'.[3]

2. Walther Zimmerli, 'Prophetic Proclamation and Reinterpretation', in Douglas A. Knight (ed.), *Tradition and Theology in the Old Testament* (Philadelphia: Fortress Press, 1977), pp. 69-100 (98).

3. Zimmerli discusses this type of reversal in which 'ancient elements of tradition' are negated in the rhetoric of the pre-exilic prophets. He argues that 'the *traditum* crumbles to pieces wherever the great pre-exilic prophets take hold of it. In their preaching it becomes the accuser of the present' ('Prophetic Proclamation and Reinterpretation', p. 98). Zimmerli's notion of '*traditum*' is essentially what I am calling the intertext, that is, the tradition taken up and interpreted by a host text. With this in mind, I would argue that the dynamic identified by Zimmerli above is at work in the

Not only does v. 12 transgress the law played upon in vv. 1-11, but it specifically absorbs and transgresses the language of v. 5. In v. 5a, the people are quoted as asking about God, 'Will he maintain [his] anger forever (הינטר לעולם)? Will he keep [it] continually?' In v. 12 YHWH addresses the former Northern Kingdom, saying, '"I will not be angry with you, for I am gracious", saying of YHWH. "I will not maintain anger" (לא אטור).' Verse 12 uses the same verbal root to answer the question of v. 5.[4]

There is also another kind of dialogue going on between vv. 5a and 12. As indicated in the discussion of v. 5a above,[5] the quoted questions addressed to God in v. 5a in all probability represent a piece of liturgy which is turned against the audience. In the context of a liturgy, the questions indicate an appeal to God for help (cf. Ps. 103.8-9), while in the context of the marriage metaphor they become an accusation against God. The tension between the legal discourse (in the metaphorical marriage relationship) and the liturgical discourse in v. 5 is resolved in v. 12. The language of v. 12 is very close to Exod. 34.6, where YHWH declares that he is 'a God merciful and gracious, slow to anger'.[6] As Fishbane says of Exod. 34.6, 'the divine attributes of forgiveness and compassion…are set against those of retributive punishment in v 7'.[7] In v. 12 YHWH is actually agreeing with the original liturgical statement contained in v. 5 and disagreeing with the way the quotation of the audience is portrayed, that is, YHWH is dissenting with the implied accusation of keeping anger forever. Whereas the quotation of the people in v. 5a implies that YHWH is

rhetoric of Jer. 3.1–4.4, where a well-known law (tradition) is negated in order to provide hope for the possibility of avoiding punishment to a people accused of wrong-doing (pre-exilic Judah) and hope to a people who already received punishment (exilic Judah).

4.   Note that it is the way in which v. 12 addresses the questions of v. 5a that convinces many commentators that v. 12 was originally the direct continuation of v. 5. Cf., e.g., William McKane, *A Critical and Exegetical Commentary on Jeremiah*. I. *Jeremiah I–XXV* (ICC; Edinburgh: T. & T. Clark, 1986), p. 72.

5.   See the section on intertextuality in vv. 1-5, pp. 46-49.

6.   Regarding v. 12, Holladay also notes that 'The theology is quite compatible with Exod. 34.6-7' (*Jeremiah 1*, p. 119). Fishbane takes the connection a step further. Positing that Ps. 103.8-9 represents a liturgical development of the statement of Exod. 34.6-7, he argues that the language of Ps. 103.9 'recalls comparable phraseology in Jer. 3.5, 12, and is a rejection of the attributes of retribution in favour of those of compassion' (*Biblical Interpretation*, p. 348).

7.   Fishbane, *Biblical Interpretation*, p. 336.

acting out of character (by keeping anger forever), here YHWH maintains instead that his character is one of graciousness (חסד) rather than anger. One of the motivations for the change from a 'No' to a 'Yes' is thus the very character of God. In the context of liturgy, YHWH's offer of return in v. 12 is thus in dialogical agreement with the liturgical sentiments of the people. In the present metaphorical marriage context, YHWH's offer also re-establishes YHWH as one who is חסיד. This intertextual connection between v. 5a and v. 12 also anticipates the liturgy in vv. 21-25: vv. 21-25 replace the wrongful liturgy of vv. 4-5 with a more appropriate liturgy acknowledging guilt.

The use of the root חסד in v. 12 also plays ironically with Jer. 2.1. There YHWH says to the people, 'I remember the loyalty (חסד) of your youth, your love as a young bride'. In contrast to the people who have not acted with חסד (2; 3.1-11), in 3.12, YHWH claims the term as part of his character: אני חסיד. Thus, the interplay between v. 12, 2.1 and 3.5 highlights the irony that the people who were supposed to act with חסד have not only done the opposite, but have accused YHWH of acting without חסד. The interplay also underscores YHWH's claim to the very quality the people are portrayed as lacking in vv. 1-11: fidelity and loving kindness.[8]

Like v. 12, v. 13 plays with the rhetoric of vv. 1-5 (and vv. 6-11 as well). In v. 3b the people are portrayed as having 'the brow of a harlot' and of refusing to be ashamed, and in v. 5b they are portrayed as turning to YHWH for help even as they committed more evil. In contrast, v. 13 requires a new attitude and new behavior: the requirement for return is an acknowledgment that their behavior has been wrong. The specifics of the required

---

8.   The root חסד has many connotations, including loyalty or fidelity (Jer. 2.1). In reference to God, the word is translated 'lovingkindness' in the sense of caring for needs (cf. Gen. 19.19; Jer. 31.3; many Psalms), or 'mercy' (cf. Num. 14.19; Ps. 145.8). It is also often paired with other terms to show God's caring for humanity: with אמת the term shows God's kindness and truth (= fidelity) (cf. Gen. 24.27; 2 Sam. 2.6; Hos. 2.21; Jer. 9.23; 16.5); with רב the term claims for God abundant mercy/loving kindness (cf. Num. 14.18; Jon. 2.13; and many of the Psalms); with גדול the term claims for God greatness of mercy/loving kindness (cf. Exod. 34.7; Num. 14.19; Jer. 32.18); and with עולם the term claims that this is an eternal characteristic of God (cf. Jer. 33.11; Pss. 100.5; 106.1; 107.1; 118; and 136). Holladay says that the term חסיד is only used of God twice in the Hebrew Bible, in this verse and in Ps. 145.17. His interpretation of the term is: 'One who is חסיד is one who does חסד…; thus Yahweh is saying, "I keep my promises"' (*Jeremiah 1*, p. 119). For a comprehensive study of the term חסד, see Katherine D. Sakenfeld, *The Meaning of Ḥesed in the Hebrew Bible* (HSM, 17; Missoula, MT: Scholars Press, 1978).

confession also accentuate the character difference between God and the people. Whereas God is חסיד, the people, in addition to being defined as deceitful by the nicknames given them in vv. 6-11, have acted deceitfully (v. 5b) and fraudulently (v. 10).

Through their interplay with Jer. 2.1 and 3.5, vv. 12-13 may provide a clue to one of the motivations behind YHWH's rhetorical overturning of the law: the need to preserve his honor and his good name.[9] YHWH cannot be identified as one who maintains anger forever. Rather, he is to be known as the embodiment of חסד in all of its connotations (loyalty, lovingkindness, mercy). In order to sustain his character, YHWH allows the people to come back. The requirement for return, the people's confession, likewise maintains YHWH's character by absolving him of any responsibility for the divorce.

To use Kristeva's terms, the law, seen in vv. 6-11 to have been absorbed as an allegorical picture, is then transgressed—overturned and reinterpreted in this new context.[10] Moreover, the actual rhetoric of the people included in Jer. 3.1-5 is transgressed. The law is used to maintain YHWH's good character (e.g. faithful and merciful instead of angry and judgmental). In these verses, then, intertextuality is used in a politically transforming way; the law is overturned in order to construct a new order, one which will be spelled out in vv. 14-18. By subverting the law and the rhetoric of the people, these verses illustrate both the subversive nature of intertextuality and the subversive nature of the rhetoric itself. In other words, the subversion of prior claims of the people and the subversion of the law are used to persuade the audience to change their self-identification and behavior.

9.   The concerns with honor and with a good name are much more clearly the motivations behind YHWH's actions in Ezek. 16 and 23, the two texts in the Hebrew Bible where the wife in the husband/wife relationship between God and Israel is dealt with in the harshest terms (cf. 16.62; 23.49). Note, too, that the reasons for YHWH's actions against Israel occur as refrains throughout the book: 'then you shall know that I am YHWH' (cf. Ezek 6.7, 13; 7.4, 9; 11.10; 16.62; 20.44; 23.49, etc.); and the references to YHWH's actions for the sake of his name (cf. Ezek. 20 and 36; and the concern for 'name' = reputation in Ezek. 16.14-15; 23.9). What is explicit in Ezekiel, however, remains implicit in Jer. 3.1–4.4.

10.   Kristeva, 'Word, Dialogue and Novel', pp. 39, 58. See also my discussion of these terms in Chapter 1.

2. *Metaphor and Gender in Jeremiah 3.12-13*

Verses 12 and 13 maintain the metaphorical relationship established between YHWH and the two kingdoms (sisters), Israel and Judah in v. 6. Here YHWH the husband addresses the sister he divorced, offering her the possibility of return (שוב), precisely what the law itself does not allow (cf. 3.1; Deut. 24.4).[11] The intertwining of the intertextual and metaphorical rhetoric allows for this overturning of the law. What is impossible in terms of human marital relations is here claimed as possible in terms of divine–human relations, and is further portrayed as a contrast between the character of God and the character of the people.

The use of a marital metaphor also necessarily involves the use of conventions of gender. In this regard, it is significant that the language shifts to that used in vv. 1-5; it switches from third person (vv. 6-11) to second person direct address. In terms of gender, the people are again being addressed in the feminine singular. In addition, the contrast between the characters of the wife and husband in vv. 12-13 plays with conventions of gender as they are interwoven with limits (boundaries). To recast the discussion above in terms of gender roles, whereas Israel the wife is characterized as one who could not (or would not) remain faithful (חסד), the husband's (God's) character is one of faithfulness and loving kindness (חסד). Verses 12-13 add to the picture of vv. 1-11 by depicting a danger that women pose to the patriarchal worldview: they cannot be relied on to act with חסד (that is, their nature is deceitful and/or treacherous);[12] therefore their sexual fidelity cannot be ensured. Thus, vv. 12-13 reveal at least one of the limits of the metaphor: if women are by nature deceitful and uncontrollable, they cannot be relied upon to change, or if they do modify their behavior, such apparent change is unstable.

The essential difference between the character of God the husband and that of his wife (Israel) illustrated in vv. 12-13 may provide a clue to one of the reasons for the shift to masculine address in the following verse

---

11. In light of the interplay between vv. 6-13 and the law of Deut. 24.1-4, the possibility of return implicitly includes remarriage (Deut. 24.4 mentions remarriage as the 'return' discussed in the law).

12. As noted above, the nicknames given to Israel and Judah in vv. 6-11 ('Turning Back' and 'Treachery') are a description of their character or nature. Their behavior as described in vv. 1-11 only confirms that deception is part of their characters. See also Prov. 7, where women are portrayed as by nature deceitful and uncontrollable. Although coming from a much later time, Ben Sira also portrays women in a similar fashion (cf. Sir. 19.2; 25.16-26 [esp. v. 24]; 42.9-14 [esp. v. 14]).

(v. 14). When describing the new order in vv. 14-18 and the conditions for repentance in vv. 21-25, 4.1-4, in which proper reverence, respect and fidelity are foundational, the marital metaphor will not work. I will argued below that eliminating the potential danger means eliminating women from the relational metaphor. Instead, a father–son metaphor, which avoids the problems of potential sexual infidelity illumined so clearly in vv. 1-13, is substituted.[13]

3. *The Application of the Rhetorical Strategies to Israel's Political and Religious Situation*

Having discussed intertextuality, metaphor and gender in these verses, it remains to address the issue of how these strategies are interwoven to address the audience's problematic religious and political involvements. The terminology used in these verses, particularly the roots שוב and פשע, apply the metaphorical relationship between Judah, Israel and YHWH to the religious and political situation being addressed through the vehicle of metaphor. Thus each term is indexed, so to speak, to all three discourses. These terms are the vehicles for the interweaving of the strategies of inter-textuality, metaphor and gender in 3.12-13. Taking the term שוב first, it is used in the call to return (v. 12), and has legal connotations within the marital metaphor: according to the law, a return in terms of remarriage is not possible. The term also has religious connotations: to return means to repent, which in v. 13 must be preceded by an acknowledgment of guilt.

In v. 13 the root פשע ('to rebel') also has connotations which inter-weave the metaphorical language with religious and political language. In the metaphorical world, the verb is associated with sexual infidelity; with regard to religious behavior, it is associated with apostasy (cf. 2.29-32; 5.6); and with regard to political and religious behavior, it is treaty language, and thus related to the covenant—פשע signifies the broken covenant between God and Israel. Verse 13b spells out in legal terms ('you have transgressed against YHWH your God'), metaphorical terms ('you scattered your ways to strangers under every leafy tree') and covenantal terms ('you have not obeyed me') how the relationship between YHWH and Israel has

---

13. Note, however, that the father–son metaphor is not wholly without its prob-lems: in v. 14, it is '"turning around" sons' who are addressed (cf. the rebellious son in Deut. 21.18-21; Prov. 10.1; 17.3, etc.). For a complete discussion of the implications of this terminology in terms of gender roles (both marital and paternal), see the discussion below, especially the section on metaphor and gender in vv. 14-18.

been broken.[14] With regard to both terms, פשע and שוב, the intertextual, metaphorical and gendered rhetoric combine to address Israel's problematic political and religious involvements.

4. *Summary*

To sum up, the climax and turning point of the chapter is reached in Jer. 3.12-13. In addition to continuing the intertextual play with the law by transgressing it, and employing conventions of gender, the terminology of vv. 12-13, particularly the roots שוב and פשע, interweave the intertextual, metaphorical and gender-specific elements of the rhetoric with the religious and political situation to which the rhetoric is addressed. The ultimate surprise in these verses is the call to return issued to someone who, by law, cannot return. What this call means in terms of the metaphorical relationship between YHWH and the people, and in terms of the people's religious and political behavior will be more directly addressed in the rest of Jer. 3.1–4.4.

---

14. Cf. Richard V. Bergren, *The Prophets and the Law* (Cincinnati: Hebrew Union College Press, 1974), pp. 114, 117.

Chapter 5

JEREMIAH 3.14-18: A MODEL FOR THE FUTURE

> When a system of power is thoroughly in command, it has scarcely need to
> speak itself aloud; when its workings are exposed and questioned, it be-
> comes not only subject to discussion, but even to change.
>
> —Kate Millett

Following Jer. 3.12-13, which establishes a new order, vv. 14-18 illustrate
how that new order will look. While the legal context is dropped in this
section, there is still concern with maintenance of proper governmental,
relational and natural boundaries. Here that concern is conveyed through
new intertexts—the Zion tradition and Isaiah, particularly Isa. 2.2-4—as
well as a new metaphor—YHWH as father or בֵאל and Judah as sons, בנים.
In keeping with the new metaphor, the form of address also shifts, to second
masculine plural. All three—intertexts, metaphor, and form of address—
embrace issues similar to those of vv. 1-13 (i.e. identity, behavior, land).
In these verses the rhetorics of intertextuality, metaphor and gender are
interwoven to portray a model picture for the future. Moreover, the same
ideals used to interweave these rhetorics in vv. 1-13 are used here (e.g.
family and proper familial relationships, creation/fertility and governmental ideals).

The following discussion will address the continuities and discontinuities of the rhetoric with the preceding verses, as well as explore the significance of the shift in metaphor and direct address. Following a translation
and discussion of general issues in Jer. 3.14-18, the analysis will be divided into two sections. The first will deal with intertextuality/intratext-
uality and the second will combine metaphor and gender, ending with the
implications of the gender construction for the passage and for the audience.

My translation of 3.14-18 is as follows:

(14) 'Return, turning back sons[1]', saying of YHWH, 'for I am your "*Baal*".[2] And I will take you, one from a city and two from a clan and I will bring you to Zion.

(15) And I will give you shepherds after my own heart and they will shepherd you [with] knowledge and insight.

(16) And it will happen that you will multiply and be fruitful in the land in those days', saying of YHWH. They will not say again, 'the ark of the house of YHWH', nor will it come to mind;[3] and they will not remember it; nor will they pay attention to it; nor will it be made again.

(17) In that day, they will call Jerusalem the throne of YHWH and all the nations will be gathered to it, to the name of YHWH, to Jerusalem. and they will no longer go after the stubbornness of their evil heart.

(18) In those days, the house of Judah will join the house of Israel, and they will come together from the land of the north to the land which I caused your fathers to inherit.

Verses 14-18 bear all the marks of a new voice added to the text. For instance, it is commonly acknowledged that the phrases, בעת ההיא (v. 17) and בימים ההמה (v. 18), are indicators of later additions to prophetic texts. Furthermore, the language itself presumes a different context than that of vv. 1-13. In contrast to vv. 1-13, several elements of vv. 14-18 may presume an exilic context. For example, v. 14b presupposes a situation in which the audience has no access to Zion (Jerusalem), as does v. 18, where Israel and Judah are pictured as returning to the land 'from the land of the north'.[4] The logical conclusion to the lack of access to the land, as

1.   While בנים may certainly refer both to sons and daughters, the shifts in imagery (from prostitution to father–son imagery to circumcision) and in address (from female to male) warrant its translation as 'sons' rather than 'children'. The significance of the address to 'sons' will be discussed in detail below.

2.   I have translated כי אנכי בעלתי בכם as 'for I am your "*Baal*"' in order to retain the word 'Baal', as well as the relational aspect of the ב in בכם. The ב may have several possible meanings: 'over', 'in', 'among'. Likewise, the root בעל may have several possible meanings (e.g. 'lord', 'master', 'husband', the god 'Baal'), each of which may be indexed to the different discourses being interwoven in these verses. The issues involved in this translation will be dealt with in greater detail below, as will the various connotations and their interplay in the rhetoric of vv. 14-18.

3.   Literally 'go up on their hearts'.

4.   With regard to v. 18, however, if the chronological date of 'the days of Josiah' (v. 6) is kept, and these verses are seen as the extension of the call to the north in vv. 12-13, then the message may be viewed as pre-exilic. In this case, the message is ostensibly addressed to the former Northern Kingdom, which had also experienced the loss of land and nation. J.J.M. Roberts holds this position (Jeremiah exegesis class, Princeton Seminary, 1985). The following analysis will take both possible situations (a

well as the assumption that people are returning from a different country, is that the people are in exile. The mention of the ark in v. 16 may also presuppose a situation of exile.[5]

Since most scholars dismiss these verses as much later additions, little attempt has been made to see their place in the context of 3.1–4.4 as a whole.[6] My analysis will address this lack by showing how the rhetoric of

pre-exilic and an exilic date) into consideration. While there are some differences in interpretation, there is extensive continuity as well.

5.   Within Jer. 3.14-18, v. 16 has generated much debate over the question of authorship and date. Some scholars consider it possible that the passage is jeremianic on the assumption that the ark disappeared in the monarchic period. M. Haran is a proponent of this view (M. Haran, 'The Disappearance of the Ark', *IEJ* 13 [1963], pp. 46-58; also Rudolph, *Jeremia*, pp. 23, 25). Similarly, J.A. Soggin posits a setting in the monarchic period, but after Israel was already in exile. His suggestion for the historical interpretation of v. 16 is provocative but unlikely, since it is based on a highly suspect syntactic change ('The Ark of The Covenant, Jeremiah 3,16', in P.-M. Bogaert [ed.], *Le Livre de Jérémie* [Leuven: Leuven University Press, 1981], pp. 215-21). Others have dated this passage after 597 on the assumption that Nebuchadnezzar took the ark, or it disappeared around this time (cf. Volz, *Der Prophet Jeremia*, p. 23; Bright, *Jeremiah*, p. 27). For our purposes the actual date is not important. The question with which we must concern ourselves is what function this verse serves in its context. As will be shown below, this verse (and the rest of 3.14-18 as well) can easily be applied either to a pre-exilic or an exilic timeframe. The message to a pre-exilic audience would be a warning against reliance on outward symbols, while the message to an exilic audience would be a message of comfort, that the outward symbols are not necessary for true YHWH worship. Thus, the reference to lack of the ark in v. 16 does not necessarily presuppose an exilic time of writing for this section.

6.   Beginning with Bernhard Stade ('Miscellen: 1. Jes. 4,2–6; 2. Jer 3,6–16; 3. Habakuk', *ZAW* 4 [1884], pp. 149-59), and since the time of Smend (*Lehrbuch der alttestamentlichen Religionsgeschichte*, pp. 247-48 n. 2), the reigning view is that these verses are exilic or post-exilic and therefore secondary. There are, however, varied approaches as to the reason for its placement. Oesterley, for example, suggests that 'it has been inserted in the collection in the place where it now stands on account of the use of the words "return" and "backsliding"...' (W.O.E. Oesterley and Theodore H. Robinson, *An Introduction to the Books of the Old Testament* [London: SPCK, 1934], p. 306). In the twentieth century, many scholars have noted the close associations of this material with Jer. 30–31 (which is dated late), and have consequently posited an early ministry for Jeremiah which was directed toward the north in the time of Josiah. According to this view, the early material dating from this time was subsequently reworked for a Judahite audience and Jer. 3.14-18 represents that reworking. Volz popularized this view (*Der Prophet Jeremia*, pp. 34, 43-49). See also Bright, *Jeremiah*, p. 27; Thompson, *Jeremiah*, p. 189; and Seitz, *Theology in Conflict*, p. 75.

these verses could function for either a pre- or post-exilic audience.[7] Whether or not one posits an exilic date for this section, it is nonetheless clear from what I have already noted above that a new voice with new concerns enters the picture. As a new voice this section reinterprets and extends the interpretation of vv. 1-5 and 6-13. In addition to dealing with the issues outlined in the introduction to this section, the following discussion will deal with the ways in which these verses appropriate and reinterpret the rhetoric of vv. 1-13.

Before proceeding to that discussion, however, a few words need to be said about the place of the root שוב in these verses. The appeal to return, this time addressed to the 'turning around' (rebellious) sons, in v. 14 uses the same root, שוב, played upon in the citation of the law in v. 1 and in the succeeding verses (vv. 2-13), but in vv. 14-18 it takes on a new connotation. Here the meaning of 'returning' is spelled out in ideal future terms. In addition to religious return to YHWH, the call to return in this section means literal return to the land. Moreover, 'turning' to YHWH will mean reversals in terms of the ideals dealt with in vv. 1-13 (legal, social, natural). Finally, as an ideal picture, these verses pave the way for a renewed appeal which sets forth the conditions under which such a return would be accepted by YHWH in reality.[8]

---

7. Mark E. Biddle's general remarks on 3.14-18 (*A Redaction History of Jeremiah 2.1–4.2*, pp. 102-103), have much in common with my own stance. He maintains that 'several particulars of this text reveal its ideological backgrounds' (p. 102). Agreeing with those scholars who date these verses late, he goes on to say: 'The eschatologist's program for the revision of Israelite religion and society emphasizes the immediate presence of Yahweh with all his people (cf Jer. 31.31ff). The old institutions for the mediation of that presence are to be obsolete in this new utopian order' (p. 103). Cf. Robert Carroll, who also dates the vv. 14-18 to the exilic period. He writes, 'The text itself is already composed of many interpretative moves and decisions. Although the text is the object we interpret, it is itself the product of interpretation' (*From Chaos to Covenant: Uses of Prophecy in the Book of Jeremiah* [London: SCM Press, 1981], p. 265). I agree that seeing this text as exilic is possible. Yet, as Biddle himself acknowledges, there are very few clues given in the text itself as to time and date, and, moreover, this state of affairs may be intentional (*A Redaction History*, pp. 31-32). An equally possible interpretation might include these verses as part of a pre-exilic program to wean the people away from the symbols of their security, and I will pursue such an interpretation below. In either case, these verses are explicitly rhetorical. Intentional or not, the lack of historical markers does allow for reinterpretation of the text, and for the text to be applicable to various historical/political circumstances.

8. Cf. Jer. 3.19–4.4.

1. *Intertextuality in Jeremiah 3.14-18*

a. *Intertextuality with the Zion Tradition*

The new order described in vv. 14-18 is based on an old theme: the gathering of all the nations to YHWH in Jerusalem. The mention of Zion (v. 14), fertility for the land and the people (v. 16), Jerusalem (v. 17), the nations coming to worship YHWH (v. 17) and a reunified Judah and Israel (v. 18) all represent ideals related to the Zion tradition in the Southern Kingdom.[9] The ideal, future movement of vv. 14-18 also resonates with this tradition, which has its clearest representation in the eighth-century prophets and the Psalms. The tenets of the tradition which are linked most closely to Jer. 3.14-18 are, among others: that YHWH chose Jerusalem for YHWH's dwelling place (cf. vv. 14, 18);[10] that the nations acknowledge YHWH's suzerainty (cf. v. 17);[11] and that the inhabitants of Zion experience blessings from YHWH which include justice, peace, prosperity and fertility for both land and people (cf. vv. 15, 16).[12] These ideals are absorbed into the picture of the new order in vv. 14-18.

A related ideal is that of the inviolability of Jerusalem. Even in the face of doom, Jerusalem is portrayed as safe from harm, as the place from which YHWH will utter judgment and salvation.[13] In the eighth century, historical circumstances had supported this view. When, in the Syro-Ephraimite War (734–32 BCE), much of the land around the city was destroyed, Jerusalem was spared. More to the point, given the comparison in 3.6-18 between the Southern and Northern Kingdoms, when the Northern Kingdom was destroyed (722 BCE), Jerusalem and Judah were spared.

---

9. Cf. J.J.M. Roberts, 'Zion in the Theology of the Davidic–Solomonic Empire', in T. Ishida and M. Sekine (eds.), *Studies in the Period of David and Solomon and Other Essays: Papers Read at the International Symposium for Biblical Studies, Tokyo, 5-7 December, 1979* (Tokyo: Yamakawa-Shuppansha, 1982), pp. 93-108; and Ben C. Ollenburger, *Zion the City of the Great King* (JSOTSup, 41; Sheffield: JSOT Press, 1987).

10. Cf. Pss. 78.68; 132.13; see also 46.5; 48.2-3, 8-9; 76.3; 87.2.

11. Cf. Ps. 2.1-3; Isa. 2.2-4.

12. Cf. Isa. 3.13-16; Pss. 24.3-4; 72. Another idea which is of great importance for 3.19–4.4 is that the people must be fit to live in God's presence (cf. Pss. 48.12-14; 101.8; 132.13-18; 133.3; 147.13; Isa. 33.17-24). A useful outline of the Zion tradition is to be found in the Roberts article, 'Zion in the Theology of the Davidic–Solomonic Empire', mentioned above. The rest of the preceding information has been taken from lectures given by Roberts in his 'Monarch to Messiah' class at Princeton Theological Seminary in 1985.

13. Cf. Isa. 24.23; 25.6-10; 31.4-5; 37.33-35.

Jeremiah 3.16 takes up this issue by announcing that the ark will no longer be a central symbol upon which the people can rely. Rather, the ark will not even be part of their vocabulary ('it will not come to mind; they will not remember it; nor will they pay attention to it; nor will it be made again'). This transgression of a central tenet of the Zion tradition acts as a warning to Judah that they cannot depend on the ark (or, implicitly, any other religious trappings) to keep them safe. In this respect, Keil's argument that the mention of the ark was in accordance with Jeremiah's aim to take away 'the false props of their confidence'[14] is very close to my own view. The sentiment presented in v. 16 is similar to that presented in Jeremiah 7, in which the people are challenged not to trust in the temple as a kind of talisman to keep them from harm (7.4), but instead to change their behavior, for if they do not, YHWH will 'cast them out' (7.14-15).[15] Both texts are arguing against reliance on physical symbols that have come to take the place of worship of YHWH. Therefore, both texts absorb specific tenets of the Zion tradition only to transgress it. This reading of 3.16 is also consonant with the systematic shattering of security begun in vv. 1-5 and continued in vv. 1-13. Even the people's central religious symbols cannot save them. Instead the people must rely on nothing besides the name of YHWH (v. 17).

J. Lust's discussion of the form of vv. 16-17 adds to this perspective. He argues persuasively for a formal link between these verses and 16.14-15, which I translate as follows: 'Therefore, behold the days are coming, saying of YHWH, when it will no longer be said, "As YHWH lives who brought the Israelites up from the land of Egypt", but "As YHWH lives who brought the Israelites from the land of the north and from all the lands where he had banished them".' With regard to both cases, Lust argues:

> The scheme is the same... A traditional popular saying is replaced with a new one. Reference is made to the past, not for its own sake, but for its value as model allowing one to interpret present and future history. The future will surpass its model. God's throne in Jerusalem will relegate the ark into oblivion (3,16-17) and the Return from the Exile will have the same effect on the Exodus (16,14-15).[16]

14. Keil, *The Prophecies of Jeremiah*, I, p. 95.

15. Cf. Jer. 26.

16. J. Lust, '"Gathering and Return" in Jeremiah and Ezekiel', in P.-M. Bogaert (ed.), *Le Livre de Jérémie: Le Prophète et son Milieu les Oracles et leur Transmission* (Leuven: Leuven University Press, 1981), pp. 119-42 (133-34).

I agree in substantial measure with Lust's argument. However, he does not take the interpretation of v. 17 far enough. Whereas he stops with the throne of YHWH in Jerusalem as the focal point of difference between the past and the future, I would argue that it is not the throne itself that is important in v. 17, but rather the idea that the name of YHWH replaces prior religious attachments. While many scholars have excised לשם יהוה (v. 17) as a gloss,[17] I propose that these words are crucial to the message of the passage and are consonant with the idea of v. 16. The placement of these words within v. 17 indicates emphasis: the people will come to or for (ל) *YHWH's* name; they will come not because of the greatness of Jerusalem, but in order to worship YHWH. This emphasis ties in with one of the themes of this passage which will be treated more fully below—the worship of YHWH and YHWH alone. These words re-emphasize that Jerusalem is not important in and of itself; rather, its importance lies in the fact that 'all the nations will come to (or "for the sake of") the name of YHWH to Jerusalem'. In other words, Jerusalem's importance lies only in its being a throne for YHWH (i.e that it is the location of God's presence); YHWH's actual presence overshadows any significance the place or the throne itself could have. Verses 16-17, then, transgress one of the central ideals of the Zion tradition, the inviolability of Jerusalem and the temple, by placing 'the name of YHWH' (v. 17) at the center of the vision of the future rather than Jerusalem, the ark, or the temple itself.

The idea of the centrality of God's name is also connected to the marital metaphor in vv. 1-13. Within a patrilineal, patriarchal society such as that of Israel, the name is of supreme importance: the control of sexuality is designed to maintain a man's name, that is, his lineage and paternity.[18] Thus, this text establishes YHWH as the archpatriarch, the one whose name is central in all areas of life.

---

17. Cf. T.N.D. Mettinger, *The Dethronement of Sabaoth* (trans. Frederick H. Cryer; Lund: C.W.K. Gleerup, 1982), p. 63. For the opposite view, see Thompson, *Jeremiah*, p. 198.

18. Cf. the levirate law of Deut. 25.5-10, as well as Pressler's discussion of it (*The View of Women*, pp. 63-74). She concludes that the law's 'overarching concern is the perpetuation of the man's name, that is, the continuation of the man's lineage, and, presumably, the continued ownership of the man's property by his male descendants' (p. 73). Similarly, Lyn M. Bechtel, using a socio-anthropological perspective, argues for the importance both of 'the perpetuation of "name"' and for a central concern in Israelite society with the heir ('Shame as a Sanction of Social Control in Biblical Israel: Judicial, Political, and Social Shaming', *JSOT* 49 [1991], pp. 47-76 [58]).

b. *Intertextuality with Isaiah*

In addition to playing intertextually with the Zion tradition as a whole, Jer. 3.14-18 plays with the message of Isaiah of Jerusalem, one of the primary biblical proponents of the Zion tradition, in particular. Many scholars have noted the connection between these verses and Isa. 2.2-4.[19] Isaiah 2.2-4 presents a picture of a glorified Jerusalem to which all nations will stream.[20] Both identify Jerusalem as Zion (cf. Isa. 2.3 and Jer. 3.14). In addition, both texts view Jerusalem as the center of the world. With regard to Isa. 2.2-4, the text pictures 'all nations' streaming to Jerusalem (v. 2), and Jerusalem as the center of God's instruction (v. 3), as well as the place of judgment and arbitration for all peoples (v. 4). Similar ideas are present in Jer. 3.14-18: in v. 14, YHWH promises to bring the people in exile to Zion; in v. 17, Jerusalem is called the 'throne of YHWH'; and also in v. 17, 'all the nations will be gathered to it', that is, 'to the name of YHWH, to Jerusalem'. In addition, v. 15 portrays the leaders as chosen by YHWH and as 'shepherding' with 'knowledge and insight'. Like Isa. 2.2-4, the picture of vv. 14-18 is clearly one in which YHWH, and more importantly, the name of YHWH (v. 17), is central both for Israel and for the nations of the world. What is also clear in both texts is that YHWH is not just a figure-head; YHWH is truly the ruler of all people.

To a large extent, then, the ideal future described in vv. 14-18 absorbs the view of the future given in Isa. 2.2-4. Where the text of Jer. 3.14-18 transgresses this view is precisely where it transgresses the Zion tradition: in the inviolability of Jerusalem and the centrality of the Temple. Whereas the broader context of Isaiah presupposes a deliverance of Jerusalem,[21] Jer. 3.14-18 presupposes an exilic audience, which has experienced the loss of Jerusalem and the destruction of the central symbol of YHWH's presence (the Temple). For such people vv. 14-18 function as a vision of hope. The ideals of the Zion tradition and the future presented by Isaiah will be fulfilled, but with a crucial difference: the future of 3.14-18 focuses on YHWH himself. This concentration on YHWH and YHWH alone will continue

19. Cf. McKane, *Jeremiah I–XXV*, p. 74; Carroll, *Jeremiah*, p. 151; and Thompson, *Jeremiah*, p. 198.

20. The dating for these verses has been the subject of controversy since the mid-eighteenth century. I follow Hans Wildberger in dating these verses to Isaiah of Jerusalem, that is, to the eighth century (*Jesaja Kapitel 1–12* [BKAT, 10; Neukirchen–Vluyn: Neukirchener Verlag, 1980 (1972)], p. 80). For an excellent discussion of the controversy itself, see pp. 78-80.

21. Cf. Isa. 1.25-26; 7; 8.

in 3.19–4.4, as will the stress on true repentance (returning) which goes deeper than the (fore)skin—to the heart (cf. v. 17).

2. *Jeremiah 3.14-18 as a New Voice*

In addition to the emphasis on the proper status of YHWH himself in the vision of the future portrayed in vv. 14-18, there is also emphasis on the proper position of the people within this vision, one which is illuminated through an intratextual link between v. 17 and the earlier verses of this chapter. This verse depicts the people's future behavior: they 'will no longer go after the stubbornness of their evil heart' (שררות לבם הרע). This behavior contrasts sharply with that described in vv. 1-13, that is, the stubbornness portrayed through the metaphor having 'the brow of a harlot' (v. 3), and turning to YHWH deceitfully (בשקר) rather than with their whole heart (בכל-לבם, v. 10). Taken together with the replacement of the ark in v. 16, v. 17 is an indication that the people's entire orientation must change. This vision of the future leaves no room for the kind of behavior exhibited by the promiscuous wife of vv. 1-5 and the promiscuous sisters of vv. 6-11; rather, the proper relationship between YHWH and the people will be restored and maintained through proper behavior, including reverence and worship of YHWH.[22]

Like vv. 16-17, the remainder of vv. 14-18 represents an absorption and transgression of the previous verses in terms of the reversal of other central themes of vv. 1-13. Whereas in vv. 1-5 the emphasis is on drought and lack of fertility, the picture of the proposed new order is one of abundance and fertility (v. 16a). Verses 14 and 17 likewise reverse the judgment and separation which one sister has experienced (exile) and which is implied for the other (vv. 6-11) by bringing both the kingdoms of Israel and Judah back to YHWH's name, to Jerusalem, and making Jerusalem once again the center of YHWH's presence and the gathering place of all

---

22. If one takes the position of J.J.M. Roberts that vv. 14-18 is viewed as an extension of the offer to the former Northern Kingdom to return during the josianic reform, these verses also have a message for a pre-exilic Judahite audience. Even while the ideal future is portrayed, there is warning that trust in the past (either in YHWH's actions in the past or in the central symbols of YHWH's actions) will not keep them from the punishment implied in vv. 6-11. Only a radical change in behavior will suffice: they are not to go to other gods (2.28; 3.13); nor to other nations (2.18, 36); neither are they to rely on religious trappings (3.16; 7; 26); rather they are to come to the presence of the Lord (3.17).

the nations. Verse 18 completes the picture of a new order by depicting the reunification of north and south, repossession of the land, and describing the land as an inheritance. These verses serve in part as a reminder that faithfulness to the name of YHWH is necessary for maintenance of the people's identity (v. 17). Thus, the fundamental issues of vv. 1-13—identity, behavior and land—are all resolved through reversal in this ideal picture of the future. What remains is to reveal how such a reversal can be accomplished. That is the task of 3.19–4.4.

3. *Metaphor and Gender in Jeremiah 3.14-18*

While the discussion of intertextuality in vv. 14-18 has focused primarily on issues of behavior and the land, it has only touched on issues of identity. The following discussion will deal primarily with the issues of identity as they are addressed in this section: through the vehicles of metaphor and gender.

Although the appeal of v. 14 repeats the invitation to return issued in vv. 12-13, the appeal is couched in more general terms. Instead of addressing Israel, the divorced sister, the prophet quotes YHWH as addressing the appeal to the 'turning back' sons. The grounds for the appeal comes next: 'for I am your (2nd masc. plur.) "*Baal*"'. Here two issues related both to identity and to power relations are central, namely, the switch to second masculine direct address, and the switch in relational metaphor. Taking the latter first, the pairing of the verb בעל with בנים is unique in the Hebrew Bible. For the most part, the verb is used without the preposition ב, and means 'to marry',[23] while in one case it is paired with אדנים to mean 'rule over'. Only in Jer. 3.14 and 31.32 is the verb בעל used with ב. In both cases the verb occurs following extended sections addressing Israel with feminine direct address and using marital imagery to portray the relationship between YHWH and Israel (3.1-13; 31.1-5, 16, 21-22). Both use the same verbal form (בעלתי) plus ב plus a masculine pronomial suffix (בכם, 3.14; בם, 31.32). Yet each is translated differently in the NRSV. While 3.14 is usually translated, 'I will be master over you'; 31.32 refers to 'the covenant which they (i.e. their fathers, אבותם) broke, though I was their husband...' (cf. RSV).[24]

23. Cf. Gen. 20.3; Deut. 21.13; 22.22; 24.1; Isa. 54.1, 5; 62.4, 5; Mal. 2.11.

24. Note that in both Jer. 3.14 and 31.32, *Tanakh* takes בעלתי as the equivalent of בחלתי, and translates, 'though I have rejected you'. There is, however, no textual evidence for such an emendation.

The translation of 31.32 highlights the potential metaphorical problems evoked by the use of the root בעל in both situations. Here the metaphor slips over its bounds, imaging men's relationship with God as marriage. In 3.14 the effect is the same: while God (as a male deity) may indeed be claiming mastership over them, God is also 'husbanding' the sons. Conventions of gender are in play here: the effect of the pairing is to 'feminize' the sons in terms of power relations. The unrestrained element in this metaphor, that is, its potential slippage, as well as the problems posed by that slippage, may be one reason for the switch explicitly to father–son imagery in 3.19–4.4.

While the metaphor may slip its bounds, there are nonetheless several ways in which the possible connotations for the root בעל interact persuasively with the various ideals already discussed in vv. 1-13 to further delineate the proper power relations between YHWH and the people. The ideal of marriage has already been mentioned: YHWH is the people's metaphorical husband. With regard to the legal and governmental ideal, the term is a reminder of the covenantal relationship between YHWH and the people. YHWH is master over them and, as such, requires fidelity and obedience. Finally, indexing the term to the issues of creation and fertility, the term may be an ironic reference to Baal worship. It is YHWH rather than Baal who is the source of fertility and the source of proper order within creation (cf. v. 16). In other words, contrary to popular belief, it is *YHWH* who is their true Baal.[25] Through the use of the verb בעל, therefore, YHWH is claiming for himself power and control over every aspect of life: social (marriage), legal/governmental (covenantal) and nature/creation (fertility).

If the root בעל establishes a certain set of power relations between YHWH and the people, the form of address (2nd masc. plur.) and the metaphor used for the people, sons (בנים), does so as well. The term 'sons' invokes yet another metaphorical relationship between YHWH and the people—a father–son relationship. Just as the marital metaphor governed vv. 1-13, this metaphor will govern the rhetoric of 3.21–4.4. Like the other relational metaphors, the father–son relationship is one of unequal power.[26]

---

25. Thompson (*Jeremiah*, p. 201) has also noted the three possibilities for the term בעל. However, he has not explored the full implications of these three meanings within the discourse and interplay of ideals in either the smaller section of 3.14-18 or the piece as a whole (3.1–4.4).

26. See, for example, the law regarding the rebellious son in Deut. 21.18-21, which assumes the authority of the male head of the household (see Pressler's discussion of

Within the familial structure, older men are privileged over younger men, and fathers over sons. As sons, the audience is portrayed as subordinate to the father, and the father requires proper reverence and obedience.

Along with the shift to בנים, the masculine direct address indicates a crucial identity shift as well. This shift implies that if the audience returns (repents) they will no longer be addressed, and therefore no longer be identified, as unfaithful wives, but rather, as sons. Yet the shift to father–son imagery is not a simple shift from negative female imagery to positive male imagery. The characterization of the sons as בנים שובבים in both v. 14 and v. 22 indicates that the sons themselves are ones who 'turn around', that is, they too are faithless. Nevertheless, to anticipate the discussion of vv. 21-25, it is as sons that God promises to heal their 'turning' (v. 22).[27] At the metaphorical level, a subtle distinction is made between being 'other' (unfaithful women, who are by very definition outside the limits) and being sons to the father (i.e. made in the [male] image of God, who represents the role of ultimate privilege). The identification of the sons with the deity also implies a certain sharing of his characteristics; they share the physical properties of the father-figure, God, and therefore, through their sex they are privileged. The very change of imagery and address exerts a subtle pressure of self-identification, not as the other, but as junior members of those who are privileged in society, who are to model their behavior after that of their (divine) father.[28]

The shift in identity and the establishment of proper power relations through the proper YHWH–son relationship are manifested in all areas of society (governmental [legal], social [familial] and natural [creation/fertility]) in the model picture of vv. 14-18. Verse 15 deals with the legal ideal through the metaphor of shepherds. It is well known that the term רעים is

this law in *The View of Women*, pp. 17-20). The Wisdom Literature also preserves such a hierarchy: the wise son is obedient and follows the father's teachings, while the foolish son acts improvidently (cf. Prov. 10.1; 17.25; 19.13).

27. Holladay rightly notes that this verse contains 'covenantal *šûbh* in a triple word-play' (*The Root Šûbh in the Old Testament*, p. 129). As the rest of Jer. 3.1–4.4 bears out, I would argue that through the establishment of the proper father–son relationship, complete with circumcision (although, to be sure, the circumcision is as metaphorical as the father–son relationship), this promise to heal the sons' 'turning' gives the sons the benefit of the doubt which is not available in the marriage metaphor.

28. The further implications of this metaphor, both in terms of gender and in terms of power relations, as well as its physical outworking in the symbol of circumcision, will be explored in detail in the final chapter, which includes my analysis of 4.1-4.

112   *Circumscribing the Prostitute*

often a metaphor for leaders.[29] In the book of Jeremiah in particular, רעים
is a term used quite often for leaders who have led the people improperly,
and who will therefore be destroyed.[30] In contrast to the improper shepherds, YHWH is here re-establishing his proper rule through the shepherds
of his choice who will be faithful to him (כלבי). Moreover, they will
'shepherd' the people. Here the Hebrew grammar allows for multiple
interpretations. The use of the direct object marker allows the root רעה to
have two different relations to the complements 'knowledge' and 'insight'.
First the shepherds themselves may act with knowledge and insight. But,
more importantly, the food they shall feed the people is knowledge and
insight.[31] Verse 15 thus invokes the legal ideal also invoked in the rhetoric
of vv. 1-13, but in this case it has the function of establishing a new,
proper, legal/governmental order with the proper power relations in place.

Verse 16 moves to the natural ideal through the image of fertility. One
of the consequences of returning as sons will be the establishment of the
proper natural order, as manifested in the multiplication and fruitfulness of
the people in the land. As a promiscuous wife, the audience polluted the
land (vv. 2, 9) and caused infertility (the withdrawing of God's seed from
the land, v. 3); but, in v. 16, a new ideal replaces the old transgressed
ideal. As sons in the proper relationship to YHWH, the audience (like the
patriarchs of old) will multiply and increase in the land. The land is no
longer polluted and infertile. Thus the natural ideal is invoked here to
establish a new, proper, natural order.

Building on v. 16, v. 17 deals with the social ideal. In this verse, the
proper social order will be restored, and all people will come to the ultimate father: 'to the name of YHWH' rather than going after 'the stubbornness of their evil heart'. Verse 18 then portrays the results for the nation as
a whole: the nation will be unified (the former Northern and Southern
Kingdoms will come together—as houses not as sisters), and the land, the
center of their identity as a nation, will be restored to them.

As can be seen from the analysis thus far, the discourse of vv. 14-18
is indexed to the same ideals dealt with in vv. 1-13 (legal, social and
natural), thus emphasizing the contrast between the model picture of the
future and the previously presented negative picture of the present. As in
vv. 1-13, the three ideals are mutually reinforcing. Combined with the

29. Cf. Jer. 23; Ezek. 34.
30. The most well-known example is Jer. 23, but see also Jer. 2.8; 10.21; 12.10;
22.22; 25.34-36.
31. Note that these are ideals associated with a just and righteous rule. Cf. Isa. 11.

switch in identity, they add to the persuasive force of the rhetoric as a whole. The implication of vv. 14-18 is that the repentance itself will allow the audience to resume their status as male subjects; but even more significantly, repentance ('turning') will restore health both to the social order, as portrayed through legal and familial ideals, and to the natural order, as portrayed through ideals of fertility.

A final rhetorical strategy, which is linked with the switch to second masculine plural in v. 14 is the fact that the description of the new order in vv. 14-18 is in the third person. As such, it is removed from the readers. Together with the markers of a future discourse ('in those days', vv. 16, 18; 'at that time', v. 17), the third person description presents a contrast between the immediacy of the direct address in metaphorical terms and the imagery here. The contrast indicates that, rather than being present reality, this description is projected as a possible future—what could happen if the people would return. Thus, the identification of the audience presented here is also a *potential* identification. Only through a behavioral change can they make this vision of wholeness a reality.

Thus far, the ways in which the actual father–son imagery works in vv. 14-18 have been explored, but not the implications of the switch from the marital metaphor to a father–son metaphor. To do so, it is necessary to give an overview of the ways in which gender constructs the whole of vv. 1-18. In these verses, an implied male audience is portrayed and addressed as a promiscuous wife who acts like a harlot. The images of overstepped boundaries in legal, social and natural terms, and the extremity of the adultery portrayed, all combine to exert subtle pressure on the audience to see their behavior as wrong, to eschew that behavior, and thereby to reverse their identification as promiscuous wives. Adultery on the part of wives, with the dilemma it poses for questions of paternity, is a potent way to indicate the threat of the audience's behavior to the entire social order. Likewise the integral connection between sexual behavior and the land indicates the danger, not only to the social order, but to the cosmic order as well (v. 3).

The change to second masculine plural direct address—as sons—in vv. 14-18 introduces a more positive image in patriarchal terms. The new father–son image avoids the potential paternity problems associated with the marital image, while at the same time representing the proper power relations between a male deity and a male audience. The combination of this image with the model of a world where the proper boundaries are in place in the legal, social and natural realms establishes a rhetorically powerful contrast to the picture of vv. 1-13. The implication of vv. 14-18 as a whole is that a return to proper actions will restore the audience's status as sons, and will also restore the proper balance to the land, to YHWH's place in the land and the relationship between YHWH and Israel.

Nevertheless, gender not only constructs Jer. 3.1-18, but also, particularly the female gender, is also constructed in this passage. In contrast to the potentially positive male images (cf. 3.21–4.4), the female images are exclusively negative. Women's marginalization in patriarchal society is exploited to portray political and religious behavior in sexual terms, terms which threaten the entire social and cosmic order. Whereas, as a harlot, the audience members are portrayed as disrupting the social order, as sons, they can resume a proper relation to the ultimate father, God, thus restoring the social order (e.g. proper worship in vv. 16-17). Moreover, that social order will have benefits not for Israel alone, but for the nations (v. 17).[32] Whereas harlotry leads to rivalry, treachery, deception and division (vv. 6-11), proper sonship leads to a reunification of the divided kingdom (v. 18). This contrast is illustrated in the cosmic sphere as well: while harlotry led to drought (v. 3), sonship leads to fertility (v. 16). In sum, whereas harlotry led to chaos, proper sonship leads to order.

What is striking after the predominance of the female imagery in Jer. 3.1-13 is the complete lack of such imagery in vv. 14-18. The world which vv. 14-18 envisions is one in which women have little or no part: it is the sons who are given the vision of an ideal future in which they are in control under the ultimate control of the father, and there are no women to threaten that control. In short, in vv. 1-18 the male gender is constructed as central to society and to its proper maintenance, while the female gender, the 'other', is the vehicle for portraying evil, disruption and chaos. The imagery and address of 3.19–4.4 will intensify these characteristics of gender construction.

---

32. This reference to blessing for the nations may be a subtle reference to the Abrahamic covenant, an allusion which is made much more overtly in Jer. 4.1-4.

Chapter 6

JEREMIAH 3.19-20:
SET AMONG THE SONS—ISRAEL AS FAITHLESS DAUGHTER

To expose and question that complex of ideas and mythologies about
women and men which exist in our society and are confirmed in our literature is to make the system of power embodied in the literature open not
only to discussion but even to change. Such questioning and exposure must
be entered into from a point of view which questions its values and assumptions and which has its investment in making available to consciousness
precisely that which the literature wishes to keep hidden.

—Judith Fetterley

The movement of Jer. 3.19–4.4 is predicated on 3.1-18 in several ways.
Jeremiah 3.19 begins a new appeal which drives home the same points as
3.1-5. Questions of repentance remain central, as do issues of identity,
behavior and the land. In addition, the intertwining of the rhetoric with a
discussion of ideals (e.g. law, family and nature/creation) will continue.
Whereas 3.1-18 introduce the question of the possibility of return, 3.19–
4.4 show what return would *mean* in terms of the changes Judah would
have to make; these verses reveal YHWH's visioning of the new order of
3.14-18. Thus, 3.19–4.4 focus on making the ideal picture of 3.14-18 a
reality. Underlying these verses as a whole is the appeal to return given in
vv. 12-13. Therefore, the argument of this section builds on and extends
that of vv. 1-18.

As with the analysis of 3.1-18, the following analysis will be structured
around the three primary rhetorical strategies employed in the piece: intertextuality, metaphor and gender. In addition to the legal citation of 3.1,
which continues to underlie 3.19–4.4, there will be two other primary
groups of intertexts discussed here. The Abrahamic promise, particularly
as presented in Gen. 22.18 (cf. Gen. 26.4), will be dealt with in relation to
Jer. 4.1-4, while various texts from Hosea will be the focus of the intertextual treatment of the whole of 3.19–4.4. Metaphorically, the text of
3.19–4.4 will continue the interplay with the husband–wife relationship in
the discussion of vv. 19-20, but will focus on the father–child relationship.

With regard to gender, the implications of the complete shift to father–son imagery and masculine plural direct address from v. 21 on will be explored in greater detail, particularly in light of the final metaphor, circumcision, which has its own implications in terms of gender for the piece as a whole.

The present chapter will focus on Jer. 3.19-20, the next will be devoted to 3.21-25, and Chapter 8 will discuss 4.1-4. Since intertextuality, metaphor and gender are inseparably intertwined in 3.19-20, the following analysis will take each verse in turn, discussing all three aspects together. It will conclude with a discussion of the implications of the rhetoric for the construction of gender in the whole of the piece, and more particularly for the switch to the masculine plural address of the rest of 3.1–4.4.

I translate:

> (19)'I thought how I would set you (fem. sing.)[1] among the sons, and give you a pleasant land, the most beautiful[2] heritage of all the nations. And I thought you[3] would call me, "My Father", and would not turn[4] from following me.
> (20)Instead, as a woman has become faithless[5] to her lover, so you (masc. plur.) have been faithless to me, O house of Israel', saying of YHWH.[6]

Jeremiah 3.19 begins with a view of YHWH's thoughts similar to that of v. 7, although this time there is no introductory frame including the prophet in the dialogue (cf. v. 6). Just as in v. 7, the reader is 'let in', so to speak, to the innermost thoughts and desires of God; that is, the audience is given insight into God's motivations. The parallel with 'the sons' in v. 19 suggests that the third feminine singular address, 'you', refers to a daughter. Thus, YHWH is pictured as a loving father, yearning to give the best to his daughter. This quotation of YHWH's thoughts is a rhetorical device, the

---

1.   The form of address is feminine singular. Many scholars, including the editors of *BHS*, wish to change the address to masculine singular. As the ensuing discussion will show, however, the feminine form of address not only recalls the earlier female metaphors for Israel, but also brings in to play issues of identity associated with YHWH's choice of Israel, and accentuates certain themes (including those of uniqueness and separation from other nations) which are central to this half of the piece.

2.   There is some question as to what צְבִי צִבְאוֹת means; most scholars read the second word as coming from the same root as the first, hence my reading of it as the superlative, 'the most beautiful'. For a thorough discussion of the possibilities, see Holladay, *Jeremiah 1*, p. 60.

3.   Reading with the *qere* as feminine singular.

4.   Again reading with the *qere* as feminine singular.

5.   Reading with the MT as qal third feminine singular (בגדה). Cf. parallel בגדתם.

6.   The reasons for this translation of אשה and מרעה will be dealt with below.

effect of which is to create a sense of intimacy, as well as to evoke sympathy for God's position *vis-à-vis* Israel. Verse 20 also uses female imagery to describe Israel's actions, thus re-presenting the situation of vv. 1-5 in new terms (a promiscuous daughter instead of a promiscuous wife). The return to feminine imagery lasts only through v. 20, however. As with 3.1-18, an identical shift in image (to father–son imagery) occurs in this section when the possibility of repentance is offered.

The first metaphor of Jer. 3.19 depicts the nation as a daughter inheriting from her father, and further, being given the best inheritance. The closest and clearest link to this image of inheritance in the Hebrew Scriptures is Deut. 32.7-9. Thus, this image evokes Deut. 32.7-9 as an intertext, where YHWH is pictured as apportioning the nations, but choosing 'Jacob' as his own portion.[7] As in Jer. 3.19, YHWH is pictured as a father (Deut. 32.7), but in Deuteronomy a father–son metaphor is used.[8] In both texts, the uniqueness of the people is emphasized, yet in slightly different ways. In Deut. 32.9, Jacob is the portion reserved for YHWH (rather than other gods), whereas in Jer. 3.19, YHWH is pictured as the sole god giving the best of the land to Israel. In both cases as well there is a contrast between YHWH's past actions and the people's behavior in response. Deuteronomy 32.7 talks of YHWH's action of choosing and apportionment as having taken place in ancient times, while Deut. 32.15-18 depicts the people's behavior in response as abandonment and mocking of God through improper worship. Similarly, in Jer. 3.19 the quotation of the motivations for YHWH's gift of the land, together with the quotation of the response he expected of the people, are contrasted with the actual behavior of the people in v. 20. Jeremiah 3.19 thus absorbs the ideas of inheritance and apportionment, the uniqueness of the nation, and the difference between YHWH's expected response and the actual response of the people.

Yet some substantial differences between Jer. 3.19 and Deut. 32.7-9 reveal how Jer. 3.19 transgresses its intertext. First, the governing metaphor is different: whereas in Deut. 32.7-9 it is the son, Jacob, who holds the land for YHWH, in Jer. 3.19, it is the daughter. Second, while the text of Deut. 32.7-9 focuses on YHWH's choice of the people and the land for himself (that is, it focuses on YHWH's election of Jacob), Jer. 3.19 assumes that Israel belongs to YHWH and focuses on the *land* as the best gift YHWH

---

7.   While the text of Deut. 32 is notoriously corrupt (cf. the *BHS* apparatus for an overview of some of the textual problems), the image portrayed in vv. 7-9 is nonetheless clear.

8.   The forms of address in Deut. 32.7-9 are masculine singular.

can give to the people whom he has chosen. These differences are especially significant as they highlight issues that we have already come to see
as central to the whole of Jer. 3.1–4.4.

The first transgression is of utmost significance for an understanding
of 3.19–4.4, and for the place of v. 19 in the context of the whole piece
(3.1–4.4). The image of the daughter inheriting in 3.19 is highly unusual in
the Hebrew Bible. The only other occasions where daughters inherit land
are the case of the daughters of Zelophehad in Num. 27.1-8 and a much
vaguer reference to Job's daughters in Job 42.15. Moreover, in Numbers
27, the daughters inherit solely because there were no sons in the family.
Further, their marriage options were restricted to men within their own
clan in order to carry forward the male line. Thus, the land would revert to
the male line through their sons. Here in Jer. 3.19, however, daughters not
only inherit with the sons, they inherit 'the most beautiful heritage of all
the nations'.

Using anthropological theory, and basing her work on evidence from
Ugarit, S. Joy Osgood[9] argues that the land belonged solely to YHWH and
that 'Israel's *naḥălâ* amounts to no more than a "gift" or grant of the right
to use that which forever remains Yahweh's possession'.[10] She argues
further that the נחלה 'was dependent upon an already established relationship between God and people. It was out of his own "rightful property" or נחלה that Yahweh granted "secondary rights of membership use"
to the people with whom he had entered into a relationship'.[11] The idea of
YHWH's ownership would aid in explaining a situation where YHWH could
banish the people from the land for disobedience or pollution, or because
of a break in the relationship.

With regard to the issue of inheritance by women, although Osgood
does not discuss Jer. 3.19 specifically, she argues compellingly that on the
other occasions in the Bible where women inherit, they inherit solely in
order to maintain the male line. If they marry, they may only marry within
their own lineage so that the property will remain within that kinship
group when their sons inherit. If they do not marry, the land reverts to the
closest male relative of their family.[12] If Osgood indeed gives the correct

---

9. S. Joy Osgood, 'Women and the Inheritance of Land in Early Israel', in George
J. Brooke (ed.), *Women in the Biblical Tradition* (Lewiston, NJ: Edwin Mellen Press,
1992), pp. 29-52.

10. Osgood, 'Women and Inheritance', p. 38.

11. Osgood, 'Women and Inheritance', p. 39. Cf. Lev. 25; Deut. 32.

12. See Osgood, 'Women and Inheritance', pp. 45-50.

anthropological basis for women's inheritance in the Hebrew Bible, then Jer. 3.19 is all the more unique. According to her research, women's inheritance occurred only when it would support and continue the male lineage in a case where there would otherwise be a disruption. Jeremiah 3.19 is quite different: rather than receiving a portion because there are no sons, the daughter here receives an inheritance among the sons. Her inheritance cannot be construed as keeping the male line of land inheritance intact.

Perhaps because it is such an unusual image, and because, at least on the surface, it makes no sense in an androcentric worldview for women to inherit among the sons, many scholars wish to change the address in 3.19 to masculine singular.[13] However, the image of the daughter inheriting is particularly apt here. Since the emphasis of the section is Israel's unique status and its separation from other nations, the father–daughter metaphor is a striking way to make the point: the fact that the daughter is the one to inherit the best portion further emphasizes her uniqueness and further separates her from the rest of the heirs (the other nations).[14] Moreover, the

---

13. This even includes the editors of the *BHS*. Cf. Bright, *Jeremiah*, p. 20; Peter C. Craigie, Page H. Kelley and Joel F. Drinkard, Jr., *Jeremiah 1–25* (WBC, 26; Dallas: Word Books, 1991), p. 64; Douglas Rawlinson Jones, *Jeremiah* (Grand Rapids: Eerdmans, 1992), p. 104. The last two works do not even mention why or how they switch from feminine to masculine address. Brueggemann avoids giving a gender to the person addressed in v. 19 completely (*To Pluck Up, To Tear Down: A Commentary on Jeremiah 1–25* [Grand Rapids: Eerdmans, 1988], p. 44). Dieter Böhler, in contrast to other scholars, sees 3.19 as ending a long monologue by YHWH comprising vv. 1-19. He argues further that this verse is key to understanding the shifts between male and female address. He argues that the feminine singular address is used to indicate times when Israel was landless (in the wilderness, after the destruction of the Northern Kingdom); conversely, when the male address is used, Böhler maintains, it refers to times when Israel held territory (Böhler, 'Geschlechterdifferenz und Landbesitz', p. 109). His argument is unconvincing, however, and does not do justice to the rhetoric of the text itself. Interestingly, the Targum removes not only the daughter image, but the image of YHWH as father as well. Verse 19 reads, 'And I said: How shall I make you prosper among the children, and give the pleasant land to you, a joyful inheritance, the glory of the nations? So I said, You shall pray before me "My Lord", and you shall not turn back from my worship.' In addition, all the sexual/harlotry metaphors are removed, as is the metaphor of circumcision. Was the sexual imagery itself problematic for early Judaism? To answer this question would be to go beyond the scope of this monograph, but it is a potentially fruitful area of further study.

14. The idea of separation from other nations is also a way to suggest that Israel has no need for those nations, that is, that Israel does not need foreign alliances, thus continuing this text's interaction with political ideals.

metaphor also accentuates the honor which YHWH bestows upon daughter Israel. These aspects of the metaphor make it rhetorically quite powerful.

The above remarks have addressed the metaphor and primary intertext of 3.19a specifically, but have not yet dealt with the second half of the verse, where YHWH discloses his expectations of Israel in response to his great gift. Here a different intertext comes into play, that of Hos. 2.18 (Eng. 16).[15] The wording of Jer. 3.19b, 'I thought you would call me "my father" and would not turn from following me', is quite similar to that of the Hosea text, which I translate: 'you will call me "my husband" and you will no longer call me "my Baal"'. The differences are significant, however. Whereas Hos. 2.18 is a statement of the future act of YHWH, Jer. 3.19b reveals the kind of loyal relationship YHWH expected from a past act of giving. Moreover, the image used in v. 19b is different (i.e. father rather than husband) reflecting the familial metaphors which govern this section as a whole. While there are statements in Jer. 3.1–4.4 which reflect the sort of division between YHWH and Baal that Hos. 2.18 indicates,[16] 3.19 highlights the yearning of YHWH which is like that of a father for his most beloved child. Verse 19b, therefore, reveals YHWH's expectations of the relationship, expectations which, as the following verse indicates, were dashed.

Verse 20 returns to the harlotry imagery so prevalent in 3.1-18 in order to emphasize the people's guilt. In v. 20 the father–daughter image is retained, but merged with the earlier image of marital promiscuity. The various English translations of v. 20 obscure the continuing reference to Israel as daughter by translating אשה as 'wife' and מרעה as 'husband' rather than the more usual 'companion' or 'friend',[17] which also indicate close association, and in the case of רעה III, an object of desire. Hence, I translate: '"Instead, as a woman has become faithless to her lover, so you have been faithless to me, O house of Israel", saying of YHWH'.

By restating or re-presenting the situation in vv. 1-5, v. 20 works intra-textually with the beginning of the piece. Verse 20 absorbs the metaphor

15. It is no accident that the primary verbal connections with Hosea occur in Jer. 3.19–4.4. The previous section, beginning with the allegorical picture of vv. 6-10, sets up the comparison between Judah and Israel that is made in v. 11. This comparison underlies 3.19–4.4 as well. Hosea's words were directed to the Northern Kingdom in the eighth century, shortly before its fall. The connections with Hosea's words would emphasize not only the dialogical relationships, but would also underline (especially in 4.4) what happened to a nation that did not heed the calls to return.

16. See especially my discussion of 3.14 in Chapter 5.

17. Cf. BDB, p. 946.

of harlotry and the accusation directed against Judah. Yet it transforms it through the merging of the father–daughter metaphor with the earlier image of sexual promiscuity. There is also an intratextual link between v. 20 and vv. 6-11. The word for the faithlessness of the daughter here is the root בגד, the very root used in Judah's nickname in vv. 6-11: 'Treachery (בגודה) Judah'. Thus, in absorbing this aspect of vv. 6-11, v. 20 implicitly identifies the daughter as Judah. Yet v. 20 transgresses vv. 6-11 in two ways. First, what the daughter has done goes beyond mere infidelity; it is a betrayal of the father. Implicit here is another issue–honor. The betrayal has shamed YHWH. Again, the danger of her behavior is stressed. Second, the behavior is the more shocking because, like the harlotry imagery within the marital context in vv. 1-5, the text uses direct accusation.[18] The audience is identified; the immediacy allows no retreat— they *are* the treacherous daughter.

If one looks at the metaphor as a father–daughter metaphor there are several implications relating to gender conventions in the rhetoric that are underscored in ways not possible with the marital metaphor alone. As with vv. 1-5, the audience is asked to identify themselves as women—this time a positive, unique identification, at least on the surface. However, in the subsequent rhetoric, the image of a daughter inheriting turns out not to be so positive. The major impact of the father–daughter imagery comes through v. 19's connection with v. 20. In v. 20, the 'positive' imagery of the daughter is problematized (just as the wife was in 3.1-5). The father–daughter metaphor (v. 19) stresses Israel's unique position among the nations, yet the metaphors of v. 20a connect the daughter's actions with transgression of sexual boundaries. Within Israelite society, as well as in other patriarchal systems, the father was accorded control of his daughter's sexuality. In economic terms, the daughter's sexual promiscuity has negative consequences for the father: he cannot marry her off, get a dowry from her, or benefit from her in any way.[19] At stake once again in this verse is

18. Verses 6-11 are in third person, allowing for some distancing. No distance is allowed in v. 20. As in vv. 1-5, the audience stands accused as promiscuous women.

19. Cf. Léonie J. Archer, *Her Price is Beyond Rubies: The Jewish Woman in Graeco-Roman Palestine* (JSOTSup, 60; Sheffield: JSOT Press, 1990), pp. 111-12, for support for this view. See also Rashkow, 'Daughters and Fathers in Genesis…', p. 254. Note, too, that a father's control over his daughter is reflected in Israelite society through the many laws circumscribing the daughter, for example, Exod. 21.7; Num. 30.4, 17; 31. Also relevant, although stemming from a much later time, is Ben Sira's discourse regarding daughters (see esp. 42.9-14). His discourse, in particular, indicates an ongoing concern with the issues raised above.

the maintenance of proper lineage and hierarchy, as well as issues sur-rounding reproduction.[20] Verse 20a thus represents the underside of the positive uniqueness of the daughter in v. 19. Her overstepping of the sex-ual boundary of virginity places her not only outside her father's control, but outside the accepted limits of society. Hence, although the daughter image is initially positive (she inherits the best portion among the sons), a shift is made immediately to undermine it in v. 20b.

Reading v. 20a as a father–daughter metaphor, however, does not ex-haust the metaphorical (and rhetorical) undertones of the language. The use of the word lover (רעה) in v. 20a causes some metaphorical slippage. Whereas the word refers to the person with whom metaphorical Israel had sexual relations, YHWH's self-comparison in v. 20b implicitly makes YHWH a lover as well. Here the metaphors of the passage have once again escaped their bounds. The image of a sexual relationship between father and daughter is problematic at best. If, however, we see this language as a merging with the marital imagery of vv. 1-11, the metaphor makes more sense. What ties both images together is the idea of overstepped bounda-ries. And, further, the overstepped sexual boundaries evoke the same issues dealt with in vv. 1-11 (e.g. faithfulness, obedience, connections between behavior and identity). These issues are thus brought into and made part of this context. Nevertheless, the slippage of the metaphor indicates its instability and the danger of using it further.

With v. 20 the metaphor has reached its limit; its inherent contradictions are revealed. On the one hand, women are chattel, goods exchanged between father and husband, and as such are representative of the men to whom they belong. On the other hand, women are the bearers of children, the necessary vehicle for ongoing life. The only way for YHWH (and men) to control life (and reproduction/fertility) is to control women's sexuality. Like vv. 6-11, the sexual promiscuity of the daughter/wife in vv. 19-20 plays on the limits of the male control of women's sexuality.[21]

By undermining the daughter image, 3.20 undermines the only 'good' role allotted to women in patriarchal society besides wife and mother. Women's sexuality, and, more to the point, any metaphorical rendering of women's sexuality, is inherently uncontrollable. Any portrayal of the future in which YHWH has complete control (even over fertility) must necessarily circumscribe women and sexual metaphors. This may be a

20. Cf. Deut. 22.13-21 and Rashkow's interpretation of it, 'Daughters and Fathers in Genesis...', p. 256.
21. Cf. the section on gender in Jer. 3.6-11 in Chapter 3.

primary reason that v. 20a marks the end of the feminine form of address. In v. 20b the negative female metaphor is merged with the male audience: 'just as a woman has been faithless to her lover, so you (masculine plural) have been faithless to me'. Once the metaphor has reached its ultimate limits, the direct address returns to the implied audience, that is, the men of Judah. Here is spelled out the message of the direct address of vv. 1-5 in a more direct manner. The wife who has stepped out of bounds is none other than the male audience. *They* have acted like unfaithful and promiscuous wives/daughters. If those listening/reading had missed the point, this verse explicitly identifies just who is being addressed by this metaphorical language. Moreover, from v. 21 onwards, the audience is finally and conclusively asked to identify themselves as sons, while God retains the position of father. The possibilities for repentance and restoration are all addressed to sons rather than to wives/daughters. The metaphorical rhetoric of sexuality itself slips over its bounds, revealing its unsustainability, requiring and explaining the switch to the father–son imagery which dominates the rest of Jer. 3.1–4.4.

Chapter 7

JEREMIAH 3.21-25: A LITURGY OF REPENTANCE

If God is male, then the male is God.

—Mary Daly

As noted in the previous chapter, Jer. 3.19-20a contains the last accusation against Judah, first couched in female metaphorical language (daughter, sexually faithless), and 3.20b introduces the masculine direct address which will characterize the rest of 3.1–4.4. Verses 21-25 of ch. 3 pick up on that masculine direct address, initiating a new metaphor, the one which will dominate the latter portion of the piece—YHWH as father and Judah as repentant son. Before discussing that metaphorical move, however, this chapter will first address the rhetoric of intertextuality in vv. 21-25. Thus, the analysis of vv. 21-25 begins with a translation followed by two sections, the first discussing intertextuality and the second metaphor and gender, including a detailed discussion of how the term 'shame' (בוש) functions in this section and in the whole of 3.1–4.4. The section on intertextuality deals with the overall frame and structure of these verses as well as their intertextual connections, while the latter section deals more specifically with the content of vv. 21-25.

Jeremiah 3.21-25 reads:

> [21]A voice is heard on the bare heights; the weeping of the supplications of the sons of Israel,[1] for they have perverted their way; they have forgotten YHWH their God.
> [22]'Return (masc. plur.) O turning back sons.[2] I will heal your (masc. plur.) apostasy.'
> 'Behold we come to you, for you are YHWH our God.

1.   While the phrase, בני שראל, is usually translated 'Israelites', I have retained the literal translation to indicate the subject's change in gender, which in turn is connected with the gender change in address in v. 22.

2.   As with v. 14, I retain the literal translation ('sons' instead of 'children') to indicate the change in gender and metaphor in these verses.

(23)Surely the hills [and] the orgies on the mountains[3] are a delusion;
Surely in YHWH our God is the salvation of Israel.
(24)But "The Shame" has devoured the toil of our ancestors from our
youth; their flocks and their cattle, their sons and their daughters.
(25)Let us lie down in our shame, and may our reproach cover us. For
against YHWH our God we have sinned; we and our ancestors, from our
youth until this day.'

With the opening words of v. 21, 'a voice is heard...', the focus shifts
for the fourth time in this piece, here moving away from YHWH's speech
to what YHWH hears—weeping. In contrast to 3.1-5, where God accuses
the people of being unrepentant, the prophet (YHWH) interprets this
voice as an acknowledgment of guilt: 'for they have perverted their
ways; they have forgotten YHWH their God'. Here the acknowledgment
of sin requested in vv. 12-13 is illustrated. Moreover, the recognition and
confession of sin engenders a dialogue in which Israel actually responds
to YHWH's appeal. In v. 22a YHWH addresses the sons of Israel in language reminiscent of v. 14, and, like v. 14, playing on the root שׁוב:
'Return (שׁוּבוּ, masc. plur.) O turning back (שׁובָב) sons. I will heal your
apostasy (מְשׁוּבָה).' Verses 22b-25 contain the sons' response to YHWH's
appeal as a quotation (in first person).

The rhetorical effect of beginning this section with 'a voice' followed
by a paraphrase rather than a quote of what is heard is not only to
shift perspectives, but to distance the reader. The immediacy of direct
address is abandoned, adding to the distancing effect. Along with the
prophet and YHWH, the audience and readers are observers of the voice
and weeping, which leads into a dialogue. In vv. 22-25 it is almost as if
the audience is now watching a play in which the main participants are
enacting what YHWH wishes for the audience to do. That this section
does not take place in real time, but rather is a prescription for the present audience is established by 4.1-4, which begins with the words, 'If
you return...' According to 4.1, the returning pictured in vv. 21-25 is
clearly not yet a reality.

---

3.   The second half of v. 23a, which I have translated here relatively literally as
'the orgies on the mountains', is problematic. While it is difficult to tell to what it
specifically refers, it is clear that it refers to some sort of forbidden worship. This
problematic phrase also echoes the nature of the offense portrayed in vv. 1-11: sexual sin. Verse 23b provides a nice juxtaposition to v. 23a. The hills and the 'orgies
on the mountains(?)' are a delusion; in contrast, the reality is that 'the salvation of
Israel lies in YHWH our God'.

1. *Intertextuality in Jeremiah 3.21-25*

The form of vv. 21-25 has been identified by Claus Westermann as a liturgy of penitence.[4] According to his schema, the people's lament is in v. 21; vv. 22b-25 are the people's turning to God 'with a confession of sins and an expression of trust'; and God's response is in 4.1-2.[5] While I see God's response as being 4.1-4 instead of 4.1-2, in the other respects I agree with Westermann's assessment of the form of this section. Here the prophet co-opts a liturgical form, a liturgy of repentance, to prescribe a model for the people's response to YHWH's appeal to return. As such, the liturgical form is absorbed and re-presented in the mouths of the people.

Not only is there an intertextual play with the form itself in these verses, but there is also an intertextual play with another text which shares the same form: Hos. 14.2-9.[6] Hosea 14.2 begins with an appeal to Israel to return (שׁוב) which closely resembles that of Jer. 3.22. The promise associated with returning also uses the same terminology: 'I will heal (רפא) your "turning back" (משובה, plus pronominal suffix)' ('their' in Hos. 14.5). In addition, both texts end with God's response (Jer. 4.1-4; Hos. 14.6-9). Hans Walter Wolff rightly notes that in Hos. 14.5 the promise phrased as 'The divine answer...is the kernel of the entire passage'.[7] Unlike Jer. 3.22, the appeal and the promise are separated in Hosea, but the promise itself functions similarly in both texts; as with Hos. 14.5, the promise in Jer. 3.22 is 'the kernel' of the whole section. Wolff also argues that the verb associated with the promise, 'to heal' (רפא), 'includes the meaning of "forgive"..., for which concept Hosea uses no other word'.[8] This meaning of the verb is absorbed by the text of Jeremiah, but in the overall context of Jer. 3.1–4.4, its meaning may be extended beyond forgiveness and healing of the people themselves. Given the importance of the land throughout the piece, and its 'sickness' portrayed in v. 3a, the term רפא may also mean healing for the land.

---

4. Claus Westermann, *Praise and Lament in the Psalms* (trans. Keith R. Crim and Richard N. Soulem; Atlanta: John Knox Press, 1981 [Ger. 1965]), p. 62.
5. Westermann, *Praise*, p. 61.
6. Westermann has also noted some connections between Hos. 14.2-9 and Jer. 3.21-25 (*Praise*, pp. 61-62).
7. Hans Walter Wolff, *Hosea* (Hermeneia; Philadelphia: Fortress Press, 1974 [Ger. 1965]), p. 233.
8. Wolff, *Hosea*, p. 123.

The fact that two prophets have co-opted this form raises the question of *Sitz im Leben*. While Westermann avoids this question, James Luther Mays addresses it in relation to the text of Hos. 14.2-9. He argues that the setting of the Hosea text 'is completely that of the prophetic message; the material does not yet have a place in the liturgical life of the people'.[9] He suggests, rather, that Hos. 14.2-4 'is a prophetic exhortation calling on Israel to return to their God...and proposing a prayer of penitence as a way of approaching him'.[10] Although I do not agree that the form must be separated so absolutely from its liturgical roots (we cannot know for sure whether this prayer represents actual liturgical use), I agree with Mays that the form itself is fully integrated into the prophetic genre in Hosea 14. Additionally, I propose that the same holds true for Jer. 3.21-25. In v. 22a YHWH issues the same appeal that was issued in v. 14 ('Return, "turning back sons"'). The appeal is then followed by an example of the kind of penitential prayer YHWH desires. Once it is established that a liturgy is indeed at the root of these texts,[11] one can see that the liturgical form is not only absorbed and re-presented, but transformed through recontextualization.[12]

The very fact that within Jer. 3.1–4.4 a text addressing the north (Hos. 14.2-9) is alluded to shortly after an appeal to the former Northern Kingdom (Jer. 3.12-13) is significant. The text of Hos. 14.2-9 is absorbed in some respects by the prophet, but the new context for which it is transformed is to be found especially in Jer. 3.6-11. Just as 'Apostasy

9.   James Luther Mays, *Hosea, A Commentary* (OTL; Philadelphia: Westminster Press, 1969), p. 185.

10.   Mays, *Hosea*, p. 184. Wolff (*Hosea*, p. 235) agrees, saying, 'Formulated in view of the promise [to heal Israel's apostasy], the prayer is spoken by the prophet as an explanation which anticipates the promise'.

11.   The discussion of vv. 5 and 12, above, has already indicated that the prophet was in dialogue with, and used liturgical forms (see also Fishbane, *Biblical Interpretation*, p. 348, for a similar assessment). It is thus likely that a liturgical form is the root of these verses.

12.   Although Hos. 14.2-9 shares a similar form with Jer. 3.21-25, its presentation is slightly different. As Westermann indicates, in addition to a petition for both forgiveness and help, the call to repent of Hos. 14.2-3 includes 'the indication of a vow of praise (v. 3)' (*Praise*, p. 62). In contrast, Jer. 3.21-25 contains neither a vow of praise nor a petition as such. The content of vv. 22b-25 is almost entirely a confession of guilt and shame. Thus, each prophet has co-opted the same form but fashioned it somewhat differently for distinct audiences and contexts. The text of Hosea was addressed to the Northern Kingdom shortly before its fall. In Jer. 3.21-25, Judah is faced with (or has experienced) a similar situation.

Israel' served as a negative example to her sister 'Treachery Judah' in
vv. 6-11, so this liturgical form alluding to a return addressed to the
Northern Kingdom serves as an example for a present Judahite audience. The fact that it is 'the sons of Israel' rather than Jerusalem or the
inhabitants of Judah weeping (v. 21) may therefore be equally significant. In a sense, the Northern Kingdom is again providing an example
for the south, although this time it is a positive example. Here, as well,
Israel is being co-opted for Judah, thus revealing another dialogical
transgression in the text as a whole. Israel's history *and* the proposed
liturgy which will bring about a return act as models (both negatively
and positively) for the actions which YHWH wishes Judah to take.

The particular contour of the transformation in Jer. 3.21-25 not only
provides an example for the audience to follow, but also addresses an
issue which has been shown to be central in the preceding verses: the
distinction between the people's words and their behavior. Like vv. 1-5,
vv. 21-25 use quotation of the people: v. 22a represents a quotation of
YHWH's appeal to those who were weeping, and vv. 22b-25 present a
quotation of those same people. However, the purpose of the quotation
in vv. 21-25 is different. Whereas in vv. 1-5 quotation is used as a basis
for indictment, here it is used as a basis for proper return. Likewise, in
contrast to the quotations of past dialogue in vv. 1-5, the quotations of
vv. 21-25 are clearly future-oriented. In both cases, however, there is an
opposition between the quoted words and present behavior. Here, rather
than being accused of inconsistency between words and behavior (cf.
v. 5), the people themselves confess that their words and their actions
have been incongruent. Indeed, I would argue that one of the purposes
of this section is to provide a framework for bringing words and behavior together.[13] The form itself is a way to move the audience from
example to action—the people can, by using this liturgy, actually return
(repent).

2. *Metaphor and Gender in Jeremiah 3.21-25*

The content and structure of the liturgy presented in Jer. 3.21-25 plays
on two issues: (1) an analysis of the multiple connotations of the root

---

13. Cf. the acknowledgment that they have been worshiping a lie (v. 23) and the
commands to swear 'in truth, justice and righteousness' (4.2); to break up the fallow
ground and not to sow among thorns (4.3); and to circumcise the *heart*, which in
Hebrew thinking is the seat of the will and therefore of behavior.

בוש as a central theme of this section; and (2) the switch in governing relational metaphor (i.e. from YHWH as husband and Israel as promiscuous wife to YHWH as father and Israel as repentant son). The discussion of this section will be divided into two parts, taking each of these issues in turn.

a. בוש *in the Rhetoric of Jeremiah 3.21-25*
The rhetoric of vv. 21-25 presents some changes in the ways in which the religious, legal, familial and creation/fertility ideals discussed in previous chapters are played on in these verses. These changes revolve around the image 'The Shame' (הבשת) in v. 24 and plays on the ways on which the root בוש is used in these verses. The following discussion will address the multiple ways the term functions as it is indexed to these ideals.

The first ideal to which to which the root בוש is indexed in vv. 21-25 is the religious ideal. In this section, a contrast is made between the people's former worship of Baal, and the present acknowledgment of the identity of the god they will henceforth worship: the people are coming to YHWH because it is he who is their God (v. 22b). The section also places in the mouths of the sons an explicit rejection of other forms of worship (v. 23a).[14] In v. 24, the quote placed in the sons' mouth: '"the Shame" has devoured us' is an oblique reference to their previous worship of Baal. The term הבשת (v. 24) refers specifically to religious worship; it is a satirical epithet for the god Baal in the Hebrew Bible.[15] This reference, together with the words placed in the mouths of the people in v. 25, 'Let us lie down in our shame', reveal that the people in vv. 21-25 acknowledge that overstepping the proper boundaries of worship has caused them shame. The designation of improper worship as a cause for shame is well documented elsewhere in the Hebrew Bible.[16]

14. It is interesting that the same root, שקר, is here used to describe the hills upon which the people worshipped, which YHWH used of Judah's return in v. 11. Whereas Judah only pretended to return to YHWH, now the people acknowledge the gods they worshipped in YHWH's place were only false gods.

15. Cf. Hos. 9.10; Jer. 11.13. See also 2 Sam 2.8 and 11.21, where בעל has been replaced by בשת or בשת as part of a personal name (for 2 Sam. 2.8 cf. 1 Chron. 8.33; for 2 Sam. 2.11 cf. Judg. 6.32) (Thompson, *Jeremiah*, pp. 109-10; cf. also McKane, *Jeremiah I–XXV*, p. 81; R.E. Clements, *Jeremiah* (Interpretation; Atlanta: John Knox Press, 1988], p. 36; and Holladay, *Jeremiah 1*, p. 125).

16. In addition to several places in Jeremiah (8.9; 10.14; 17.13; 51.17 [= 10.14]), see Isa. 1.29; 42.17; 44.9, 11; 65.13; Hos. 4.19; 10.6. See also Margaret S. Odell,

The designation of proper worship of Y<small>HWH</small> as a means of avoidance of shame is equally well documented.[17] The term 'shame' is thus used to convey the sense of overstepped boundaries, in this case the boundaries of proper worship.

The acknowledgment of shame and the return to the proper boundaries in this section are intertwined with the covenantal (i.e. legal/governmental) ideal as well. In covenantal terms, the people are here stepping back within the bounds of proper reverence and fidelity to Y<small>HWH</small> their overlord. Yet, the return within proper boundaries is accomplished by means of the liturgical portrayal of their acknowledgment of the falsity of their previous actions (v. 23a), their statements acknowledging Y<small>HWH</small> as their God and the salvation of Israel (v. 22b, 23b), and their actual confession of sin (v. 25). Thus, in addition to religious ideals, the legal ideal is invoked and actualized for this group of people through the vehicle of a liturgy of repentance.

There is yet another ideal played upon in these verses through the verb בוש—the creation/fertility ideal. The Hebrew Bible contains several texts that connect shame with creation/fertility, most notably Hos. 13.15, Joel 2.26 and Jer. 14.3-7. The first of these, Hos. 13.15, indicates that as a result of sin, Ephraim's 'spring shall be parched'. The word translated 'parched' here, is בוש (מבוש מקורו), literally, 'his spring shall be shamed'. This phrase is the second of two phrases in synthetic parallelism. The first may be translated, 'his fountain shall dry up'. Thus, in Hos. 13.15 the term בוש can be read on two levels, one indexing it to the natural ideal through the 'natural' consequences of disobedience

---

'An Exploratory Study of Shame and Dependence in the Bible and Selected Near Eastern Parallels', in K. Lawson Younger, Jr, William W. Hallo and Bernard F. Batto (eds.), *The Biblical Canon in Comparative Perspective* (Scripture in Context, 4; Lewiston, NY: Edwin Mellen Press, 1991), pp. 217-33. Other work on shame, however, in the Hebrew Bible is scanty. See M.A. Klopfenstein, *Scham und Schande nach dem Alten Testament* (Zürich: Theologischer Verlag, 1979); H. Seebass, '*Bosh; Bushah; Bosheth; Mebhushim*', in *TDOT*, II, pp. 50-60; F. Stolz, 'Bosh zuschanden werden', in *THAT*, I, pp. 269-72; J. Pedersen, 'Honour and Shame', in *idem, Israel: Its Life and Culture* (4 vols.; London: Oxford University Press, 1962), II, pp. 213-44; D. Daube, 'The Culture of Deuteronomy', *Orita* 3 (1969), pp. 27-52; and Bechtel, 'Shame as a Sanction of Social Control'.

17. Cf. Isa. 45.17; 49.23; 50.7; Pss. 119.6; 127.5, and many other Psalms from all periods where proper worship of God is the grounds for supplication and avoidance of shame (see, for e.g., Pss. 25.2, 3; 65.6). See also Bechtel, 'Shame as a Sanction of Social Control', pp. 70-71.

(drought = 'parched'), and the other indexing it to the ethical consequences of disobedience (shame).

A second text, Joel 2.26, links fertility both with proper worship and
with avoidance of shame. In a picture of restoration, YHWH promises
Israel, 'You shall eat in plenty and be satisfied, and praise the name of
YHWH your God, who has dealt wondrously with you. And my people
shall never again be shamed.' Here fertility is pictured as the result of
proper worship, which in turn results in avoidance of shame. In this
case, בוש is indexed to two ideals, the natural consequences of obedience (fertility) and the covenantal and religious ideal (proper reverence
and worship), through the vehicle of the ethical ideal (never again being
shamed).

In Jeremiah shame is also associated with infertility and/or drought.
In 14.3 the people are ashamed because they find no water, and in 14.4
the farmers are ashamed because there has been no rain. Here the reverse
of an ethical ideal (shame) is paired with the reverse of a natural ideal
(drought). In v. 7, they are connected with the religious ideal through
the acknowledgment of sin.

Finally, 3.1–4.4 has already provided an example of the link between
shame and drought. Already in 3.3 the people experience drought but
'have a harlot's brow' and 'refuse to be ashamed'. In this case, social
ideals (as expressed through overstepped sexual boundaries) and the
natural ideal (drought) are expressed through the vehicle of shame.
According to v. 3, the people who have done these things should clearly
be ashamed, but they are not.

Building upon the rhetoric of v. 3, a similar indexing is present in
3.21-25. In v. 24 the people indicate that by worshipping 'The Shame'
(Baal), they have reaped, instead of the abundance YHWH would have
given them, only shame. There is an irony here which connects these
verses with the rain imagery of v. 3: the very god who was supposed to
guarantee fertility and abundance has devoured everything for which
they and their ancestors labored. Verse 25 finally expresses the shame
Israel would not admit in vv. 1-5. This verse also portrays the acknowledgment of sin for which YHWH asked in v. 13. By acknowledging their
shame, the people are not only stepping back within the bounds of
proper worship, they are stepping back within the bounds of the natural
order. Their statement implies an acknowledgment that YHWH alone is
the true source of fertility and abundance. In addition to being indexed
to the natural ideal (fertility), the term בוש in these verses is also indexed

to the covenantal and religious ideal (fidelity to and worship of YHWH
alone). Through the acknowledgement of shame and sin the people are
admitting that any hope for the future rests with YHWH—not with Baal
and not on the hills where they formerly worshipped. By making YHWH
their Baal (cf. v. 14), they step back within the proper legal, covenantal, religious and natural boundaries, and rely upon YHWH's promise of
healing (v. 22a). All of these ideals are intertwined in this portrayal of
repentance.

A fourth ideal, which is somewhat obscured by the explicit connections between shame and improper worship, is the ethical ideal. By
acknowledging sin in addition to their shame in v. 25, the people are
also acknowledging improper ethical behavior. In 6.15 and 8.9, 12, the
fact that the people do not deal justly with others results in their being
put to shame. In 2.26 YHWH promises the people that they will be put to
shame because of their unjust actions. Similarly, later in ch. 2, after portraying their unjust behavior (vv. 33-35), YHWH quotes the people as
saying 'I have not sinned' (v. 35) and counters with the promise that
they will be put to shame (v. 36). Jeremiah 3.25 reverses the quotation
of 2.36 ('we have sinned against YHWH our God'), thus connecting the
rhetoric of vv. 21-25 with ethical behavior. In this way, the covenantal/
legal ideal invoked here is also linked to and intertwined with the ideal
of proper ethical behavior.[18]

Finally, the familial ideal is also intertwined in this portrayal, again
through the root בוש. Verses 1-20 portray metaphorically how the
people's behavior pushed beyond legal, ethical, natural and social (as
portrayed through sexual) boundaries. What is at stake is honor: by
behaving improperly, they have shamed themselves. As many recent
socio-anthropological studies have pointed out, shame is a method of
social control.[19] Dealing with selected examples of shaming in judicial,
political and social contexts, Lyn M. Bechtel argues that shaming 'functions primarily as (1) a means of social control which attempts to re-
press aggressive or undesirable behavior; (2) as a pressure that preserves
social cohesion in the community through rejection and the creation of

18. For a further connection with ethical behavior, see 4.1-4.
19. Two studies dealing with this issue with regard to the Hebrew Bible are
Bechtel, 'Shame as a Sanction of Social Control', and Odell, 'An Exploratory
Study'. Bechtel's study, however, is much more thorough in its documentation of
the psychological and socio-anthropological background to this issue.

social distance between deviant members and the group; and (3) as an important means of dominating others and manipulating social status'.[20] While Bechtel's work deals entirely with how shame works within societal structures, I would argue that the same issues apply to 3.1–4.4. In fact, the prophet goes one step further by portraying God as the one doing the shaming, thus providing the pressure to return within boundaries which will unite the people as a group under his rule. To illustrate how this is played out in the text itself: in vv. 6-10 one type of social control was shown to be exerted (the example of what happened to one 'sister' [Israel], was to act as a deterrent to the other 'sister' [Judah]). In a similar manner, although through a completely different vehicle, that is, by putting words acknowledging shame into the mouths of the sons (v. 25), and using a public form, a liturgy, to phrase that shame, vv. 21-25 act rhetorically to exert public social control. Verses 21-25 imply that the audience's repentance will have to include an acknowledgment that their actions have shamed them. It is only through this confession, which admits to overstepped (legal, covenantal, ethical and familial) boundaries, that the people step back within the bounds of society.

b. *The Father–Son Metaphor in Jeremiah 3.21-25*
While the other ideals have primarily been associated with behavior, however, the familial ideal is also integrally associated with identity through a change in metaphor—the shift to a father–son metaphor. As noted in the previous chapters, vv. 1-11 and 19-20a ask the (primarily male) audience to identify themselves as an adulteress/prostitute; it is that strategy which makes the audience's behavior of infidelity to YHWH clear. Verses 21-25 present a crucial change, however. Although the language of v. 21 at first designates no subject ('*A* voice is heard') and is followed by a third person description of what is heard, the language of v. 22a is direct address. The direct appeal to the 'turning back' sons to return introduces a new, if related metaphor to this half of the piece: YHWH as a father in dialogue with his wayward sons. In addition to issues of identity, two things are significant about this change in address. For the first time Israel actually responds to the appeal of vv. 12-13, and for the first time healing/forgiveness is promised. Second, the imagery of repentance in the rest of the passage is exclusively male, as is the

---

20. Bechtel, 'Shame as a Sanction of Social Control', p. 76.

direct address. With the possibility of repentance, the imagery of prostitution fades and is finally written out.[21]

With regard specifically to issues of identity, from v. 21 onwards it is through asking the audience to identify themselves as repentant sons that the pressures of identification are made clear.[22] Through the model prescribed in vv. 21-25, pressure is exerted on the audience to return to their primary (and positive) self-identification as sons through change of behavior. The text has claimed for God the authoritative position of patriarchal father and has attempted to discredit the people's religious, social and political actions by showing that they push the audience's behavior beyond legal, ethical and natural boundaries. In vv. 21-25 it is the public vehicle of social control (that is, honor vs. shame) within a male-dominated public context (the form of a liturgy) which ties the various ideals together in such a way as to create rhetorically powerful pressure for change of behavior. The switch to male imagery, with its attendant play on shame, illustrates this dynamic. The male audience as husbands (present, past or future) and as sons have a stake in maintaining the order, the status quo. In short, the audience, as sons, have a stake in maintaining a positive (male) identity precisely *as* sons.

As has been shown through the rhetoric of vv. 1-20, when women take control by transgressing the boundaries (sexual or otherwise) that men have set, the entire social and natural order (creation, legal, ethical, religious, etc.) is challenged. Such behavior leads to dishonor. Through identifying themselves as sons, through repentance and change of behavior, the audience is able to return to the proper relationship with God which will enable them to avoid such danger, thus returning them

21. The implications of this switch in terms of gender conventions will be addressed in the following chapter.

22. Here I am in disagreement with Diamond and O'Connor, who seek to read the children, in analogue with Hos. 2, as the wife's children of Jer. 3.1-5 ('Unfaithful Passions', pp. 297-98, 306-307). In making this move, they rightly see some major connections between Jer. 3.1–4.4 and Hos. 2, but wrongly read the larger constellation of images into Jeremiah from Hosea. They see YHWH turning to the sons in vv. 21-25 when the mother will not repent (their interpretation of vv. 12-13) (p. 307). However, their reading neglects the fact that the appeal to the north in v. 12 is already addressed to a male audience (second masculine plural direct address coupled with second masculine plural suffixes). Instead, I see this change of address, and therefore metaphor, as part and parcel of the pressures of identification asserted throughout this text.

to the proper boundaries of nature and society. The reasons for and implications of this change to a father–son metaphor and male direct address will become clearer in my discussion of the final section of the piece, Jer. 4.1-4.

Chapter 8

JEREMIAH 4.1-4: THE REQUIREMENTS FOR RETURN

Strictly speaking, 'women' cannot be said to exist.
—Julia Kristeva

Jeremiah 4.1-4 presents the closing rhetorical arguments of the whole of 3.1–4.4.[1] Scholars have traditionally not considered the links between these verses and the rest of 3.1–4.4; rather, vv. 1-4 are usually treated on their own or discussed in the context of source criticism.[2] In contrast, I see this section as integral to an understanding of the previous verses. Together they present a powerful rhetorical argument for Judah to return to YHWH. My analysis will combine all the rhetorical threads described previously, including the ways in which ideals of nature, law and family/ sexuality are integrated into the rhetoric, to round out the picture of what true turning must entail. The analysis will be divided into two subsections: intertextuality, followed by metaphor and gender.

I begin with my translation:

(1)'If you return, Israel', saying of YHWH, 'it is to me you shall return'.[3] 'If you remove your idols from before me and do not wander;

1. As noted in the Introduction, pp. 3-5, one of the issues in scholarship related to these verses is whether the larger passage ends at 4.2 or 4.4. For the reasons for ending the text at 4.4, see the discussion there.

2. Bernhard Duhm, for example, sees 4.1-4 as a section of text belonging to Jeremiah's early ministry (*Das Buch Jeremia*, p. 15). See also, Rudolph, *Jeremia*, p. xiv; Craigie, Kelley and Drinkard, *Jeremiah 1–25*, p. 67; McConville, *Judgment and Promise*, p. 40; and Unterman, *From Repentance to Redemption*, pp. 31-32. Some exceptions to this atomistic treatment include Brueggemann, *To Pluck Up, To Tear Down*, pp. 46-47; Carroll, *Jeremiah*, pp. 156-57.

3. There are several possible translations of the second half of v. 1a (see Thompson, *Jeremiah*, p. 211, for a list of possibilities). However, the syntax places the emphasis on אֵלַי. Hence this translation.

(2)And you swear "as YHWH lives" in truth, in justice and in righteousness, then the nations shall be blessed in him, and in him shall all the nations glory.'[4]

(3)For thus says YHWH to each man of Judah and to Jerusalem:

'Break up your fallow ground and do not sow among the thorns.

(4)Circumcise yourselves to YHWH and remove the foreskins of your heart, each man of Judah and inhabitants of Jerusalem; or else my anger will go forth like fire and burn and nothing will quench it because of the evil of your deeds.'

1. *Intertextuality in Jeremiah 4.1-4*

As a final response by YHWH to the pictured repentance of Jer. 3.21-25, these verses conclude the interplay with the law of Deut. 24.1-4 and the play with the citation of the law in Jer. 3.1-5 by resolving decisively the question of the overturning of the law for those living in Jerusalem and Judah. Following up on the play with שוב begun in 3.1, these verses open with a conditional statement; according to v. 12, YHWH will overturn the law *if* the people return (שוב) to him. The 'if' (אם) of 4.1 reiterates the conditional nature of return and follows up with the specifics: the bounds of behavior necessary for return are laid out in vv. 1b-4. Not only is the legal context invoked through the question of return, but the legal ideal is also invoked through concrete connections with covenant terminology. For example, the phrase חי־יהוה is an oath formula which connects the people to the covenant.[5] Furthermore, all three of the terms of v. 2a (אמת, משפט, צדקה) are covenantal terms which relate these verses specifically to the deuteronomic covenant.[6] Part of keeping the covenant in Deuteronomy is to live justly and righteously. Whereas previously the people had not kept the covenant,[7] they are now expected to do so. The oblique reference to the covenant in v. 2 implies all the obligations that go with it. A tension is thus emphasized between what Israel had done in the past and what they are expected to do now. Moreover, the rhetoric of this section pairs words (swearing by YHWH) and actions (breaking up, circumcising

4.   Translation issues concerning this verse will be dealt with in the intertextual discussion below.

5.   The term חי יהוה is an oath formula used most often in narrative texts (cf. 1 Sam. 20.3; 25.26; 2 Kgs 2.2, 4, 6; 4.30). Moshe Greenberg discusses the dispute over the meaning of this phrase, concluding that the phrase 'joins an oath to "the life of Y"' ('The Hebrew Oath Particle *ḤAY/ḤĒ*', *JBL* 76 [1957], pp. 34-39 [37]).

6.   Cf. Deut. 6.25; 16.19-20.

7.   Cf. Jer. 2.34.

their hearts). The emphasis placed on bringing their words and their actions together, as well as on true as opposed to false return, reinforces the picture of repentance (return) in vv. 21-25 by making explicit precisely what sort of behavior YHWH expects. Thus, in these verses the law cited in Jer. 3.1 receives its final transformation. YHWH can and will overturn the law if the people return to a proper covenantal relationship with YHWH. Also, connections with the other issues surrounding the law, namely, land and identity, are made specifically through intertextual play with the covenant to the patriarchs (v. 2b) and through the symbol of circumcision (vv. 3-4). While the latter two will be discussed below, it is important for now to note that these verses round out the overarching concern of the entire piece with all three issues: behavior, land and identity.

In addition to the continuing interplay with the law, Jer. 4.1-4 plays with several other intertexts: Hos. 14.2-9 (especially vv. 6-9), the patriarchal promise as contained in Gen. 22.18 and 26.4, Hos. 10.11-13, the broader patriarchal covenant including the symbol of circumcision, and Deut. 10.16 and 30.6. The following discussion will take each in turn.

a. *Hosea 14.6-9*
Jeremiah 4.1-4 builds on the repentance liturgy of 3.21-25 by presenting YHWH's answer to the people's confession and statement of penitence. In this respect, the primary intertext for vv. 21-25, Hos. 14.2-9, remains an intertext for this section as well.[8] Hosea 14.6-9 represents the response of YHWH corresponding to Jer. 4.1-4. Unlike God's answer in Hos. 14.6-9, which Claus Westermann rightly notes as 'an unconditioned and very full proclamation of salvation, almost approaching the apocalyptic pictures of salvation',[9] I propose that the proclamation of salvation in Jer. 4.1-4 is both conditional and lacks the vision of wholeness of its intertext.[10] Most scholars place Hosea 14 shortly before the fall of Samaria, when there was no hope that the people would be spared the judgment proclaimed in the

---

8.   Cf. the intertextuality section of Chapter 7, pp. 126-28, for verbal connections between Hos. 14.2-9 and Jer. 3.21–4.4, as well as for the specific ways the Hosea text acts as an intertext with vv. 21-25.

9.   Westermann, *Praise and Lament in the Psalms*, p. 62.

10.   The conditional nature of the proclamation of salvation in Jer. 4.1-4 may account for presence of the other Hosean intertext (Hos. 10.12) in Jer. 4.3. Hos. 10.12 is part of an oracle of judgment, thus providing the balance needed for the very different literary situations of Hos. 14 and Jer. 3.1–4.4 (see the discussion of Hos. 10.12 as an intertext below).

earlier chapters.[11] Hence, such a promise of wholeness and newness would be appropriate hope for the future in the face of unavoidable judgment.

For an exilic audience, the use of Hos. 14.2-9 as an intertext for Jer. 3.1–4.4 would imply similar hopes in the face of judgment already experienced. This is the situation of Jeremiah 30–31, which, while sharing many similarities with 3.1–4.4,[12] is specifically set during the exile (i.e. its literary setting is exilic). There the unconditional promise and pictures of complete restoration are clear (cf. 31.27-40).[13] Here, however, the literary setting (3.6) places this section before the exile, when, according to this text, the people still have a possibility of avoiding their fate. Thus a picture of wholeness and restoration would be inappropriate. While 3.21–4.4 absorbs certain aspects of its intertext, then, it also transgresses it by excluding those aspects which do not fit the (literary) context. The unconditionality and wholeness of Hos. 14.6-9 are replaced by a conditional return (vv. 1-4a) ending with a warning of what will happen if the audience does not return (v. 4b).

b. *The Patriarchal Covenant: Genesis 22.18; 26.4*
The second intertext for this section is the promise to the patriarchs, particularly in its formulations in Gen. 22.18 and 26.4.[14] Following up on the covenant terminology mentioned above, Jer. 4.2b, through citing the patriarchal promise, describes the blessing which will result if the audience's behavior is changed. There is some question as to the sense of the hithpael (i.e. reflexive or passive) in all three passages.[15] It is not crucial

---

11. Cf. Wolff, *Hosea*, p. 234; Mays, *Hosea*, p. 185.

12. Cf. the discussion of Smend in the Introduction, pp. 6-7.

13. Another link is a dialogue between YHWH and the people in 31.15-22 (cf. 3.21-25). All this is good evidence that Jer. 3.1–4.4 is the primary intertext for Jer. 30–31. While this intertextual dimension is beyond the scope of the present study, it is a subject for further investigation, and, moreover, one which may have implications for the long-debated structure of the book of Jeremiah.

14. As with previous intertexts, some scholars have noted a connection between the language of Jer. 4.2 and the patriarchal covenants. The most recent is Biddle, *A Redaction History of Jeremiah 2.1–4.2*, p. 179. Yet, as with previous intertexts, little attention has been paid to the ways in which they interact.

15. The discussion regarding whether to translate the hithpael as reflexive or passive is most thorough with regard to the texts in Genesis. For the passive nuance of the hithpael, see Gerhard von Rad, *Genesis* (OTL; Philadelphia: Westminster Press, 1961), p. 156. For the reflexive, see E.A. Speiser, *Genesis* (AB, 1; Garden City, NY: Doubleday, 2nd edn, 1978 [1964]), p. 86 (cf. the discussion in Claus Westermann,

to answer that question, however. What is crucial is the fact that the patri-archal covenantal blessing is cited here. By citing it, the promises of land and descendants that go with the promise are also included in this con-text.[16]

A second translation question reveals how the promise of Gen. 22.18 and 26.4 is transgressed for the new context of Jer. 3.1–4.4. The *BHS* pro-poses emending the MT בו of Jer. 4.2, here translated as 'in him' to 'in you' (בך). The proposed change may have as its basis the text's allusion to the promises in Gen. 22.18 and 26.4 where the nations will bless themselves or be blessed 'in your seed' (בזרעך). In both cases, the descendants of the patriarch will be the agents of blessing to the nations. It is fitting, however, that the prophet does not make the people or their descendants the agents of blessing, but rather makes 'him' the agent of blessing. Given the tenor of the discussion of Jer. 3.1–4.4 thus far, the third person pronominal suffix ('him') most likely refers to YHWH. If this is so, 3.2 both absorbs the promise to the patriarchs and transforms it. Now it is YHWH, rather than the descendants themselves, who is the agent of blessing for all people.

A final transgression of the Genesis texts concerns the type of promise given to Abraham and Isaac. The promise to Abraham and Isaac is uncon-ditional. By juxtaposing the promise with conditional covenantal terms and placing the whole within a legal/covenantal context revolving around questions of the possibility of an ongoing relationship with YHWH, the text of Jer. 4.1-4 transgresses the unconditional promissory nature of Gen. 22.18 and 26.4. The promise given to Abraham and Isaac will only be actualized if the people speak and act a certain way (vv. 1b-4); and even then, it will be actualized through YHWH and not through the people themselves. Rhetorically, the interplay with the promise to the patriarchs reminds the people of their special and unique relationship with YHWH. Yet the juxtaposition of this idea with the imposition of conditions for remaining within that special relationship is a powerful incentive to live up to the choice. The tension between the attractiveness of preserving their uniqueness and the responsibility of the conditionality associated with maintaining the unique relationship creates a powerful rhetorical argument for fulfilling the conditions set out for true return to YHWH.

Genesis 12–36: A Commentary [Interpretation; trans. John J. Scullion; Minneapolis: Augsburg, 1985 (Ger. 1981)], p. 151).

16. Verses 3-4 deal more specifically with the ramifications of this absorption in terms of metaphor and gender, and the discussion below will take up these issues.

Thus far, only the intertextual connections between Jer. 4.1-2 and other texts have been discussed. Jeremiah 4.3-4 bring out yet more interplays with other texts and traditions, but also *intra*textual connections with previous verses of 3.1–4.4. The new introductory formula of 4.3 addresses the people of Judah and Jerusalem, for the first time including them specifically in the invitation to return. Thus, this verse resolves the question of whether YHWH's invitation 'to the north' in vv. 12-13 would also be extended to the present audience. In vv. 3b-4 two new stipulations are added, stipulations that link with the accusation that 'Treachery Judah' is more guilty than 'Turning Back Israel' (3.11). Whereas 'Turning Back Israel' was offered the possibility of return through the mere acknowledgment of their wrongdoing (vv. 12-13), 'Treachery Judah' must fulfill more conditions. The added stipulations imply that because of the deeper nature of the treachery more radical means are needed to restore the relationship with YHWH.[17] Two intertexts also connect with these stipulations.

c. *Hosea 10.12 (11-13a)*

The first intertext, Hos. 10.12, shares with Jer. 4.3 the command to 'break up the fallow ground for yourselves' (נירו לכם ניר).[18] In contrast to 4.3, however, Hos. 10.12 is part of an oracle of judgment. Whether one sees Hos. 10.11-13a as a section by itself[19] or as a subsection of a larger oracle of judgment (vv. 9-15),[20] I propose that in addition to the command of v. 12, vv. 11-13a have several themes in common with Jer. 4.1-4. The verb 'to sow' (זרע) is included both in Jer. 4.3 and in Hos. 10.12. Whereas in Jer. 4.3 it is a negative command ('do not sow among thorns') parallel to a

---

17. Many scholars have not included 4.3-4 with Jer. 3.1–4.2. Cf. Biddle, *A Redaction History of Jer 2.1–4.2* (note that even his title indicates the division he assumes between 4.2 and 4.3); Cornill, *Das Buch Jeremia*, p. 45; Unterman, *From Repentance to Redemption*, pp. 31-32; Craigie, Kelley and Drinkard, *Jeremiah 1–25*, p. 67; and Thompson, *Jeremiah*, p. 214. A dissenter is Carroll, who states that Jer. 4.3-4 is 'an appropriate conclusion to the liturgy of turning in 3.21–4.2' (*Jeremiah*, p. 157). My own work has led me to take the same position. Indeed, I wish to take the argument a step further: by connecting these verses specifically with the earlier rhetoric of Jer. 3.1–4.4 I hope to broaden the discussion and show how these verses both interplay with and resolve the issues raised in the rhetoric of the piece as a whole.

18. Again, as with other allusions, scholars have noted the textual connection, but to my knowledge none has drawn out the interplay between the texts. For example, in his exhaustive commentary, Holladay says merely, 'There is a strong likelihood that Jrm intended the words as a reminiscence or quotation of Hosea' (*Jeremiah 1*, p. 29).

19. Mays, *Hosea*, pp. 144-47.

20. Wolff, *Hosea*, p. 182.

positive command ('break up the fallow ground'), in Hos. 10.12 it is a positive command linking it specifically to covenantal behavior ('sow righteousness for yourselves; reap the fruit of חסד'). Moreover, the shared phrase already mentioned above, נירו לכם ניר, is also connected to covenantal behavior in the intertext. James Luther Mays' translation of Hos. 10.12b is 'Break up new ground for yourselves; it is time to seek YHWH'.[21] Taken together with the command for proper return in 4.1, and the command to swear in truth, justice and righteousness in 4.2, the command to 'break up the fallow ground' in 4.3 is also integrally linked with covenantal ideals. When the allusion to Hos. 10.12 is added to the concern with covenantal ideals of the context of Jer. 4.3, it is clear that the text of 4.3 also absorbs the covenantal ideal addressed in the Hosea text.

Not only is the covenantal ideal of Hos. 10.12 absorbed by Jer. 4.3, but an intertwining of the covenantal ideal with other ideals is also absorbed. Though Mays does not even mention Jer. 4.1-4, he alludes to the kind of intertwining of two ideals in the Hosea text for which I have been arguing with regard to 3.1–4.4: the natural and the covenantal ideals. To use his terms, 'The language of agricultural work is woven together with the normative terms for covenantal life'.[22] The Jeremiah text, too, absorbs both the idea of intertwining ideals of the proper relation to nature (agricultural work) with the proper relation to covenant.

There is yet another way in which Jer. 4.3 absorbs the ideas of its intertext. Mays suggests that Hos. 10.11-13a portray 'the contrast between expectation [vv. 11-12] and result [v. 13a]'.[23] A similar contrast, this time using sisters Israel and Judah (north and south), and indicating a contrast between the expectation that Judah would learn from Israel's example, and the result (Judah did not learn) was made clearly in Jer. 3.1-13. In both cases, YHWH expected fidelity which was not forthcoming. Furthermore, in the intertextual dialogue Hosea's words are directed to the north; in 3.1-13 the fate of the north has been used as an example of what happens when a people does not heed YHWH's call. Jeremiah 4.3 absorbs this connection with the north, as well as the agricultural terminology originally addressed to the north ('break up your fallow ground'), and transforms it into a message for Judah. Moreover, in the final warning of Jer. 4.4, the warning implied through the play with an oracle of judgment originally directed to the north (Hos. 10.11-13a), is absorbed and made explicit. This

---

21. Mays, *Hosea*, p. 144.
22. Mays, *Hosea*, p. 146.
23. Mays, *Hosea*, p. 147.

connection in turn makes the warning implied in Jer. 3.11 manifest—what happened to the north will happen to Judah if they do not change their behavior. Thus, 'the contrast between expectation...and result' in Hos. 10.11-13a is both absorbed and transformed to fit the contrast between north and south in the larger context of Jer. 4.1-4.

d. *The Image of Circumcision*
The final major intertext for Jer. 4.1-4, the broader allusion to the Abrahamic covenant through the use of the metaphor of circumcision, unites many of the intertextual plays discussed above. Yet, it too is modified by connections with the deuteronomic covenant. The following discussion will address the metaphor of circumcision first, and then address the deuteronomic intertexts associated with it.

The use of the metaphor of circumcision alludes to the sign of YHWH's covenant with Abraham (cf. Gen. 15 and 17). In this respect, the call to 'circumcise [them]selves to YHWH' (niphal המלו) absorbs the larger context of the Abrahamic covenant by including its attendant sign, circumcision. This absorption has much the same function rhetorically as does the specific allusion to the covenant itself: it highlights the chosenness and uniqueness of this group of people, and makes them heirs (cf. 3.19) to a long stream of tradition which sets these people apart physically as belonging to YHWH. The second phrase of the verse, however, represents a transgression of the Abrahamic covenant. Rather than merely requiring physical circumcision as YHWH did of Abraham, the Jeremiah text adds a command to 'remove the foreskins of your heart', thus setting up circumcision of the heart as a final stipulation for returning to YHWH. The additional command emphasizes the radical change in behavior that YHWH requires of this people. It also re-emphasizes the conditionality of this call to uniqueness as opposed to the unconditionality of the original covenant with Abraham and his descendants. Moreover, the call to circumcise the heart connects this text with the conditional covenantal relationship between YHWH and the people portrayed in Deuteronomy through two specific references to circumcision of the heart (Deut. 10.16 and 30.6). Before discussing the deuteronomic intertexts, however, it is important to note that, just as with every other intertext, certain aspects of the Genesis tradition have been absorbed and others, specifically the unconditionality of that covenant, have been jettisoned.

Moving to the connections between circumcision of the heart in Jer. 4.4 and Deuteronomy, in Deut. 10.16 Moses tells the people to 'circumcise the foreskin of your heart' (ומלתם את ערלת לבבכם). The second phrase of the verse, 'do not be stubborn any longer' (literally, do not make your necks stiff any longer') opposes circumcision of the heart to stubbornness, thus contrasting previous behavior with the new behavior expected of them in the present. Moreover, the new behavior being advocated is worship of YHWH alone: the remainder of Deuteronomy 10 deals with worship of YHWH, and in Deut. 10.20 Moses declares that the people shall worship only YHWH. The same contrast was already made in Jer. 3.17, where YHWH's vision of the future includes a similar change in behavior: worshipping YHWH alone, and 'no longer following after the stubbornness of their evil hearts'. While there is no verbal connection between the second phrase of Deut. 10.16 and Jer. 4.4, the idea that circumcision of the heart is a reversal of the people's previous stubbornness is nevertheless present in the broader context of Jer. 3.1–4.4.

In addition, Deut. 10.16 is set in the context of a list of what YHWH requires from the people about to enter the land, and follows directly on the idea already alluded to in 3.19: that YHWH chose this people from among all peoples (Deut. 10.15).[24] In a similar fashion, following emphasis on the people's uniqueness and chosenness, Jer. 4.1-4 sets out the requirements for a continuing relationship with YHWH. The juxtaposition of the covenant of Abraham with a command resonating so much with the conditional deuteronomic covenant absorbs the conditionality, as well as the contrast between previous behavior and expected present behavior of the deuteronomic text. This juxtaposition also links the command to be circumcised to the idea that this people is chosen and set apart.

The second deuteronomic text that refers to circumcision of the heart is Deut. 30.6, which reads, 'YHWH your God will circumcise your heart and the heart of your descendants so that you will love YHWH your God with all your heart, and with all your being (נפשׁ) and with all your strength'. It is important to note that the purpose given for this circumcision is that they will worship God properly (30.6b). Moreover, circumcision of the heart is linked with obedience in 30.8, and with prosperity, fertility and abundance in 30.9. Deuteronomy 30.6 also appears in a context where the people are asked to make a decision 'between life and prosperity, death and adversity' (30.15). After setting out the blessings and curses associ-

---

24. M. Weinfeld makes a similar assessment of Deut. 10.16, arguing that the verse 'is uttered against the background of the election of the patriarchs *and of their descendants after them* (זרעם אחריהם v. 15)' ('Jeremiah and the Spiritual Metamorphosis of Israel', *ZAW* 88 [1976], pp. 17-56 [34] [original emphasis]). However, he does not mention Jer. 3.1–4.4 in his discussion of circumcision of the heart.

ated respectively with fulfilling or not fulfilling the people's obligations in their covenantal relationship with YHWH (Deut. 27–28), and portraying the consequences of the people's turning away from YHWH (Deut. 29), Deuteronomy 30 discusses what will happen when the people remember the blessings and curses and return (שוב) to YHWH (Deut. 30.1-2; cf. Jer. 4.1). The specific choice is between obeying and worshipping YHWH and experiencing life and prosperity (Deut. 30.16), or serving other gods and experiencing death and adversity (30.17-18). YHWH promises to bring them back from the lands where they were exiled (30.3) and restore the land of their ancestors to them (30.4-5). Thus, these verses present a picture of the future much like that of Jer. 3.14-18.

As with the text of Deuteronomy 10, apart from the reference to circumcising the heart, it is primarily ideas rather than verbal links which interplay with Jer. 3.1–4.4. The first link, as noted above, is with 3.14-18, where the vision for the future, like that of Deuteronomy 30, associates worship of YHWH with life, prosperity and fertility. A second link is with Jer. 4.4 itself, where, similarly to Deuteronomy 30, the people are given the choice between life and death; in Jer. 4.4, the people must either remove the foreskins of their hearts or they will face YHWH's destructive anger. Thus these aspects of the larger context of Deut. 30.6 are absorbed in the text of Jer. 4.4.

However, there is a crucial transgression. In Deut. 30.6, it is *YHWH* who will circumcise their hearts (much as in Jer. 31.31-34, it is YHWH who will write his law on their hearts), while in 4.4 it is clearly the *people's* responsibility to make the behavioral changes. In keeping with the entire piece's emphasis on the people's responsibility and on change in behavior, they themselves must remove the foreskins of their hearts, with all that image entails in terms of proper religious and political fidelity to YHWH. The final warning of the piece, 4.4b, underlines conclusively the conditional nature of the return, thus emphasizing the radical nature of the call to circumcise the heart. No longer is the mere outward sign of circumcision enough. A radical change of conduct is necessary.

The foregoing discussion has made clear that although the verbal intertextual allusions in Jer. 4.1-4 are primarily to the patriarchal covenant, the actual terms according to which YHWH will let the people return are more closely allied with the covenant as presented in Deuteronomy.[25] The closer

25. Cf. also Deut. 30.6. Weinfeld also links this text 'with the notion of a "new covenant"' in Jer. 31 ('Jeremiah', pp. 34-35). The other connections with Jer. 30–31 mentioned above make this a likely notion.

connection with the deuteronomic covenant is fitting, given the ways in which the law as presented in Deut. 24.1-4 has been in dialogue with the whole of Jer. 3.1–4.4.

Yet there is significance in the fact that it is the patriarchal covenantal blessing rather than any other which is the primary intertext of 4.2, and that its attendant sign, circumcision, is also used. For example, it is important, given the undermining of the Royal Zion theology in 3.14-18, as well as the stance against relying on the outward trappings of religion there, that the Davidic covenant was not chosen. It is fundamental that the sign of Israel's identity is not the king, but rather a sign of separation and uniqueness—circumcision. The metaphor of circumcision, moreover, connects with two of the overarching themes of Jer. 3.19–4.4 in particular: uniqueness as represented in 3.19, and separation as represented both through the liturgy of repentance in 3.21-25 and through the specific conditions of 4.1-2, which would separate the people from worship of other gods.

There is another significance as well. The background of the larger context, including ch. 2, is the exodus/wilderness traditions. The lines of argument in 2.1–4.4 all point to the fact that the people have not lived up to the covenant established in the wilderness. By concluding with the patriarchal covenant, the writer goes back to earlier beginnings,[26] thus paving the way for the new covenant which will be established in Jeremiah 30–31. Going back to the people's prior origins also highlights issues of uniqueness and identity in a way the exodus/wilderness traditions cannot. For a pre-exilic audience this language is a powerful encouragement for change. By conforming to YHWH's requirements, they take their place as the heirs (sons) of Abraham, inheriting as well the promise of blessing given to Abraham, while if they refuse to conform they lose that chosen,

---

26. Biddle also sees significance in these earlier beginnings: 'Those texts which have in mind an initial period of Israel's faithfulness frequently center upon the period of the patriarchs (Ne 9; Is 63; Ps 106), often naming the covenant with Abraham, Isaac, and Jacob as the grounds for YHWH's past action on Israel's behalf or as grounds for his sought-after intervention in the present (Ps 105.7ff; Ne 9.6f; cf Ps 106.4, 45 and Is 63.11, where Moses replaces the patriarchs)' (*A Redaction History*, p. 179). He writes of Jer. 2.1–4.2 specifically, 'If the hand responsible for Jeremiah 2.2b-3 was to find a means to contramand the charges leveled against Israel…he found it necessary to harken to a generation before the "fathers". Jeremiah 2.2b-3 (and 4.1f) introduce(s) a new historical period, that of Israel's beginning, into the discussion of Israel's sin and hopes for a future' (p. 180).

unique relationship with YHWH. For an exilic audience the argument is equally powerful if somewhat different. The allusion to the Abrahamic covenant may remind them of the wandering of Abraham, as well as YHWH's election and blessing of the original ancestor, all in a foreign land. Thus, while the piece ends with a warning, an exilic audience may draw hope from the implicit lines established between YHWH's dealings with the people and the Abrahamic covenant. As with the law of Deut. 24.1-4, something of the broader context is absorbed and transformed here as well.

To summarize the study of intertextuality in this section, Jer. 3.19–4.4 contains further play on the law cited in 3.1, particularly on the ramifications of its overturning in vv. 12-13. The intertextual plays in this section give primary emphasis to the issues of uniqueness, separation, true rather than false turning, and the need for a radical change in behavior. Issues of identity and the land continue to play a significant part in the rhetoric, but the land becomes an underlying rather than a primary theme in these verses. Just as with the intertexts of the previous sections, the intertexts of this section are absorbed and transgressed, transforming them for a message in a new situation. Such a message has been revealed to shatter security. The final warning of 4.4 makes it perfectly clear that if the people do not change their ways, they will experience judgment. While this statement presupposes the literary context of pre-exile, the message functions equally as well for an exilic audience. It provides theological justification for exile, and focuses on issues of uniqueness, separation and proper worship which were essential for maintaining their identity in a foreign land. Jeremiah 3.19–4.4 thus portrays what is necessary to make the ideal picture with which 3.1-18 ended a reality.

2. *Metaphor and Gender in Jeremiah 4.1-4*

While identity has been mentioned in connection with the intertextual rhetoric of this section, it is in the metaphors and their interaction with gender conventions that the issue of identity finds both its focus and its resolution. Moreover, it is at the metaphorical level that the ideals dealt with earlier in the piece are interwoven and tied together in the final demands for the Judahite audience. As was the case with those ideals in the first two sections (3.1-5, 6-11), in these verses they are held together by the common thread of the verb שוב. The above section discussed the ways in which the verb שוב related to the covenantal relationship, thus expressing the legal ideal for return. The verb also indicates the religious ideal, referring both to repentance and proper worship (v. 1b). The rest of the verses spell out what return means using metaphors which intertwine with the other ideals (natural, social/sexual).

Just as with what has gone before, the conditions and promises for repentance in Jer. 4.1-4 reveal the concern for order by their connection with boundaries. The imperatives, 'return to me', 'do not wander', 'swear "as YHWH lives"', indicate bounds within which repentance must take place. The concern with order is also indicated in the intertwining of legal, natural, social and religious boundaries. The legal/covenantal order has been discussed above, and is especially visible in the ethical command to swear 'in truth, in justice and in righteousness' (v. 2). Likewise, through the allusion to proper worship in v. 1, these verses are concerned with religious order; this text is concerned with true worship of YHWH and YHWH alone. The agricultural metaphors of v. 3, as will be shown below, reveal a concern for order by insisting on the proper relationship between humans and the land. Finally, concern for the social order (as well as identity) is represented both through the exclusively male terms of this section and the ways in which the agricultural metaphors and the metaphor of circumcision play on conventions of gender, particularly conventional sexual boundaries.

In addition to the continued metaphorical play on the verb שׁוּב, another metaphor introduced earlier in the chapter, that of fertility (seed), is also picked up again in these verses. This metaphor, too, plays on the ideals and concern for order in various realms just mentioned. Although the term זֶרַע does not occur in Jer. 4.1-4, the intertext alluded to in v. 2, that is, the promise to Abraham in Gen. 22.18 and then to Isaac in Gen. 26.4, explic-itly associates fertility with seed: 'All the nations of the earth shall gain blessing for themselves in your זֶרַע'. The term is nevertheless evoked through the allusion to the promise and through the metaphorical associa-tions in the piece as a whole (e.g. sexual promiscuity, which blurs the line of descent by mixing seed) as well as in 4.3-4 in particular (the agricul-tural/sexual metaphors). Moreover, as mentioned above, the re-presen-tation of this promise places the audience in the line of descent from Abraham. The special place which the audience holds in relation to YHWH, together with the imperatives addressed directly to the sons, returns us to the issue of identity. Verse 2 implies that if the audience takes up the sub-ject position of sons, it (the current sons) will be the agents of the blessing promised to the patriarchs.

Issues of land and descendants, absorbed in the intertextual play between v. 2 and Gen. 22.18 and 26.4, are also brought up metaphorically in vv. 3-4. Specifically, I propose that in vv. 3-4 the agricultural metaphors merge the foregoing seed and sexual metaphors. The Hebrew Bible contains numerous analogies between human fruitfulness and agricultural fruitfulness. The most explicit associations occur extensively in Ezekiel,[27] but also in Ps. 128.3 and Isa. 56.3-6.[28] Other texts compare human and agricultural yields in various ways. For instance, firstborn children are viewed as the first yield (Ps. 105.35; Deut. 18.4; 21.17); children are called the 'fruit of the womb' (Gen. 30.2); and the descendants of David who are to carry on the royal line are referred to in agricultural terms: 'stump', 'twig', 'branch', and so on (cf. Isa. 11.1; Jer. 23.5; 33.15; Zech. 6.12-13).[29] The clearest example of the type of merging of metaphors for which I am arguing for Jer. 4.3-4, however, is Samson's accusation against the Philistines in Judg. 14.8: 'If you had not plowed with my heifer, you would not have found out my riddle'.

With this evidence in mind, I propose that the agricultural metaphors of Jer. 4.3-4, that is, breaking up the fallow ground and not sowing among thorns, refer just as much to proper sexual practice and fidelity as they do to fertility.[30] As with the previous sections of Jer. 3.1–4.4, then, in this section the natural ideal, as represented by the restoration of the proper human relationship with the land, is interwoven with the sexual ideal, representing proper sexual relations.

Although most commentators emphasize the agricultural aspects of the metaphors in Jer. 4.3-4,[31] I would stress the sexual aspects since they

27. Cf. Ezek. 15.6; 17.1-24; 33.3; 34.26-31; 37.16-19.

28. Cf. Isa. 65.

29. Howard Eilberg-Schwartz, in his *The Savage in Judaism: An Anthropology of Israelite Religion and Ancient Judaism* (Bloomington: Indiana University Press, 1990), argues compellingly for even more extensive analogies (see pp. 145-61, esp. pp. 156-60). Although he does not include any part of Jer. 3.1–4.4 in his argument, he concludes, 'the themes of harvesting a fruit tree and the ripening of fruit are treated as analogous to the harvesting of a woman and the maturing of one's children' (p. 159). With regard to Jer. 4.3, I would argue that the analogy is taken one step further, setting the boundaries as to what type of soil/woman a man can plow/sow. I submit that these ideas underlie the rhetoric of Jer. 3.1–4.4 in addition to the texts he discusses.

30. Although it uses different imagery, Prov. 5.15 ('Drink water from your own cistern...') uses a similar structure of comparison through sexual punning.

31. Thompson puts it best when he says, 'Judah's own field was so infested with the thorn seeds of past evil deed that her only hope was to reclaim new ground. The

resolve several issues raised in the preceding material. Here the effects of using the harlotry imagery on men are played out.[32] Through addressing a primarily male audience as promiscuous women, not only women's sexual behavior, but their (the men's) sexual behavior was called into question. If they are now to be identified as YHWH's sons rather than as promiscuous women, they must be careful where they sow their seed. Hence the command: 'Break up your fallow ground' (i.e. virginal ground) and 'do not sow among thorns' (i.e. do not have sexual relations with those foreigners [in all its senses]). Since paternity and proper relationships are the stakes of the imagery of 3.1–4.4, proper use of seed is an essential part of those stakes. Here the proper sexual as well as natural boundaries are set for the sons. As with the rhetoric of 3.1-25, in these verses it is the sexual ideal, here expressed through the agricultural metaphors, which interweaves and binds the other ideals (covenantal, religious and creation/fertility) together in a mutually reinforcing manner, thus creating a powerful rhetorical strategy for change in behavior.

But women are implicated in the agricultural/sexual metaphors as well. In their roles as wives and mothers, they must be the fallow ground, the ground with no thorns. If promiscuous, they *are* the thorns. The boundaries, however, are to be maintained and controlled by the men. These metaphors make the classic equation of women and nature. Like the earth, their potential for reproduction is harnessed and controlled.[33] Hence the necessity of the change to masculine imagery here. If male sexual behavior is being addressed in these verses, male control over women's sexuality is presumed. Male behavior is prescribed while female behavior is circumscribed in this text.

3. Circumcision: The Synoptic Metaphor for Jeremiah 3.1–4.4

The centrality of the sexual ideal is made clearer in Jer. 4.4, which continues the link to the patriarchs and resolves the issue of the uniqueness and separation of Israel raised in 3.19. In the final image of 4.1-4, that of

whole future was threatened by the legacy of the past, and only a complete and radical new beginning would suffice to save the nation' (*Jeremiah*, p. 215). Note, however, how Thompson's use of 'her' for Judah muddies the metaphorical waters: what is a male address (second masculine plural) in the text, he transforms to a feminine singular.

32. I am grateful to George Hall for suggesting that I look for the implicit male side of the harlotry imagery in this section.

33. Like the earth, women are receptacles for the seed. Cf. Delaney, *The Seed and the Soil*, pp. 30-42.

circumcision, the issues of identity, inheritance, paternity, and maintaining uniqueness and separateness coalesce. Just as the promise to the archpatriarch, Abraham, is linked with a physical sign of separation and uniqueness (circumcision), so in 4.4, the sons are reminded of that sign and called to extend the sign by circumcising their hearts to YHWH. Moreover, the links between sexuality, seed and circumcision return us to the issue of identity, both cultic identity and political allegiance, with which the passage began. As I have argued previously, these issues, summed up in the necessity of a pure line of descent, underlie the whole of the piece. An indication that this is the case is the preoccupation of the rest of the text with sexual matters. In the first part of the piece, Israel the wife's main offense is that her sexuality is uncontrolled (she lies in wait 'like an Arab in the desert', 3.2) and uncontrolled by YHWH, her husband/father (3.1-11/19-20). These concerns are summed up and resolved in the (male) symbol of separation *par excellance*, circumcision.

Above I discussed the need for male and divine control over women's reproductive potential, as well as the connections between divine seed in Jer. 3.3 and the promise to the patriarchs and circumcision in 4.1-4. I shall argue that these images are linked together in 4.4 in such a way as to re-establish divine male control where such control was lost, and that they are linked together through the metaphor of circumcision.

Both Howard Eilberg-Schwartz[34] and Gerda Lerner[35] justify a symbolic link between fertility and circumcision. Using anthropological studies, Eilberg-Schwartz argues persuasively for a connection between circumcision and both fertility and genealogy in the Hebrew Bible. An illustration of this link is the content of the covenant.[36] As my intertextual work above has shown, the covenantal promise to the patriarchs is intimately connected with issues of fertility through the covenantal importance on descent, particularly with a male line of descent.[37] The covenant and its symbol, circumcision, are connected in several other important ways as well. The covenant with Abraham sets him apart from all others, as does circumcision. Abraham is different from all who came before. Those who bear this mark are likewise set apart. Yet those who bear the mark are

34. Eilberg-Schwartz, *Savage*, pp. 141-76.

35. Gerda Lerner, *The Creation of Patriarchy* (New York: Oxford University Press, 1986), pp. 191-93.

36. See especially Gen. 17 and Eilberg-Schwartz' argument in *Savage* (pp. 145-48).

37. See also Eilberg-Schwartz, *Savage*, p. 147. Other passages where this connection is made include Gen. 12.1-3; 17.4-6; 28.3; 35.11; 48.3.

linked with each other in several ways. First, those who bear the mark will be fruitful (they are promised many descendants). Second, those who are circumcised are related. Circumcision is thus a symbol of kinship.[38]

Eilberg-Schwartz also notes an opposition between circumcision and women. When carried out at birth, as it is in the Hebrew Bible, 'circumcision is a postpartum ritual associated with the separation of a male child from the impurity of his mother'.[39] He also notes a correspondence between circumcision and sacrifice. Through his study of Leviticus 12 he argues that 'circumcision...removes the male from the realm of death through the shedding of his own blood, just as the sacrifice of an animal eventually removes the boy's mother from the impurity caused by the birth process (Lev. 12.6-7)'.[40] He concludes that 'circumcision and sacrifice...have overlapping functions'.[41]

In a similar vein, Nancy Jay makes a compelling argument for the connection in patrilineal societies between sacrifice in general and the continuity of the (male) social order. Founding her work on cross-cultural studies, she sees participation in blood sacrifice as a way of incorporating men into kinship, and as a means of preserving descent lines. More importantly, such participation provides a means to overcome the problem of women's part in procreation, as well as a means to overcome the problem of lack of complete certainty as to paternity:

> When the crucial intergenerational link is between father and son, for which birth itself cannot provide sure evidence, sacrificing may be considered essential for the continuity of the social order. What is needed to provide clear evidence of jural paternity is an act as powerful, definite, and available to the senses as birth. When membership in patrilineal descent groups is identified by rights of participation in blood sacrifice, evidence of 'paternity' is created that is as certain as evidence of maternity, but far more flexible.[42]

It seems to me that circumcision, as an act of shedding blood, functions in much the same way with regard to the patriarchal covenant as does blood

---

38. See Eilberg-Schwartz, *Savage*, pp. 162-63.
39. Eilberg-Schwartz, *Savage*, p. 174.
40. Eilberg-Schwarz, *Savage*, pp. 174-75. See pp. 174-76 for the full argument.
41. Eilberg-Schwartz, *Savage*, p. 175.
42. Nancy Jay, 'Sacrifice as Remedy for Having Been Born of Woman', in C.W. Atkinson, C.H. Buchanan and M.R. Miles (eds.), *Immaculate and Powerful: The Female in Sacred Image and Social Reality* (Boston: Beacon Press, 1985), pp. 283-309 (291). See also Jay's *Throughout Your Generations Forever: Sacrifice, Religion, and Paternity* (Chicago: University of Chicago Press, 1992), p. 36.

sacrifice. However, it functions not just on the human level, but, at least in the prophets, on the divine level as well. Circumcision is the symbol not only separating Israel from other nations, but establishing a unique relationship with the deity. The fact that each new generation of boys must be circumcised (and at birth, rather than at puberty), sets up a divine line of descent where women are passed by. Circumcision, therefore, could be the symbol of blood sacrifice which enables men once and for all to transcend women's reproductive power. Or, similarly, circumcision may be the symbol *par excellance* which serves, to use Jay's phrasing, as the 'remedy for having been born of a woman'.[43]

Bringing together issues of identity, fertility, descent and kinship, as well as addressing the reason for the fact that it is the male sexual organ which is the site of the symbol of the covenant, Eilberg-Schwartz sums the above line of thought best:

> The association between the male organ and the idea of kinship made the penis doubly appropriate as the spot for the symbol of God's covenant. God had promised to make Abraham fertile and provide him with a successful progeny…the removal of the foreskin symbolizes the fertility of the organ. But the cut also suggests that this lineage, represented by the penis, is set apart from all others. In this way, circumcision symbolizes and helps create intergenerational continuity between men. It graphically represents patrilineal descent by giving men of this line a distinctive mark that binds them together.[44]

He continues, 'Since circumcision binds together men within and across generations, it also establishes an opposition between men and women'.[45]

To connect the above discussion specifically with Jer. 4.1-4, issues of seed, paternity, fertility, identity and descendants are all issues carried through the whole of 3.1–4.4. My intertextual work with the Abrahamic covenant and the metaphor of circumcision already highlighted these aspects in 4.1-4 itself. When one also takes into account the work of Eilberg-Schwartz and Jay linking circumcision with fertility, genealogy, and setting up a system of descent in which men are related to each other in a powerful physical and symbolic way, and in which women are passed by, the rhetorical power of the image of circumcision in this text becomes clear. This imagery functions antithetically to the harlotry imagery.

---

43. This quote is a reference to the title of Jay's article, 'Sacrifice as Remedy', cited in the preceding footnote.

44. Eilberg-Schwartz, *Savage*, p. 171.

45. Eilberg-Schwartz, *Savage*, p. 171.

Circumcision as a metaphor functions to set up the proper divine line of descent. It continues the pressure of identification: the members of the audience are not only to be proper sons, but they are the ones who will continue the line. Hence they are God's representatives: each generation, through circumcision, sets up the line of the patriarchs, who in turn reflect the deity.

To illustrate how this imagery works to resolve the problems which the imagery of sexual promiscuity posed to the social order, let us review how the whole of Jer. 3.1–4.4 has dealt with issues of paternity and identity through the lens of sexuality. First, where women's sexuality is not controlled, chaos threatens and the land is polluted (3.1-5). The consequence of such pollution for the land is portrayed through withholding of the deity's seed (drought, 3.3). Proper sexual behavior and circumcision are the answers to restoring the proper relationship, in this case through a proper father–son relationship. The consequence of this restoration is fertility: God will make them fruitful (vv. 14-18). God is nevertheless in control, even (perhaps especially) over the sons, who are to be the new patriarchs. The imagery of 4.1-4 effectively writes out ('exscribes') the woman (along with all the dangers associated with her, reproductive and otherwise) and puts in its place the 'fertile patriarch'.[46]

In the Hebrew Bible, the metaphor of circumcision not only sets in place the ideal gender relations, but also incorporates the other ideals through which the rhetoric of Jer. 3.1–4.4 has worked. The covenantal ideal was already dealt with in the intertextual section. Here let me append that the idea of circumcision setting up a kinship relation and preserving a pure line of descent only adds to the idea of a legal and/or covenantal boundary separating this people from all others. Moreover, in 4.4 this legal/covenantal boundary is interwoven with sexual ideals. Writing regarding analogies

46. The term 'fertile patriarch' comes from J. Cheryl Exum, who describes a similar dynamic at work in the patriarchal stories themselves. She argues, 'If permitting conception is the prerogative of God, impregnating women is the work of males. The counterpart to the sterile matriarch is the fertile patriarch, whose procreative role is enhanced through an implicit association of reproduction with circumcision, the mark of the covenant' (*Fragmented Women*, p. 124). Although the case for a 'sterile matriarch' cannot be established for Jer. 3.1–4.4, Exum's argument regarding this phenomenon in Genesis deals with many of the same issues raised by the language of Jer. 3.1–4.4. It may just be that the same dynamic, that is, replacement of the sterile matriarch by the fertile patriarch, is at work here as well. (For her complete argument, see pp. 107-24 [111, 120-24]).

between circumcision and other organs in the Hebrew Bible,[47] Eilberg-Schwartz argues:

> Israelite writers equated the lack of circumcision with the improper functioning of a human organ. Uncircumcised hearts, ears, and lips are organs that cannot do what God intended them to do. By extension, the removal of a man's foreskin symbolically enables the penis to more effectively discharge its divinely allotted task. That task, as suggested by the content of the covenant, is to impregnate women and produce offspring.[48]

The call to circumcision of the heart specifically interweaves the covenantal and sexual ideals by calling for the people to do (both covenantally and sexually) what YHWH has intended for them. The call to circumcise the heart thus radicalizes the image of circumcision itself, cutting to the center of both identity and behavior. Through circumcision of the heart, the people maintain their unique, separate relationship with YHWH and with each other, and modify their behavior to that which YHWH has commanded.

Another ideal which is incorporated within the metaphor of circumcision is the agricultural (natural) ideal, (as represented through the ideal of the proper relationship between humans and the land). Eilberg-Schwartz has argued that the priestly tradition extends the metaphor of circumcision to the agricultural realm.[49] Referring specifically to Lev. 19.23-25, which mentions 'uncircumcised' fruit trees, he discusses the significance of this extension: 'the priestly writings suggest an analogy between an uncircumcised male organ and an immature fruit tree. They thus associate the circumcision of the male with pruning juvenile fruit trees; like the latter, circumcision symbolically readies the stem for producing fruit'.[50] Immediately following as it does agricultural metaphors (4.3), the call to circumcise themselves to YHWH in 4.4 incorporates a similar link. Circumcision, as with fruit trees, symbolically readies the sons to 'break up the fallow ground' and not to 'sow among thorns'. In addition to connecting the agricultural ideal with the metaphor of circumcision in 4.3-4, circumcision as

---

47. Analogies between circumcision and other organs include hearts (Lev. 26.41; Deut. 10.16; Jer. 9.25; Ezek. 44.7, 9), ears (Jer. 6.10) and lips (Exod. 6.12, 30). See Eilberg-Schwartz, *Savage*, p. 149.

48. Eilberg-Schwartz, *Savage*, p. 149.

49. Cf. Eilberg-Schwartz, *Savage*, pp. 149-54.

50. Howard Eilberg-Schwartz, 'People of the Body: The Problem of the Body for the People of the Book', *Journal for the History of Sexuality* 2 (1991), pp. 1-24 (8); cf. *Savage*, pp. 149-54.

a symbol of readiness to produce fruit is also interwoven with the establishment of the proper social order. Circumcision affects the identity of the people. Through circumcision, they will not just be agents of the patriarchal promise, but they themselves will become the next generation of the patriarchs. The image of circumcision therefore brings together the major ideals played with in the whole of 3.1–4.4 by absorbing the agricultural and natural, social, sexual and covenantal ideals, and being interwoven with them in the rhetoric of 4.1-4 as a whole.

4. *Powers of Persuasion: Issues of Identity*

a. *Male Identity*

Together with the other images of Jer. 4.1-4 (patriarchal covenant and agricultural metaphors), the image of circumcision addresses issues of uniqueness, separation and identity. While uniqueness and separation have been dealt with adequately above, the following will sum up how these images coalesce to provide a rhetorically persuasive device pressuring the audience to identify themselves as sons. Through this imagery, the listeners are not just to be sons, but, through proper sexual behavior and circumcision; they are to take their places as patriarchs. The unspoken message is one of power, as well as of identity. As patriarchs they will be fertile, receive their inheritance and maintain their distinctiveness as a community. The patriarchal symbolic order may be maintained or re-established through stopping their promiscuous behavior (metaphorically speaking, their promiscuous sexual behavior, but speaking politically and in terms of religious fidelity, their 'promiscuous' worship of other gods and making of political alliances), and by preserving their uniqueness as sons. Once they have identified with and rejected the negative female metaphors, they return to the comfortable subject position of sons to God's father in the patriarchal symbolic order. They are called no longer to identify themselves as promiscuous women/worshipers of other gods/makers of foreign alliances, but can now identify themselves as new Abrahams, worshipping YHWH alone and preserving their distinction from other peoples.

This final picture is an exclusively male picture. Not only has female direct address been abandoned, but female imagery has been abandoned as well. Just as blood sacrifice and circumcision bypass women's roles and power in issues of descent and kinship, so has the prophetic rhetoric of Jer. 3.1–4.4. As such, this imagery and rhetoric reinforce an exclusively male view of proper power relations both between the deity and humans, but also between men and women.

b. *Female Identity*
While this language has strong rhetorical power in fashioning male identity, I would also argue that the ways in which gender has been played
upon in the text as a whole have implications for female identity as well.
As J. Cheryl Exum argues, this language has

> destructive implications for gender relations... It cannot be dismissed by
> claiming that it is only 'metaphorical', as if metaphor were some kind of
> container from which meaning can be extracted, or as if gender relations
> inscribed on a metaphorical level are somehow less problematic on a literal
> level.[51]

The power of the rhetoric exploiting gender conventions relies on the fact
that at some level the metaphors regrading sexual and social identity
reflect life. In other words, at some level, readers see these metaphors as
true of what sexual and social relations should (or should not) be. As noted
above, much of the power of the gendered imagery of Jer. 3.1–4.4 lies in
the fact that its roots are embedded in the patriarchal social system of
Israel, as well as in the fact that the listeners to which it is addressed
(implicitly men) would have a stake in maintaining the social structures on
which the metaphors were based.

This text reflects a societal structure in which the norm for humanity
was male, and in which, ideally, men had political, social and sexual
control over women.[52] The use of gendered imagery, specifically gendered
imagery in which women are portrayed negatively, as overstepping the
proper bounds of male-controlled sexuality, bolsters the view that women
must be controlled or they get out of hand. Both the image of Jer. 3.2, the
harlot lying in wait for lovers, and that of Jer. 3.19-20, in which the
(initially) positive daughter imagery is immediately undermined by her
seeking lovers, reflect and reinforce the view that women should not be
autonomous. In the case of v. 2, women are portrayed as being insatiable,
and incapable of controlling their sexual urges; in the case of vv. 19-20,
the daughter's behavior is evidence that women should not own land or
have control of their own bodies for they will not reward the giver with
faithfulness, but with treachery (בגד).

51. Exum, 'Prophetic Pornography', p. 119.
52. A quick look at the narrative portions of the Hebrew Bible, however, indicates
that women did exert political and social power within a circumscribed sphere. A few
narratives even indicate places where women step out of that sphere (e.g. Tamar in
Gen. 38 and the Shunnamite woman in 2 Kgs 4).

Carol Newsom notes that any symbolic thinking which uses a specific group of people cannot simply be symbolic—it also has an implication for the behavior of that group of people.[53] This is especially true in a text that uses symbolic language referring to women. By assigning female gendered imagery an exclusively negative place in the rhetoric, the author objectifies and marginalizes women. This text not only assumes a male-dominated societal structure, but in asking the reader to make the metaphorical connections which the images represent, it asks the reader to assent to the imagery itself. This in turn implies an assent to the societal structure which this text assumes. In this text it means that repentance, identity and the status of future generations are exclusively male. The final allusions to the patriarchal covenant and to circumcision make an undeniably exclusively male statement. Although the circumcision is radicalized (it is circumcision of the heart), it is nonetheless an exclusively male metaphor which effectively bars women from a place in structuring identity, descent or kinship. Women, by definition, are excluded from the positive symbols of this text.

Such rhetoric and use of imagery have political implications. Women who read this text, by identifying with and assenting to the female imagery, become defined by it. It becomes the 'natural' way to view reality. According to this text the natural role for women is that of loyal wives and mothers, while the unnatural role is that of the harlot or sexually promiscuous wife/daughter. There are no other roles allotted to women in this kind of thinking. Apart from sowing among thorns, which is unnatural agricultural practice, there is no explicit unnatural role for men here, except perhaps when they act like promiscuous women. The natural role for men is that of the good son to the father (God), who will maintain proper identity through proper behavior (sexual [4.3] and otherwise), and thus continue the pure patriarchal line of descent through the generations. To the extent that these views are perceived as 'natural' they will be invisible both to women and men in society.[54]

This invisibility has consequences for both genders in society, but particularly for women. Women who assent to this view deny themselves full membership in society, as well as a separate identity of any kind. As long as only the males in society enter into public roles, one does not notice such implications. Once, however, women enter into the public domain,

---

53. Carol Newsom, 'Woman and the Discourse of Patriarchal Wisdom', Day (ed.), *Gender and Difference in Ancient Israel*, pp. 142-60 (155).

54. See Lerner, *Creation of Patriarchy*, p. 10.

both through taking on public roles and through identifying themselves as individuals, the symbolic language becomes confused. When a woman reads this text, she 'cannot occupy the same symbolic relation to herself that she does to man'.[55] In short, this text functions ideologically to circumscribe women.

As a subordinate social group, women have a different relationship to language.[56] Although the language is disguised as neutral (the devoted wife is the 'natural' order of things, sexually promiscuous women have transgressed the 'natural' boundaries), it nevertheless acts ideologically to exert pressure on female readers to be a faithful wife, mother and daughter, the only positive roles allotted to them within the boundaries created by this type of social structuring. Because harlotry metaphors can be applied to real women, women are forever connected with the evil actions of the male citizens, with the defeat of Israel, with its inevitable demise. It is but a step to turn this imagery against women themselves.[57] The consequences for women who overstep the boundaries are the same as they were for the male audience: punishment. Yet women remain to a large extent excluded in this text, both through the shifts to the masculine address when the conditions and promises for repentance are offered, and through the use of the metaphor of circumcision. The entire symbolic world of the discourse operates to marginalize women and women's interests. Yet, while there is a way out for men (change of behavior/circumcision of the heart), there is no redeeming escape for women.

5. *Seeds of Deconstruction*

Or is there? Just as with the metaphors of sexuality which contained uncontrollable slippage, so the metaphor of circumcision also has unrestrained elements. Even if women are symbolically erased and the patrilineal bond created through circumcision is a replacement for the sexual bond between YHWH as husband and Israel as wife, the imagery of circumcision cannot dispose of the necessity of women and sexuality completely. Fathers and

55. Newsom, 'Woman and Patriarchal Wisdom', p. 155.
56. Moi, *Sexual/Textual Politics*, p. 154.
57. A recent illustration will suffice to show how this text continues to function to bolster patriarchal views of gender roles today. When I taught a Sunday school class on Jeremiah in a downtown Atlanta church, the men in the class interpreted the metaphors as applying literally to women's behavior. According to them, the message of the text was that women should 'watch out', that is, women should be careful to act in a modest and sexually moral way.

sons cannot self-reproduce or reproduce through each other. Without women, fathers and sons cannot perpetuate the line; without women there is no line of descent. Sexuality must return, albeit dominated and controlled by men (4.3). While the text seeks to constrain or circumscribe women's role, particularly through the agricultural metaphors of 4.3, where the classic equation between women and nature is made in which women are reduced to mere receptacles for the seed, as fields to be cultivated (dominated), the necessity of women for reproduction still maintains the necessity both of women and of sexuality. As soon as women are part of the picture in any way that includes sexuality, however, the possibility of uncontrolled behavior, of women's breaking out of male sexual control, also returns. Women's power in procreation cannot be completely erased. The imagery of circumcision, while symbolically potent, does not entirely deal with the problems 'avoided' by the change to exclusively masculine imagery and address. Thus, the imagery contains slippage that undermines itself. The very fact that women, and women alone, have the ability to carry and give birth to children, reveals the engendering power of women which this text would like to 'exscribe'. The world portrayed here cannot be sustained without women and female sexuality. Yet such an evaluation does not negate the rhetorical power of the passage as a whole, which acts to prescribe as well as reflect a certain view of male and female identity and conventions governing their relationships with each other, but also acts as a powerful argument for a change in religious and political behavior.

Chapter 9

NEW SIGHTS FROM AN OLD SEER:
RHETORICAL STRATEGIES AND JEREMIAH 3.1–4.4

> Re-vision—the act of looking back, of seeing with fresh eyes, of entering
> an old text from a new critical direction—is for us more than a chapter in
> cultural history: it is an act of survival. Until we can understand the
> assumptions in which we are drenched we cannot know ourselves. And this
> drive to self-knowledge, for woman, is more than a search for identity: it is
> part of her refusal of the self-destructiveness of male-dominated society. A
> radical critique of literature, feminist in its impulse, would take the work
> first of all as a clue to how we live, how we have been living, how we have
> been led to imagine ourselves, how our language has trapped as well as
> liberated us; and how we can begin to see—and therefore live—afresh.
>
> —Adrienne Rich

This study has been an attempt at the kind of re-visioning Adrienne Rich[1]
recommended. I have looked at an old text from several new critical directions, directions that intersect and interweave. Theologically speaking, the
Bible in general and this text in particular, has been taken 'as a clue to how
we live, how we have been living, how we have been led to imagine ourselves...' Specifically, this exegetical study of Jer. 3.1–4.4 has explored
the interweaving of three rhetorical strategies, intertextuality, metaphor
and gender, which have been used to paint a picture of Israel's religious
and political infidelity and its consequences, as well as a picture of what it
would take to re-establish a proper relationship with YHWH which would
give the people a secure and prosperous future. In this chapter I seek to
draw together the conclusions of the previous chapters, look at implications of the methods used, indicate the usefulness of such an interweaving
of approaches for other biblical texts and suggest some ways forward, both
for this text and for interpretation of the prophets in general.

---

1. Adrienne Rich, 'When We Dead Awaken: Writing as Re-Vision', *College
English* 34 (1972), pp. 18-25 (18).

The Introduction set the literary and historical contexts for a detailed analysis of Jer. 3.1–4.4. Although this text has been the subject of intense study and the focus of several ongoing debates in the last 150 years, it was found that little had been done with regard to a view of the rhetoric as a whole. Indeed, the general consensus was that this text could not be read as a coherent whole. In contrast, I proposed that a study of the rhetorics of intertextuality and metaphor, with particular attention to conventions of gender as they are played with in this text, would yield a coherent and persuasive reading of the whole. Thus, this study was framed around the following issues: the ways in which the intertextual and metaphorical aspects of the piece act persuasively to form a cohesive argument, as well as the ways in which gender both constructs and is constructed by this text.

Chapter 1 discussed intertextuality as a rhetorical strategy, applying it specifically to the connections between Jer. 3.1-5. The work of Mikhail Bakhtin provided the foundation for this approach to intertextuality, although insights from several other theorists were incorporated, most notably those of Julia Kristeva in her early work and Jonathan Culler. Kristeva and Culler provided several of the terms to be used when exploring intertextual allusion and citation—namely, re-presentation, absorption, transgression, transformation—while Bakhtin's work provided the more general questions to explore, including identification of different voices in the text, and the ways in which each voice enters into dialogue with others, adding to or changing the rhetoric of the whole. It was followed by a second reading of 3.1-5 in Chapter 2, which focused on the conventions of gender. Several feminist appropriators of Bakhtin's work provided access to the issues of gender with which this study was concerned, for instance, the ways in which gender images reflect and refract power dynamics at work in the text, and the ways in which gender roles are played upon, and often reinforced, by the literary devices of a text.

Chapter 3, focused on the rhetorical strategy of metaphor, was devoted to Jer. 3.6-11, using primarily the work of David E. Cooper, Donald David-son and Wayne Booth. This chapter argued for a functional theory of metaphor which would address such questions as the ways the metaphors and metaphorical language function in the text of 3.1–4.4, the conventions with which the metaphors themselves interact, and the ways in which the metaphors may or may not slip their bounds, so to speak, and thus provide an opening for evaluation from a contemporary perspective. The rest of the chapters, each devoted to a portion of the rest of the text, dealt with all three rhetorical strategies either separately or together. The resulting book is an extended analysis of Jer. 3.1–4.4 revolving around the rhetorics of intertextuality, metaphor and the ways in which both interact with conventions of gender.

The intertextual rhetoric of Jer. 3.1–4.4 is one way in which this text is 're-visioned' for a new audience. The piece as a whole was shown to be centered around the citation of the law in Jer. 3.1 which is also found in Deut. 24.1-4. The law is re-presented in the form of a rhetorical question, which in turn acts as a springboard for a discussion of the applicability of this law to the relationship between YHWH and Israel. Issues of identity, land and behavior, raised by the interplay with the law, were shown to be the vehicles by which the text deals with the question of whether YHWH could re-establish his relationship with the people after they had failed to fulfill the obligations of their part of the relationship. The goal of such discourse was to persuade the audience to change its behavior: to worship YHWH alone, rather than other gods, to ally themselves politically with YHWH alone, rather than with Egypt or Babylon, and to act in justice and in truth.

In addition to the law contained in Deut. 24.1-4, other intertexts were demonstrated to address the primary issues raised by the citation of the law in various ways. The ideal future portrayed in Jer. 3.14-18, for example, plays with the Zion tradition and with several texts in Isaiah, on the one hand, in such a way as to deny the centrality and inviolability of Jerusalem or the classic symbols of the people's religious connection with YHWH (e.g. the Temple or the ark, v. 16), but on the other, incorporates many aspects of their future vision into the ideal picture of return. The intertexts of this section were revealed to deal primarily with the issues of land and behavior. The people will be brought back to the land, and they will come to Jerusalem to worship YHWH. Verses 21-25, which form a rhetorical intertext with Hos. 14.2-9, address primarily the issue of behavior by providing a model for proper repentance. Finally, the intertexts of Jer. 4.1-4, namely, Hos. 14.6-9 and 10.11-13a, Gen. 22.18 and 26.4, along with the interplay with the traditions regarding circumcision, bring issues of land and behavior together with the issue of identity by re-establishing the earliest covenant which sets the people apart, identifies them as belonging to YHWH, and provides them with both the land and fertility for land and people. At the same time the final intertexts establish this covenant as conditional, with behavioral stipulations which must be met for the people to return to YHWH.

Judith Fetterley talks about the act of re-reading and re-visioning texts as being an act of political change.[2] This act of re-reading the traditions to apply to a contemporary political situation is one of the primary tasks of the prophets. Intertextuality, dialogue with the tradition, both absorbing it and transforming it, at times even transgressing it, is a rhetorical strategy used in Jer. 3.1–4.4 to enact political change. Through changing the framework, through a re-reading, a re-interpretation of the ancient traditions, a new way of behaving is placed before the audience. As such, the very act of re-reading the ancient traditions is an act of political change. In the end, change is effected through YHWH's actions: YHWH overturns the law in terms of divine–human relations, albeit conditionally—the people must fulfill YHWH's requirements in order to return to YHWH.

Likewise, the prophet, through the persuasive use of metaphor, 're-visioned' the text. Metaphorically, the text of Jer. 3.1–4.4 deals with the issues of identity, land and behavior primarily through gender-specific relational metaphors. To summarize the metaphorical movement of the piece, the text opens with a marital metaphor, YHWH as husband and Israel as a sexually promiscuous wife who acts like a harlot (3.1-5). The rest of the text spins out the metaphors introduced in vv. 1-5 in two separate appeals. The first is directed to the Northern Kingdom and represents the ideal scenario (3.6-18). The second is broader in scope, containing a repentance liturgy, which accentuates the need for true rather than false repentance and incorporates the Southern Kingdom into the call to return (3.19–4.4). When the ideal view of return is introduced (v. 14), the metaphor switches from a marital metaphor to another familial metaphor, that of father and son. This metaphor in turn is the focus of the picture of repentance in 3.21–4.4. The switch in metaphors is accompanied by the insistence that a change in behavior and identity is necessary for the (re)establishment of proper relations between YHWH and the people. The relational metaphors work to persuade the people that their identity as individuals, as a community of faith and as a nation rests in their relationship to God. The metaphors also illustrate that proper relationship to God entails responsibility on several levels. Religiously, it involves responsibility to God in the form of proper worship. It also entails ethical responsibility, including the establishment of proper relationships on the human level. The relational metaphors, together with multiple uses of the word שוב, the verb 'to return', work together to portray these ideas.

2.   Judith Fetterley, *The Resisting Reader: A Feminist Approach to American Fiction* (Bloomington: Indiana University Press, 1978), p. xxiii.

The metaphorical language also plays with various ideals to set out the proper boundaries for return. These ideals include: (1) the legal/covenantal ideal, as represented by the legal citation of v. 1 and its outworkings in the text, and by the covenantal terminology and allusions throughout the piece; (2) the natural/creation ideal, as represented by images of drought, fertility and agriculture; (3) the sexual ideal, as represented by the metaphor of prostitution, the move to father-son imagery and the culminating metaphor of circumcision; and (4) the religious ideal, which is indirectly represented by all of the above ideals, as well as directly presented through calls to follow YHWH alone. These ideals, as well as concerns with boundaries, are interwoven throughout the piece to present a mutually reinforcing persuasive picture of return.

There are several common threads interweaving the ideals as well as the metaphorical representation of Jer. 3.1–4.4. The first has already been mentioned: the root שוב in all its shades of meaning; the whole piece revolves around the possibility of return (religious, political and, metaphorically speaking, sexual, legal, and natural return as well). Another common thread is the focus on identity through the use of direct address and the use of the relational images (husband–wife, father–son). A third is the emphasis pervading the piece on the idea that return involves a radical change in behavior. The ways in which these threads are interwoven allow the text to be interpreted from various perspectives and to be applied to various situations. The metaphorical language, with its inherent ambiguity, aids in this versatility.

In terms of the metaphorical rhetoric of the piece, the citation of the law was not left as a rhetorical question, but rather, was applied in metaphorical terms to the relationship between YHWH and Israel. This re-visioning of the relationship in terms, first of sexual promiscuity, then of the proper father–son relationship with its attendant sign of circumcision, was itself another strategy enacting political change. The very pressure of identification, that is, the pressure to change behavior so as not to identify oneself as a sexually promiscuous woman, but rather to identify as the son who will continue the patriarchal line, I have argued, would place pressures on behavior as well. The very fact that these texts have been retained as part of several theological traditions (e.g. Judaism and Christianity), as well as the fact that YHWH faith continued past the largest crisis ever to face the people of Israel and Judah, the Babylonian exile indicates the measure of success the prophet had in applying the ancient traditions to new situations, and in creating political change.

The final strategy, the interaction with conventions and ideals of gender relations, functions through the use of relational metaphors to portray the present relationship between the people and YHWH (they are promiscuous wives while YHWH is the devoted, loving husband), as well as the proposed future relationship between YHWH and the people (they are to become obedient, loyal sons in relationship to YHWH the father and arch-patriarch). With regard to gender, both the limits of the negative female imagery and the necessity of change to a different relational metaphor, that of father and son, were addressed. It was also shown that the use of gender, in combination with direct address in keeping with the gender of the metaphors themselves, places dual pressures on a primarily male audience: first, when accusing them, to identify themselves as promiscuous wives, an identification which they would surely resist; and second, when setting out the possibility of repentance and return, to identify themselves as sons who will confess and repent (3.21-25), who will return to the earliest covenant with YHWH, and who will bear the mark of identity, circumcision, both on their bodies and on their hearts (that is, they will not only identify themselves as sons, but behave as proper sons should). The latter identification would be far more attractive and therefore persuasive. Last, the imagery and its shifts were explored in terms of both male and female identity. This imagery was shown to implicate the identity not only of the male audience, but of women as well. Male behavior is prescribed while female behavior is circumscribed by this text. However, the imagery itself contains the seeds of its own undermining. While circumcision symbolically excludes women, there remains the need for women and female–male sexuality for reproduction. The symbolic system cannot completely dominate or control women's place and reproductive power, however much it may seek to do so. Thus, a re-visioning in the sense of 'looking at an old text from a new critical direction' was also undertaken in this study.

Although this study has been confined to one text, Jer. 3.1–4.4, I see the investigation of rhetorical strategies, particularly those employed in this monograph, that is, intertextuality, metaphor and gender rhetoric, to be a fruitful avenue of exploration for the prophets in general. While Jeremiah may have been a master metaphorist, there are indications that others were as well. Ezekiel, for example, takes the language of Jer. 3.1–4.4 to its vituperative extreme.[3] Even the imagery of Daughter Zion in second Isaiah, for example, may fruitfully be explored through such a method. Such

---

3. See my articles, 'Multiple Exposures' and 'An Abusive God?'.

exploration would include several other passages from Jeremiah (e.g. chs. 30–31), as well as some from the earlier prophets (e.g. Hosea).

Among other results, a broader exploration of the gendered imagery as interwoven with intertextuality and metaphor would yield a larger picture of the conventions of gender at work in these texts, their power as persuasive tools their own historical context, as well as their continuing power in the contemporary context. In addition, future study may uncover alternative images to those deemed ultimately harmful for women in general, as well as provide a new vision of non-hierarchical and mutual male–female relations in particular. I would hope, along with Rich, that such study would not only serve 'as a clue to how we live, how we have been living, how we have been led to imagine ourselves, how our language has trapped as well as liberated us', but would also provide a new vision: 'how we can begin to see—and therefore live—afresh'.

BIBLIOGRAPHY

Albertz, Rainer, 'Jer 2–6 und die Frühzeitverkündigung Jeremias', *ZAW* 94 (1982), pp. 20-47.

Archer, Léonie J., *Her Price is Beyond Rubies: The Jewish Woman in Graeco-Roman Palestine* (JSOTSup, 60; Sheffield: JSOT Press, 1990).

Bakhtin, Mikhail, *The Dialogic Imagination: Four Essays* (ed. Michael Holquist; trans. Michael Holquist and Caryl Emerson; University of Texas Press Slavic Series, 1; Austin: University of Texas Press, 1981).

—'Discourse in the Novel', in *idem, The Dialogic Imagination*, pp. 259-422.

—'Forms of Time and Chronotope in the Novel', in idem, *Dialogic Imagination*, pp. 84-258.

—*Problems of Dostoevsky's Poetics* (ed. and trans. Caryl Emerson; Minneapolis: University of Minnesota Press, 1984).

Bakhtin, Mikhail, and Pavel Medvedev(?), *The Formal Method in Literary Scholarship: A Critical Introduction to Sociological Poetics* (trans. Albert J. Wehrle; The Goucher College Series; Baltimore: The Johns Hopkins University Press, 1978).

Barthes, Roland, 'De l'oeuvre au texte', *Revue d'esthétique* 23 (1971), pp. 225-32.

Barton, John, 'History and Rhetoric in the Prophets', in Martin Warner (ed.), *The Bible as Rhetoric: Studies in Biblical Persuasion and Credibility* (London: Routledge, 1990), pp. 51-64.

Bauer, Angela, *Gender in the Book of Jeremiah: A Feminist-Literary Reading* (New York: Peter Lang, 1999).

Bauer, Dale M., and Susan Jaret McKinstry, 'Introduction', in Bauer and McKinstry (eds.), *Feminism, Bakhtin, and the Dialogic*, pp. 1-6.

Bauer, Dale M., and Susan Jaret McKinstry (eds.), *Feminism, Bakhtin, and the Dialogic* (Albany: SUNY, 1991).

Bechtel, Lyn M., 'Shame as a Sanction of Social Control in Biblical Israel: Judicial, Political, and Social Shaming', *JSOT* 49 (1991), pp. 47-76.

Benveniste, Emile, *Problems in General Linguistics* (trans. Mary Elizabeth Meek; Coral Gables: University of Miami Press, 1971).

Bergren, Richard V., *The Prophets and the Law* (Cincinnati: Hebrew Union College Press, 1974).

Biddle, Mark E., *A Redaction History of Jeremiah 2.1–4.2* (ATANT, 77; Zürich: Theologisher Verlag, 1990).

Bird, Phyllis A., '"To Play the Harlot": An Inquiry into an Old Testament Metaphor', in Day (ed.), *Gender and Difference in Ancient Israel*, pp. 75-94.

Black, Max, *The Labyrinth of Language* (New York: New American Library, 1968).

—*Models and Metaphors* (Ithaca, NY: Cornell University Press, 1962).

—'More About Metaphor', in A. Ortony (ed.), *Metaphor and Thought* (Cambridge: Cambridge University Press, 1979), pp. 19-43.

Bogaert, P.-M. (ed.), *Le Livre de Jérémie: Le Prophète et Son Milieu les Oracles et Leur Transmission* (Leuven: Leuven University Press, 1981).

Böhler, Dietrich, 'Geschlecterdifferenz und Landbesitz: Stukturuntersuchungen zu Jer 2,2–4,2', in Walter Gross (ed.), *Jeremia und die 'deuteronomistische Bewegung'* (Weinheim: Beltz Athenäum, 1995), pp. 91-127.

Booth, Wayne, 'Metaphor as Rhetoric: The Problem of Evaluation', in Sacks (ed.), *On Metaphor*, pp. 47-70.

—'Ten Literal "Theses"', in Sacks (ed.), *On Metaphor*, pp. 173-74.

Bright, John, *Jeremiah* (AB, 21; Garden City, NY: Doubleday, 1965).

Brinkley, T., 'On the Truth and Probity of Metaphor', in M. Johnson (ed.), *Philosophical Perspectives on Metaphor* (Minneapolis: University of Minnesota Press, 1981), pp. 136-53.

Brueggemann, Walter, 'Israel's Sense of Place in Jeremiah', in J.J. Jackson and M. Kessler (eds.), *Rhetorical Criticism: Essays in Honor of James Muilenberg* (Pittsburgh: Pickwick Press, 1974), pp. 149-65.

—'Jeremiah's Use of Rhetorical Questions', *JBL* 92 (1973), pp. 358-74.

—*To Pluck Up, To Tear Down: A Commentary on Jeremiah 1–25* (Grand Rapids: Eerdmans, 1988).

Burnett, Fred W., 'Postmodern Biblical Exegesis: The Eve of Historical Criticism', in Gary A. Phillips (ed.), *Poststructural Criticism and the Bible: Text/History/Discourse* (Semeia, 51; Atlanta: Scholars Press, 1990), pp. 51-80.

Butler, Judith, *Gender Trouble: Feminism and the Subversion of Identity* (New York: Routledge, 1990).

Camp, Claudia V., 'What's So Strange about the Strange Woman?', in David Jobling, Peggy L. Day and Gerald T. Sheppard (eds.), *The Bible and the Politics of Exegesis: Essays in Honor of Norman K. Gottwald on His Sixty-Fifth Birthday* (Cleveland: Pilgrim Press, 1991), pp. 17-31.

Carmichael, Calum M., *Law and Narrative in the Bible* (Ithaca, NY: Cornell University Press, 1985).

—*The Law of Deuteronomy* (Ithaca, NY: Cornell University Press, 1974).

Carroll, Robert P., *From Chaos to Covenant: Uses of Prophecy in the Book of Jeremiah* (London: SCM Press, 1981).

—*Jeremiah* (OTL; Philadelphia: Westminster Press, 1986).

Cazelles, Henri, 'Jeremiah and Deuteronomy', in Perdue and Kovacs (eds.), *A Prophet to the Nations*, pp. 89-112.

Childs, Brevard S., *Introduction to the Old Testament as Scripture* (Philadelphia: Fortress Press, 1979).

Clements, R.E., *Jeremiah* (Interpretation; Atlanta: John Knox Press, 1988).

Clifford, Gay, *The Transformations of Allegory* (London: Routledge & Kegan Paul, 1974).

Cohen, Ted, 'Metaphor and the Cultivation of Intimacy', in Sacks (ed.), *On Metaphor*, pp. 1-10.

Cooper, David E., *Metaphor* (Oxford: Basil Blackwell, 1986).

Cornill, Carl Heinrich, *Das Buch Jeremia* (Leipzig: Chr. Herm. Tauchnitz, 1905).

Craigie, Peter C., *The Book of Deuteronomy* (NICOT; Grand Rapids: Eerdmans, 1976).

Craigie, Peter C., Page H. Kelley and Joel F. Drinkard, Jr, *Jeremiah 1–25* (WBC, 26; Dallas: Word Books, 1991).

Culler, Jonathan, 'Presupposition and Intertextuality', in *idem*, *The Pursuit of Signs: Semiotics, Literature, Deconstruction* (rev. rep.; Ithaca, NY: Cornell University Press, 1981), pp. 100-18.

Daniels, Dwight R., 'Is there a "Prophetic Lawsuit" Genre?', *ZAW* 99 (1987), pp. 339-60.

Daube, D., 'The Culture of Deuteronomy', *Orita* 3 (1969), pp. 27-52.

Davidson, Donald, 'What Metaphors Mean', in Sacks (ed.), *On Metaphor*, pp. 29-45.

Davis, Ellen, *Swallowing the Scroll: Textuality and the Dynamics of Discourse in Ezekiel's Prophecy* (JSOTSup, 78; Bible and Literature Series, 21; Sheffield: Almond Press, 1989).

Day, Peggy L. (ed.), *Gender and Difference in Ancient Israel* (Minneapolis: Fortress Press, 1989).

Delaney, Carol, *The Seed and the Soil: Gender and Cosmology in Turkish Village Society* (Berkeley: University of California Press, 1991).

Diamond, A.R. Pete, and Kathleen M. O'Connor, 'Unfaithful Passions: Coding Women Coding Men in Jeremiah 2–3 (4.2)', *BibInt* 4 (1996), pp. 288-310.

Donovan, Josephine, 'Style and Power', in Bauer and McKinstry (eds.), *Feminism, Bakhtin, and the Dialogic*, pp. 85-94.

Douglas, Mary, *Purity and Danger: An Analysis of Concepts of Pollution and Taboo* (New York: Praeger, 1966).

Duhm, Bernhard, *Das Buch Jeremia* (Tübingen: J.C.B. Mohr [Paul Siebeck], 1901).

Durlesser, James A., 'The Rhetoric of Allegory in the Book of Ezekiel' (unpublished doctoral dissertation, University of Pittsburgh, 1988).

Eilberg-Schwartz, Howard, 'People of the Body: The Problem of the Body for the People of the Book', *Journal for the History of Sexuality* 2 (1991), pp. 1-24.

—*The Savage in Judaism: An Anthropology of Israelite Religion and Ancient Judaism* (Bloomington: Indiana University Press, 1990).

Erbt, Wilhelm, *Jeremia und Seine Zeit* (Göttingen: Vandenhoeck & Ruprecht, 1902).

Ewald, H., *Die Propheten Des Alten Bundes*, II (3 vols.; Göttingen: Vandenhoeck & Ruprecht, 2nd edn, 1868 [1841]).

Exum, J. Cheryl, 'Prophetic Pornography', in *idem*, *Plotted, Shot, and Painted: Cultural Representations of Biblical Women* (JSOTSup, 215; Gender, Culture, Theory, 3; Sheffield: Sheffield Academic Press, 1996), pp. 100-28.

Exum, J. Cheryl, and Johanna W.H. Bos (eds.), *Reasoning with the Foxes: Female Wit in a World of Male Power* (Semeia, 42; Atlanta: Scholars Press, 1988).

Fetterley, Judith, *The Resisting Reader: A Feminist Approach to American Fiction* (Bloomington: Indiana University Press, 1978).

Fewell, Danna Nolan, and David M. Gunn, *Gender, Power, and Promise: The Subject of the Bible's First Story* (Nashville: Abingdon Press, 1993).

Fineman, Joel, 'The Structure of Allegorical Desire', in Greenblatt (ed.), *Allegory and Representation*, pp. 26-60.

Fishbane, Michael, *Biblical Interpretation in Ancient Israel* (Oxford: Oxford University Press/ Clarendon Press, 1985).

— *Text and Texture: Close Readings of Selected Biblical Texts* (New York: Schocken Books, 1979).

—'Torah and Tradition', in Knight (ed.), *Tradition and Theology in the Old Testament*, pp. 275-300.

Fogelin, Robert J., *Figuratively Speaking* (New Haven: Yale University Press, 1988).

Frymer-Kensky, Tikva, *In the Wake of the Goddesses: Women, Culture, and the Biblical Transformation of Pagan Myth* (New York: Free Press, 1992).

—'Law and Philosophy: The Case of Sex in the Bible', *Semeia* 45 (1989), pp. 89-102.

—'Pollution, Purification, and Purgation in Biblical Israel', in C. Meyers and M. O'Connor (eds.), *The Word of the Lord Shall Go Forth: Essays in Honor of David Noel Freedman* (Winona Lake, IN: Eisenbrauns, 1983), pp. 399-414.

—'Virginity in the Bible', in Victor H. Matthews, Bernard M. Levinson and Tikva Frymer-Kensky (eds.), *Gender and Law in the Hebrew Bible and the Ancient Near East* (JSOTSup, 262; Sheffield: Sheffield Academic Press, 1998), pp. 79-96.

Fuchs, Esther, '"For I Have the Way of Women": Deception, Gender, and Ideology in Biblical Narrative', *Semeia* 42 (1988), pp. 68-83.

Furman, Nelly, 'The Politics of Language: Beyond the Gender Principle?', in Gayle Green and Coppélia Kahn (eds.), *Making a Difference: Feminist Literary Criticism* (New Accents; London: Routledge, 1985), pp. 59-79.

Graf, Karl Heinrich, *Der Prophet Jeremia* (Leipzig: T.O. Weigel, 1862).

Graffy, Allan, 'The Literary Genre of Isa 5,1-7', *Bib* 60 (1979), pp. 400-409.

Greenberg, Moshe, 'The Hebrew Oath Particle *ḤAY/ḤĒ*', *JBL* 76 (1957), pp. 34-39.

Greenblatt, Stephen J. (ed.), *Allegory and Representation: Selected Papers from the English Institute, 1979–80* (Baltimore: The Johns Hopkins University Press, 1981).

Haran, M., 'The Disappearance of the Ark', *IEJ* 13 (1963), pp. 46-58.

Herrmann, Siegfried, *Jeremia: Der Prophet und das Buch* (Erträge der Forschung, 271; Darmstadt: Wissenschaftliche Buchgesellschaft, 1990).

Hertzberg, H.W., 'Jeremia und das Nordreich Israel', *ThLZ* 77 (1952), pp. 595-602.

Hitzig, F., *Der Prophet Jeremia* (Leipzig: Weidmannsche Buchhandlung, 1841).

Hobbs, T.R., 'Jeremiah 3.1-5 and Deuteronomy 24.1-4', *ZAW* 86 (1974), pp. 23-29.

Holladay, William L., *The Architecture of Jeremiah 1–20* (London: Associated University Press, 1976).

—*Jeremiah 1* (Hermeneia; Philadelphia: Fortress Press, 1986).

—*The Root Šûbh in the Old Testament: With Particular Reference to its Usages in Covenantal Contexts* (Leiden: E.J. Brill, 1958).

Honig, Edwin, *Dark Conceit: The Making of Allegory* (Evanston: Northwestern University Press, 1959).

Horwitz, W.J., 'Audience Reaction to Jeremiah', *CBQ* 32 (1970), pp. 555-64.

Huffmon, H.B., 'The Covenant Lawsuit in the Prophets', *JBL* 78 (1959), pp. 285-95.

Hyatt, J. Philip., 'Jeremiah and Deuteronomy', in Perdue and Kovacs (eds.), *A Prophet to the Nations*, pp. 113-27.

Jacobs, Deborah, 'Critical Imperialism and Renaissance Drama: The Case of *The Roaring Girl*', in Bauer and McKinstry (eds.), *Feminism, Bakhtin, and the Dialogic*, pp. 73-84.

Janzen, J. Gerald, *Studies in the Text of Jeremiah* (HSM, 6; Cambridge, MA: Harvard University Press, 1973).

Jay, Nancy, 'Sacrifice as Remedy for Having Been Born of Woman', in C.W. Atkinson, C.H. Buchanan and M.R. Miles (eds.), *Immaculate and Powerful: The Female in Sacred Image and Social Reality* (Boston: Beacon Press, 1985), pp. 283-309.

—'Sacrifice, Descent and the Patriarchs', *VT* 38 (1988), pp. 52-70.

—*Throughout Your Generations Forever: Sacrifice, Religion, and Paternity* (Chicago: University of Chicago Press, 1992).

Jones, Douglas Rawlinson, *Jeremiah* (Grand Rapids: Eerdmans, 1992).

Kaufman, Stephen A., 'Rhetoric, Redaction, and Message in Jeremiah', in Baruch A. Levine, Jacob Neusner and Ernest S. Frerichs (eds.), *Judaic Perspectives on Ancient Israel* (Philadelphia: Fortress Press, 1987), pp. 63-74.

Keil, C.F., *The Prophecies of Jeremiah*, I (2 vols.; Edinburgh: T. & T. Clark, 1873).

172   *Circumscribing the Prostitute*

Klopfenstein, M.A., *Scham und Schande nach dem Alten Testament* (Zürich: Theologischer Verlag, 1979).

Knight, Douglas A. (ed.), *Tradition and Theology in the Old Testament* (Philadelphia: Fortress Press, 1977).

Kristeva, Julia, *The Kristeva Reader* (ed. Toril Moi; New York: Columbia University Press, 1986).

—'Word, Dialogue and Novel', in *idem*, *The Kristeva Reader*, pp. 34-61.

Lerner, Gerda, *The Creation of Patriarchy* (New York: Oxford University Press, 1986).

Lincoln, Bruce, *Discourse and the Construction of Society* (New York: Oxford University Press, 1989).

Long, Burke O., 'Recent Field Studies in Oral Literature and their Bearing on Old Testament Criticism', *VT* 26 (1976), pp. 187-98.

Lundbom, Jack R., *Jeremiah: A Study in Ancient Hebrew Rhetoric* (Missoula, MT: Scholars Press, 1975).

Lust, J., '"Gathering and Return" in Jeremiah and Ezekiel', in Bogaert (ed.), *Le Livre de Jérémie*, pp. 119-42.

Man, Paul de, 'The Epistemology of Metaphor', in Sacks (ed.), *On Metaphor*, pp. 11-28.

—'Pascal's Allegory of Persuasion', in Greenblatt (ed.), *Allegory and Representation*, p. 1.

Martin, James D., 'The Forensic Background to Jeremiah III 1', *VT* 19 (1969), pp. 82-92.

Mays, James Luther, *Hosea, A Commentary* (OTL; Philadelphia: Westminster Press, 1969).

McConville, J.G., *Judgment and Promise: An Interpretation of the Book of Jeremiah* (Winona Lake, IN: Eisenbrauns, 1993).

McKane, William, *A Critical and Exegetical Commentary on Jeremiah. I. Jeremiah I–XXV* (ICC; Edinburgh: T. & T. Clark, 1986).

Medvedev, Pavel, and Mikhail Bakhtin(?), *The Formal Method in Literary Scholarship: A Critical Introduction to Sociological Poetics* (trans. Albert J. Wehrle; Baltimore: The Johns Hopkins University Press, 1978).

Merendino, Rosario Pius, OSB, *Das Deuteronomisches Gesetz* (Bonn: Peter Hanstein Verlag, 1969).

Mettinger, T.N.D., *The Dethronement of Sabaoth* (trans. Frederick H. Cryer; Lund: C.W.K. Gleerup, 1982).

Miller, Patrick, *Deuteronomy* (Interpretation; Louisville, KY: John Knox Press, 1990).

Moi, Toril, *Sexual/Textual Politics: Feminist Literary Theory* (New Accents; London: Routledge, 1985).

Morgan, Thaïs, 'The Space of Intertextuality', in Patrick O'Donnell and Robert Con Davis (eds.), *Intertextuality and Contemporary American Fiction* (Baltimore: The Johns Hopkins University Press, 1989), pp. 239-79.

Morson, Gary Saul, and Caryl Emerson, *Mikhail Bakhtin: The Creation of a Prosaics* (Stanford: Stanford University Press, 1990).

Mowinckel, Sigmund, *Zur Komposition des Buches Jeremia* (Norske Videnskapsakademie, Oslo. Hist.-Filos. Klasse, Skrifter 1913, No. 5; Oslo: J. Dybwad, 1914).

Muilenberg, James, 'The Terminology of Adversity in Jeremiah', in Harry Thomas and W.L. Reed Frank (eds.), *Translating and Understanding the Old Testament: Essays in Honor of Herbert Gordon May* (Nashville: Abingdon Press, 1970), pp. 49-63.

Nasuti, Harry P., 'Identity, Identification, and Imitation: The Narrative Hermeneutics of Biblical Law', *Journal of Law and Religion* 4 (1986), pp. 9-23.

Newsom, Carol, 'A Maker of Metaphors—Ezekiel's Oracles Against Tyre', *Int* 38 (1984), pp. 151-64.

—'Woman and the Discourse of Patriarchal Wisdom: A Study of Proverbs 1–9', in Day (ed.), *Gender and Difference in Ancient Israel*, pp. 142-60.

Nicholson, Ernest W., *Preaching to the Exiles: A Study of the Prose Tradition in the Book of Jeremiah* (Oxford: Basil Blackwell, 1970).

O'Connor, Kathleen M., 'The Tears of God and Divine Character in Jeremiah 2–9', in Tod Linafelt and Timothy K. Beal (eds.), *God in the Fray: A Tribute to Walter Brueggemann* (Minneapolis: Fortress Press, 1998), pp. 172-88.

O'Day, Gail R., 'Jeremiah 9.22-23 and 1 Corinthians 1.26-31: A Study in Intertextuality', *JBL* 109 (1990), pp. 259-67.

Odell, Margaret S., 'An Exploratory Study of Shame and Dependence in the Bible and Selected Near Eastern Parallels', in William W. Hallo, K. Lawson Younger, Jr, and Bernard F. Batto (eds.), *The Biblical Canon in Comparative Perspective* (Scripture in Context, 4; Lewiston, NY: Edwin Mellen Press, 1991), pp. 217-33.

Oesterley, W.O.E., and Theodore H. Robinson, *An Introduction to the Books of the Old Testament* (London: SPCK, 1934).

Ollenburger, Ben C., *Zion the City of the Great King* (JSOTSup, 41; Sheffield: JSOT Press, 1987).

Orr, Mary, *Claude Simon: The Intertextual Dimension* (University of Glasgow French and German Publications; Somerset: Castle Cary Press, 1993).

Osgood, S. Joy, 'Women and the Inheritance of Land in Early Israel', in George J. Brooke (ed.), *Women in the Biblical Tradition* (Lewiston, NJ: Edwin Mellen Press, 1992), pp. 29-52.

Overholt, Thomas W., 'Jeremiah 2 and the Problem of "Audience Reaction"', *CBQ* 41 (1979), pp. 262-73.

Pedersen, J., 'Honour and Shame', in, *idem, Israel: Its Life and Culture* (4 vols.; London: Oxford University Press, 1962), II, pp. 213-44.

Perdue, Leo G., and Brian W. Kovacs (eds.), *A Prophet to the Nations: Essays in Jeremiah Studies* (Winona Lake, IN: Eisenbrauns, 1984).

Pressler, Carolyn, *The View of Women Found in the Deuteronomic Family Laws* (BZAW, 216; Berlin: W. de Gruyter, 1993).

Rad, Gerhard von, *Deuteronomy: A Commentary* (trans. Dorothea Barton; OTL; Philadelphia: Westminster Press, 1966).

—*Genesis* (OTL; Philadelphia: Westminster Press, 1961).

Raitt, Thomas M., *A Theology of Exile: Judgment and Deliverance in Jeremiah and Ezekiel* (Philadelphia: Fortress Press, 1977).

Rashkow, Ilona, 'Daughters and Fathers in Genesis... Or, What is Wrong with this Picture?', in J. Cheryl Exum and David J.A. Clines (eds.), *The New Literary Criticism and the Hebrew Bible* (JSOTSup, 143; Sheffield: JSOT Press, 1993), pp. 250-65.

Rich, Adrienne, 'When We Dead Awaken: Writing as Re-Vision', *College English* 34 (1972), p. 18.

Ricoeur, Paul, *The Rule of Metaphor: Multi-Disciplinary Studies of the Creation of Meaning in Language* (trans. Robert Czerny, Kathleen McLaughlin and John Costello; Toronto: University of Toronto Press, 1977).

Rietzschl, C., *Das Problem der Urrolle: Ein Beitrag zur Redaktionsgeschichte des Jeremiabuches* (Gütersloh: Gerd Mohn, 1966).

Roberts, J.J.M., 'Zion in the Theology of the Davidic–Solomonic Empire', in T. Ishida and M. Sekine (eds.), *Studies in the Period of David and Solomon and Other Essays: Papers Read at the International Symposium for Biblical Studies, Tokyo, 5-7 December, 1979* (Tokyo: Yamakaw-Shuppansha, 1982), pp. 93-108.

Roche, Michael de, 'Yahweh's *Rîb* Against Israel: A Reassessment of the So-Called "Prophetic Lawsuit" in the Preexilic Prophets', *JBL* 102 (1983), pp. 563-74.

Rofé, A., 'The Arrangement of the Book of Jeremiah', *ZAW* 101.3 (1989), pp. 390-98.

Rosenberg, Joel, *King and Kin: Political Allegory in the Hebrew Bible* (Bloomington: Indiana University Press, 1986).

Rudolph, Wilhelm, *Jeremia* (HAT, 12; Tübingen: J.C.B. Mohr [Paul Siebeck], 3rd edn, 1958).

Sacks, Sheldon (ed.), *On Metaphor* (Chicago: University of Chicago Press, 1978).

Sakenfeld, Katherine D., *The Meaning of Ḥesed in the Hebrew Bible* (HSM, 17; Missoula, MT: Scholars Press, 1978).

Savran, George, *Telling and Retelling: Quotation in Biblical Narrative* (Bloomington: Indiana University Press, 1989).

Schmitt, John J., 'The Gender of Ancient Israel', *JSOT* 26 (1983), pp. 115-25.

—'Israel and Zion—Two Gendered Images', *Horizons* 18.1 (1991), pp. 18-32.

Seebass, H. , '*Bosh; Bushah; Bosheth; Mebhushim*', in *TDOT*, II, pp. 50-60.

Seitz, Christopher R., *Theology in Conflict: Reactions to the Exile in the Book of Jeremiah* (BZAW, 176; Berlin: W. de Gruyter, 1989).

Setel, T. Drorah, 'Prophets and Pornography: Female Sexual Imagery in Hosea', in Letty M. Russell (ed.), *Feminist Interpretation of the Bible* (Philadelphia: Westminster Press, 1985), pp. 86-95.

Shields, Mary E., 'An Abusive God? Identity and Power/Gender and Violence in Ezekiel 23', in A.K.M. Adam (ed.), *Postmodern Interpretations of the Bible—A Reader* (St.Louis: Chalice Press, 2001), pp. 129-51.

—'Circumcision of the Prostitute: Gender, Sexuality, and the Call to Repentance in Jeremiah 3.1–4.4', *BibInt* 3 (1995), pp. 61-74.

—'Circumscribing the Prostitute: The Rhetorics of Intertextuality, Metaphor, and Gender in Jeremiah 3.1–4.4' (doctoral dissertation, Emory University, 1996).

—'Multiple Exposures: Body Rhetoric and Gender Characterization in Ezekiel 16', *JFSR* 14 (1998), pp. 5-18.

Simon, U., 'The Poor Man's Ewe Lamb', *Bib* 48 (1967), pp. 207-42.

Smend, Rudolf, *Lehrbuch der Alttestamentlichen Religionsgeschichte* (Freiburg: J.C.B. Mohr, 2nd edn, 1899).

Smith, George Adam, *Jeremiah: Being the Baird Lecture for 1922* (New York: G.H. Doran Company, 1922).

Snodgrass, Klyne, 'What Method Should be Used?', in *idem, The Parable of the Wicked Tenants* (WUNT; Tübingen: J.C.B. Mohr [Paul Siebeck], 1982), pp. 12-30.

Soderlund, Sven, *The Greek Text of Jeremiah: A Revised Hypothesis* (JSOTSup, 47; Sheffield: JSOT Press, 1985).

Soggin, J.A., 'The Ark of the Covenant, Jeremiah 3,16', in Bogaert (ed.), *Le Livre de Jérémie*, pp. 215-21.

Soskice, Janet Martin, *Metaphor and Religious Language* (Oxford: Clarendon Press, 1985).

Speiser, E.A., *Genesis* (AB, 1; Garden City, NY: Doubleday, 2nd edn, 1978 [1964]).

Stade, Bernhard, 'Miscellen: 1. Jes. 4,2–6; 2. Jer 3,6–16; 3. Habakuk', *ZAW* 4 (1884), pp. 149-59.

Stolz, F., 'Bosh zuschanden werden', in *THAT*, I, pp. 269-72.

Thiel, Winfried, *Die deuteronomistische Redaktion von Jeremia 1–25* (Neukirchen–Vluyn: Neukirchener Verlag, 1973).

Thompson, J.A., *The Book of Jeremiah* (NICOT; Grand Rapids: Eerdmans, 1980).

Unterman, Jeremiah, *From Repentance to Redemption: Jeremiah's Thought in Transition* (JSOTSup, 54; Sheffield: JSOT Press, 1987).

Vanhoozer, Kevin J., *Biblical Narrative in the Philosophy of Paul Ricoeur: A Study in Hermeneutics and Theology* (Cambridge: Cambridge University Press, 1990).

Vološinov, V.N., *Marxism and the Philosophy of Language* (trans. L. Mateja and I.R. Titunik; Cambridge, MA: Harvard University Press, 1973).

Volz, D. Paul, *Der Prophet Jeremia* (KAT, 10; Leipzig: A. Deichertsche Verlagsbuchhandlung, 2nd edn, 1928 [1920]).

Weems, Renita J., *Battered Love: Marriage, Sex, and Violence in the Hebrew Prophets* (Overtures to Biblical Theology; Minneapolis: Fortress Press, 1995).

Weinfeld, M., 'Jeremiah and the Spiritual Metamorphosis of Israel', *ZAW* 88 (1976), pp. 17-56.

Weiser, A., *Der Prophet Jeremiah* (ATD, 20/21; Göttingen: Vandenhoeck & Ruprecht, 1960).

Wenham, G.J., 'The Restoration of Marriage Reconsidered', *JJS* 30 (1979), pp. 36-40.

Westbrook, Raymond, 'The Prohibition on Restoration of Marriage in Deuteronomy 24.1-4', in Sara Japhet (ed.), *Studies in Bible* (Scripta Hierosolymitana, 31; Jerusalem: Magnes Press, 1986), pp. 387-405.

Westermann, Claus, *Genesis 12–36: A Commentary* (Interpretation; trans. John J. Scullion; Minneapolis: Augsburg, 1985 [Ger. 1981]).

—*Praise and Lament in the Psalms* (trans. Keith R. Crim and Richard N. Soulen; Atlanta: John Knox Press, 1981 [1965]).

Wieder, Arnold A., 'Josiah and Jeremiah: Their Relationship According to Aggadic Sources', in Michael A. Fishbane and Paul R. Flohr (eds.), *Texts and Responses* (Festschrift Nahum N. Glatzer; Leiden: E.J. Brill, 1975), pp. 60-72.

Wildberger, Hans, *Jesaja Kapitel 1–12* (BKAT, 10; Neukirchen–Vluyn: Neukirchener Verlag, 1980 [1972]).

Wolff, Hans Walter, 'Das Zitat im Prophetenspruch', in *idem*, *Gesammelte Studien Zum Alten Testament* (Munich: Chr. Kaiser Verlag, 2nd edn, 1973 [1964]), pp. 36-129.

—*Hosea* (Hermeneia; Philadelphia: Fortress Press, 1974 [Ger. 1965]).

Yaron, R., 'The Restoration of Marriage', *JJS* 17 (1966), pp. 1-11.

Yee, Gale, 'Spreading Your Legs to Anyone Who Passed: The Pornography of Ezekiel 16', (unpublished paper presented at the 1990 Annual Meeting of the SBL in New Orleans).

Zakovitch, Yair, 'The Woman's Rights in the Biblical Law of Divorce', *JLA* 4 (1981), pp. 28-46.

Zimmerli, Walther, 'Prophetic Proclamation and Reinterpretation', in Knight (ed.), *Tradition and Theology in the Old Testament*, pp. 69-100.

INDEXES

INDEX OF REFERENCES

INDEX OF AUTHORS

Wenham, G.J. 31, 32
Westbrook, R. 32
Westermann, C. 126, 127, 138
Wieder, A.A. 81
Wildberger, H. 107
Wolff, H.W. 47, 126, 127, 139, 141

Yaron, R. 30, 32
Yee, G. 14

Zakovitch, Y. 32
Zimmerli, W. 93

JOURNAL FOR THE STUDY OF THE OLD TESTAMENT
SUPPLEMENT SERIES